Grief Diaries

Surviving Loss by Overdose

True stories about surviving loss
of a loved one from an overdose

LYNDA CHELDELIN FELL
with
SHANNIE JENKINS
WHITNEY O'BRIEN

FOREWORD BY
ELAINE FAULKNER, SUDP

Grief Diaries
Surviving Loss by Overdose – 1st ed.
Lynda Cheldelin Fell/Shannie Jenkins /Whitney O'Brien
Grief Diaries www.GriefDiaries.com

Cover Design by AlyBlue Media, LLC
Interior Design by AlyBlue Media LLC
Published by AlyBlue Media, LLC

ISBN: 978-1-950712-07-6
AlyBlue Media, LLC
Ferndale, WA 98248
www.AlyBlueMedia.com

PRINTED IN THE UNITED STATES OF AMERICA

Testimonials

"CRITICALLY IMPORTANT . . . I want to say to Lynda that what you are doing is so critically important." –DR. BERNICE A. KING, Daughter of Dr. Martin Luther King

"STUNNING . . . Grief Diaries treats the reader to a rare combination of candor and fragility through the eyes of the bereaved. A stunning read full of comfort and hope." —DR. GLORIA HORSLEY, President, Open to Hope Foundation

"HOPE . . . These stories reflect the authentic voices of individuals at the unexpected moment their lives were shattered and altered forever. Moments of strength in the midst of indescribable pain, resilience in the midst of rage; hope while mired in despair." —SHERIFF SADIE DARNELL, Chair, Florida Cold Case Advisory Commission

"INSPIRATIONAL . . . Grief Diaries is the result of heartfelt testimonials from a dedicated and loving group of people. By sharing their stories, the reader will find inspiration and a renewed sense of comfort as they move through their own journey." -CANDACE LIGHTNER, Founder of Mothers Against Drunk Driving

"DEEPLY INTIMATE . . . Grief Diaries is a deeply intimate, authentic collection of narratives that speak to the powerful, often ambiguous, and wide spectrum of emotions that arise from loss. I so appreciate the vulnerability and truth embedded in these stories." —DR. ERICA GOLDBLATT HYATT, Chair of Psychology, Bryn Athyn College

"BRAVE . . . The brave individuals who share their truths in these books do it for the benefit of all." —CAROLYN COSTIN, Founder of Monte Nido Treatment Centers

"HOPE AND HEALING . . . You are a pioneer in this field and you are breaking the trail for others to find hope and healing." —KRISTI SMITH, Bestselling Author & International Speaker

"A FORCE . . .The writers of the Grief Diaries anthology series are a force to be reckoned with. I'm betting we will be agents of great change."
—MARY LEE ROBINSON, Author and Founder of Set an Extra Plate initiative

"MOVING . . . In Grief Diaries, the stories are not only moving but often provide a rich background for any mourner to find a gem of insight that can be used in coping with loss." —DR. LOUIS LAGRAND, Author of Healing Grief, Finding Peace

"HEALING . . . Grief Diaries can heal hearts and begin to build community and acceptance to speak the unspeakable." —DIANNA VAGIANOS ARMENTROUT, Poetry Therapist & Author of Walking the Labyrinth of My Heart: A Journey of Pregnancy, Grief and Infant Death

"INCREDIBLE . . .Thank you so much for doing this project, it's absolutely incredible!" —JULIE MJELVE, Founder, Grieving Together

"WONDERFUL . . .Grief Diaries is a wonderful computation of stories written by the best of experts, the bereaved themselves. Thank you for building awareness about a topic so near and dear to my heart." —DR. HEIDI HORSLEY, Adjunct Professor, School of Social Work, Columbia University, Author, Co-Founder of Open to Hope Organization

Dedication

In loving memory
of all our loved ones
who died too soon

Contents

BY ELAINE FAULKNER, CDP

Foreword

You are not alone! Help has arrived. We understand how much you tried to help your loved one. I tried to help my loved one, as well. We cajoled, threatened, suggested, made plans, educated ourselves, spent money, and stayed awake countless nights. In the end, it was enough. You cared enough, loved enough, and cried enough. The disease of addiction is stronger than you or me.

The brain changes that caused our loved one's demise overpowered their logic, willpower, and survival instincts. The complex brain changes due to substance use changes our loved ones and their behavior in ways we could not have imagined. Vulnerabilities from genetic predisposition, societal messages, overprescribing doctors, peers, and other influences, were beyond our power to control.

Traumatic experiences may have increased their risk, but it was also their perception of the trauma and their life experiences that created their need to hide out in an alternate chemical reality.

At times, we are still angry at them, sometimes at ourselves. Now that they have passed, we can own those feelings, but we can also hold them in our hearts with compassion and love. They did the best they could. We did the best we could. They tried. We tried. We did not fail.

I am proof that knowledge is **not** the key to knowing what to do about our addicted loved ones. I had firsthand experience counseling thousands of people in active substance abuse, drug dependence, and their families. My son Jacob had the benefit of hearing many lessons and the latest research on drugs and drinking. Some of those lessons hit home. Some didn't, and he would say "Don't counsel me, Mom!"

I know from working as a chemical dependency professional that there is no stigma, there is no shame. Our loved ones were ill. We don't need to hide ourselves or our feelings. Speak proudly of your loved one and the gifts they shared with the world.

Focusing on Jacob's life instead of his death has been valuable to my healing. My hope is that you, too, will feel the same about your loved one.

My husband Jack had an insightful comment two days after Jacob died. He said to our small family, "We have to do this together. We will never be able to do this alone."

This is my charge to us all: let's share our stories. Sharing will bring us together; we will not be alone!

Blessings,

ELAINE FAULKNER, SUDP

Jacob's Mom

BY LYNDA CHELDELIN FELL

Preface

Overdose. Addiction. Drugs. It's anywhere and everywhere. An ugly villain disguised as pills, capsules, liquids, and powders. Tiny yet powerful, its only aim is to destroy everyone in its path.

Drugs are rampant in today's world, yet nobody has answers. We only have stories. Our stories. The stories of our intelligent, kind and promising loved ones who fell victim to a villain.

By sharing our stories, we help each other feel less alone. We give each other the compassion that's often denied in a stigmatized death. These stories also serve to educate society. They open the dialogue, raise awareness and understanding, and invite humanity to see the journey through our eyes—the first step toward removing the stigma.

Further, our stories hold the power to advocate. With research dollars often granted to the noisiest advocacy groups, it is through these stories that we advocate for past, present, and future loved ones. These narrations can be used by researchers and professionals to study the villain and work with us toward better support.

If someone you love has died by overdose, the following stories are written by people who share your path and know exactly how you feel. Although no two journeys are identical, we hope you'll find comfort in these stories and the understanding that you aren't truly alone, for we walk ahead, behind, and right beside you.

Wishing you healing and hope from the Grief Diaries village.

Warm regards,

Lynda Cheldelin Fell

Creator, Grief Diaries
INTERNATIONAL GRIEF INSTITUTE
www.InternationalGriefInstitute.com | www.LyndaFell.com

BY REV. ROLAND JOHNSON

Introduction

The true victims of overdose death are not the deceased but the living. The parents, children, siblings, spouses, lovers, partners, close relatives and friends who remain behind to wonder and to grieve. The survivors face terrible loss that's often complicated and shrouded in social stigma. Support networks are thin and inadequate. Specialized training is severely lacking and only others experiencing the same type of loss seem to have the ability to sympathize. Moving forward in life holds more questions than answers, and society blames the survivors for the "inadequate whatever" that led to the drugs in the first place.

Drug overdose is killing people. Many people. Today, it seems as though everyone has lost someone to overdose.

During the last few years of my teaching career in academia, death by overdose was reducing my student rosters at an increasing rate. As an ordained minister, I held the bereaved and mourned their loss with them. As a police chaplain in a busy urban department, I saw and served death on the frontline. As a crime victims' liaison for the state, I comforted and counseled while seeking justice for the bereaved.

I watched as our nation drowned in overdose deaths.

In 2017, an eleven-year-old girl waited for her dad to pick her up. He was running late for their visit, and her mom was getting upset. Angry and griping, the mother called his cell again and again but no answer. Exasperated, she decided to drive her daughter to her dad's, even though she didn't like his roommates. As she pulled up to his house, she was greeted first by police and then by a chaplain. There would be no visit tonight, nor ever again. Dad is dead. Syringe, heroin, spoon, lighter and tie tell the story of his evening.

In the U.S., her dad was just one of the 70,237 drug overdose deaths to opioid derivatives, analogs and synthetics compounds alone (National Center for Health Statistics, 2018).

In 2018, a twenty-one-year-old woman died from methamphet-amine toxicity, the technical term for overdose. A popular high school cheerleader, homecoming queen and gymnast, she weighed just eighty-two pounds when she died.

A couple days later, a young mother gave birth in her home and then disappeared. She was found behind a shed four blocks away, dead from an overdose of "ice," a pure, extremely potent methamphetamine that had arrived in town. More deaths would follow.

Come spring 2019, someone I spent years moving from addiction to success overdosed and died. His story is personal. Like an adopted son, Mark and I walked through all the misery and pain of his life to see a new day. Though a little older than many, he went to college, settled into a career, and began to support his daughter and become a dad. He repaired his relationship with his ex-wife enough to share genuine warmth. He graduated with honors and entered his new life.

Five years clean and accepted into the medical profession, he was hired by one of the most prestigious hospitals in the country. He was to begin in one week.

So excited, Mark planned to reward himself with a celebration and tropical vacation. While celebrating, he ran into old friends who whipped out some heroin just for old times' sake. Mark did a small amount and was dead within minutes.

Mark's ex-wife asked me to write a letter to his daughter for when she's older, explaining who her dad was, how he had a good heart and soul, and how much he loved her. I still haven't found the right words.

Come fall 2019, a college freshman went to a crowded party. A stellar student and star athlete, the popular young man was having fun when someone pulled out powder cocaine. "Come on, time to party like a college kid!"

It was his first—and last—time. Life ended shortly after. A coffin instead of a college dorm is now his resting place. Nothing will console his mom, dad, and little sister.

Opioid and opioid derivatives have their own category of recorded death by the Center for Disease Control. Codeine, morphine, hydrocodone, and oxycodone are natural and semisynthetic opioids. Fentanyl, fentanyl analogs, and tramadol are synthetic opioids.

Cocaine, methamphetamine, ecstasy, and other toxic recreational drugs drive the parties of our society, and produce a death count not easily calculated and not uniformly recorded.

Death from any drug overdose deprives us all of so much talent and promise. Drugs harvest lives before they reach fruition. And the stories of loss and grief grow exponentially.

Statisticians keep count. Politicians pass laws. Police are overwhelmed. Preachers condemn. Doctors medicate. Businesses look at the bottom line. And, academia is stymied. The war on drugs is an abysmal failure.

All the excuses and explanations do nothing to slow the flood of heartache and sorrow. As a sociologist, I call for greater academic study and involvement. As a pastor, I call for compassion and better instruction and training for all who touch the grieving.

Social scientists collect all the demographics, analyze all the data, and publish the statistics on drug overdose. But statistics are not people, and it is people who grieve. To study the grief, to find the similarities and the differences in post-loss trauma, is an academic endeavor that is mostly avoided.

Causation for the grief is known: death of a loved one by drug overdose. But the effects are not easily predictable and do not lead to clear results. Too many variables influence the personal loss to drugs. Sadly, the data on grief from death by drug overdose can only be gathered from those who grieve.

This book is the beginning. It explores grief and loss to overdose from the narratives written by the survivors, those living the loss. These are the personal stories of individuals, of real people in real time with real loss.

This book challenges many social ideas on the loss that comes from drug overdose. It lays bare a reality of the death of indignity many feel at the hands of the professionals, from the first responders to the final funeral participants, from the clergy to counselors. Very few really know what to say or do.

Current instruction is inadequate to accommodate the needs of this growing community of profound grief. Today's culture is not trained to understand grief, loss, or the pain of surviving loss by overdose. A starting point is necessary if we, as a collective society, are going to address an issue that frightens and repels most everybody.

This book is a starting point for exploration, research, and most importantly, academic expansion of training for bereavement and grief specialists.

This book is a goldmine for students pursuing careers in the social science and counseling professions, and serves as an excellent resource for practicing medical and grief professionals. With proper education, learning and training, light can begin to permeate a very dark place. With education and learning, wisdom is possible. With competent training of career professionals, educators, counselors, clergy, and so many others, survival, coping and eventual thriving of the living is obtainable.

Whether you are grieving a loss to drug overdose or trying to console or counsel someone who is, this book provides a catalog of issues faced by the grieving. May these real life accounts assist and challenge you to explore and develop effective strategies for the living as we struggle as a nation to cope with our loss.

REV. ROLAND JOHNSON, III
Sociologist & police chaplain
www.OutsideWalls.org

CHAPTER ONE

The Beginning of our Journeys

A lifetime is not enough to KNOW someone else.
~ SIMON MCBURNEY

Every journey starts at the beginning, and so do our stories. In this chapter, writers share what life was like before that pivotal moment when life as they knew it ended and a new one began, forever defining their calendar to before and after.

*

KIMBERLY CALAIS
Kim's 23-year-old daughter Emily died from a multiple drug overdose including heroin and methamphetamine in 2016

January 5, 2016 at 3:16 a.m. This was the exact moment my life changed forever. The official beginning of the worst days of my life. This was the moment I received that call . . . the one you hear people elude to never wanting to receive. The call that I fearfully dreaded receiving for the past four years. And a call that I absolutely did not expect, as I believed the worst was over. Rock bottom had been reached. A corner had been turned. A new page awaited. I was wrong. That one call turned my entire world upside down, throwing me into the darkest part of the depths of hell imaginable.

It was the call where I was told that my daughter, Emily, was gone. Gone? Gone. A scream left my body that came from a place inside me I did not know existed. It was primal. I have since decided that place was a part of my soul, the place that holds every memory, every sensation of knowing, raising and loving my daughter. The place that held the hope for every moment of her life since I discovered I was pregnant with her, and all the moments yet to be. It's where I held the dreams of her life. All the hope. All the yet to be's. Gone. Her voice. Her smile. The silkiness of her hair. The sound of her laughter. The touch of her skin. The softness of her kisses. The warmth of her hugs. Gone.

Gone.

It was also the moment that marked a new beginning. One I did not sign up for nor wanted to take. It was—is—the journey of horrific, unrelenting grief.

Of understanding the incomprehensible. Of performing an autopsy of my daughter's life to try to comprehend how this could have happened. Of learning so much more about drugs, addiction, mental health, and the ever-present stigma placed by society which makes the most horrific pain of learning of your child's death even more debilitating as it seems no one understands…or cares. The death of a child is already a difficult topic for others to address. Death by drugs somehow makes it dirty or deserved in the opinion of others. That is not acceptable to me. Those who died from an overdose are someone to many.

This moment marked the beginning of my journey of getting to know my daughter—who I believed I knew better than any other person on this earth—in reverse.

That call came by way of a text message from Emily's dad in California. I had gotten up early and thought about going downstairs to the gym. I picked up my phone from its charging base and saw a text from my former husband asking me to call him as soon as I received his message on either his home or cell, and that it is was important. All at once I felt my stomach drop.

I had last spoken to Emily the morning of January 1, 2016, New Year's Day. She was on her way to work but asked if I could send her twenty dollars for an Uber as she wanted to take more time getting ready for work that day. Her boss was in and she was going to ask for a raise. She said that if that didn't work, she was going to look at getting a second job, as it was expensive living in the Bay area.

She sounded upbeat, happy and motivated. I sent her the money. Since I usually received text notifications from the bank when the transfer was accepted, I was not happy to read that she didn't accept it until late that night when she was already off work. I was not pleased at her apparent lie, and contemplated writing her an email about it, but decided to wait until we could speak.

The next morning, she sent me a text message, writing "A friend of mine died."

I responded immediately. "Who? How?"

Given our three-hour time difference, my message was sent a couple hours after her message. No response. That wasn't unusual so I assumed she was busy.

I was wrong.

I didn't want to call her dad back. I felt sick. If I didn't call, I reasoned, the reality of whatever potentially awful news he had wouldn't be real if I didn't hear it. I pondered this for about a minute, took a deep breath and dialed his number. He answered quickly. Without even a hello, I asked, "What's wrong?" which was something I often said when getting urgent messages in the night from Emily.

Then he said the words that are forever burned in my soul. "Emily's gone."

Emotions were like knives, attacking and cutting me, killing me. Disbelief. Shock. Denial. Fear. Anger. And all simultaneously. I immediately felt my blood run cold and I could swear my heart stopped beating. I listened to him speak, but I couldn't hear his words.

And then came that scream.

I spoke with the coroner a few hours later. She told me Emily was found in the locked bedroom of a house she shared with three other friends/coworkers. An initial blood analysis determined that there were drugs in her system, and she was found with paraphernalia around her that was consistent with an overdose death. I asked if this was intentional. She said that she would know more after the autopsy was performed.

An autopsy? On my little girl? Why are people saying these things to me?

I needed to know as much as I could about what happened. Since I paid for her cellphone, I went to my bill and looked at her activity. I saw that she was actively texting up and until the morning of January 2. She received my text and exchanged texts with another number a half hour later. The bill also reflected her receiving many more messages for the next two days. But there were no more outgoing messages from her. I couldn't catch my breath and I felt dizzy as I processed—and visualized—what this meant. Her door was locked and although she shared a house with three other people, she often stayed in her room. I was convinced that she would not have been dormant in communicating via her phone. She was constantly on her social media as she was a prolific selfie taker. I was always asking her to watch her data use and her phone bill was always very high.

The coroner asked me about her state of mind and any history she had with drugs. My sigh and momentary silence represented the flood of memories from the past years.

In September 2014, Emily called me and told me she needed help. "I'm addicted to heroin, Mom. I need help."

I put aside my initial reaction of absolute horror and asked what she meant. She told me she had been doing heroin for about four months and was addicted. I asked her if she took this intravenously. She said yes.

She went on to tell me she was having sex with strangers to get drugs. She was going to dangerous neighborhoods in Oakland to buy drugs in the middle of the night. She told me she had shared needles with some girl and now had an open hole in her arm. I calmly told her that I would get her help and that everything would be okay.

Since I live in Canada and she lived in California, I told her I would contact her dad. He lived in the Bay area and carried her health insurance coverage. She told me she would be seeing him the next day and was afraid of his reaction. I told her I would talk to her dad and we would figure things out. I told her I loved her, how proud I was of her for telling me about this as I knew this took a lot of courage, and that everything would be okay. We hung up. I dropped my phone in my lap and started to cry uncontrollably.

My relationship with Emily's dad at the time was strained and I decided to send him a text message to start the conversation, so our past issues didn't get in the way of dealing with this devastating news.

What followed was the beginning of our journey to help Emily get the help she said she wanted for herself, help that she wanted on her terms as she believed she was smarter and stronger than all those other people.

She was wrong.

The coroner's report was received sometime later and indicated that she had passed away from multiple drug toxicity. She had heroin and methamphetamine in her system at potentially toxic levels. There was also cocaine, morphine, benzodiazepines, codeine and the chemical compound for marijuana in her system.

I remember thinking "Jesus, Emily...what were you thinking?!" Once again, I wondered if this was intentional. Did she want to end her life this way?

A few weeks earlier while I was out in California during the holidays, we were driving back to my hotel, arguing, and she said, "If you drop me off at my house, I'm going to go out and buy a bunch of heroin."

She had been clean for some time, so I considered this comment another attempt at manipulation. She was very skilled at manipulating people, especially me. Usually the goal was to get money in some way or another, and she almost always got her way eventually.

Every conversation we had was now under a microscopic review in my mind. I became obsessed in my investigation of everything that had transpired after we had spoken for what would be the very last time.

I started with the numbers on her phone bill. I called and left a message for the person she was texting. A recording indicated that the number was not in service at that time. This bothered me.

I spoke to her employer who told me he had seen her at work on New Year's Day, but she hadn't asked him for a raise. This confused and disturbed me greatly.

I spoke to her coworker who told she was having a very bad day at work, was visibly upset and told him that her friend had died. He told me he offered to take her home after they finished their day on January 1, and she asked him to drop her off at a friend's house in a not too nice part of San Francisco. This frightened me to my core.

I spoke to her roommate who told me that she had last seen and spoken to Emily after midnight on January 1. She said Emily told her about a friend who had just died, and she seemed, in her words, out of it. She asked her to stay up with them, but Emily said she was tired and went into her room. This cut me deeply.

I spoke to her other roommate who tried calling her numerous times and grew concerned when she didn't return his calls. Her phone appeared to have died as his messages went straight to voicemail after a day or so. This roommate eventually gained access into her locked bedroom, saw her body, and called 911. This destroyed all of me.

I spoke to the coroner's investigator several times to express my thought that she had duped me into giving her money as she didn't ask for a raise, and that my earlier remarks about her being in a good place in life was incorrect. To this day, the thought that the twenty dollars I sent her for the Uber was used to buy drugs that took her life takes my breath away and makes me sick to my stomach. There are no words for what this did and continues to do to me.

Two days after receiving the call, I boarded the plane to go back home and join Emily's dad and our older daughter to begin the ride on the most hideous and vile rollercoaster through blackness imaginable. The world as I knew it was gone. I prayed for that plane to crash.

*

SUSAN CARLYON
Susan's 22-year-old son Adam died from
an overdose of carfentanyl in 2016

I have always wanted to be a mom and I was blessed with two wonderful children, a daughter and a son. Adam was the youngest of my two children. He was a wonderful, kind, sweet, and caring person. He could do the best voice imitations. You couldn't help but smile and laugh when you spent time with Adam.

He was very polite and responsible. He was an employer's dream; the workplace always ran better when Adam was scheduled. He was also a teacher's dream student; never absent, earned straight As, never missed an assignment.

Adam would help out any friend when needed, no matter how big the favor was and without expecting anything in return. Adam was a loving son, brother, grandson, and nephew. His bright blue eyes, sparkling genuine smile, and infectious laugh could not only light up a room, but also your heart.

Adam loved video games, baseball, Star Wars, Pokémon, Airsoft, movies, history, Indian Guides, and the beach. We were a very close-knit family and we also had strong relationships with extended family and friends. We were the family who was always involved and went all out. We attended every sporting or school event our children were in. We volunteered both at their schools and with their sports teams.

The kids had amazing birthday celebrations every year with great themes and dozens of special extra touches. The four of us had so many traditions that meant so much to all of us. Christmas was a magical time with traditions galore for weeks.

Every summer we enjoyed such happy and fun times together at our favorite beach. Even the little things such as game nights, movie nights, special dinners, or going out to get ice cream at night were filled with love.

In March 2014, when Adam was nineteen, I noticed that something was just not right. He was attending Kent State University while living at home. As a mom, I knew something was wrong, but didn't know what. It would turn out to be something that I never would have guessed.

I made numerous appointments for Adam with psychologists and doctors. Adam seemed to be sick all the time, and he was very moody, emotional, and angry. I worried daily. What was wrong with my son?

A month later I was still looking for answers. One night at the end of April, Adam came to his dad and I and said he had to tell us something. He asked us to still love him and to not kick him out of the house. He then told us he was taking drugs. We were in total shock! My husband asked him what drugs he was using. He replied, "Heroin."

Adam said our neighbor had given him some heroin to snort and he had. After that one time, he was addicted. Everyone makes mistakes. Adam's bad decision would ultimately end his life. That night ended our lives as we had once known them. Adam started calling rehab places and help lines immediately, with us right by his side supporting him. This continued throughout the night. Adam was so frustrated. He kept asking us, "Why won't people help me when I am asking for help and wanting it?"

Adam told us he kept trying to quit on his own, but he couldn't, and he knew he needed help. When morning came, Adam asked us to drive him to the emergency room, as he was going through severe withdrawal. At the emergency room, we learned that it wasn't easy as we thought it would be to get help. After many disappointments, Adam registered at a free detox facility and waited in the parking lot for a bed to open. Thankfully, a bed became available that afternoon.

Watching the staff take Adam through the locked doors with his approved belongings, and knowing that we could have no contact with each other for a week, broke my heart. Adam spent a week going through their detox program and when released, returned home. He was extremely angry and didn't want to talk about drugs or what had happened. He returned to school the next day and took his final exams of the year. Our lives at home had changed. While Adam was angry, we were scared. We constantly worried that Adam would relapse. We were always wondering where he was, who he was with, and what he was doing. Adam did not want to go to any meetings, counseling, or outpatient programs. He said he was fine. And he was...for eighteen months.

In the fall of 2015, I started worrying about Adam again. He was sick all the time. He agreed to see a new doctor and have tests run. All the tests came back fine, but Adam was not acting like himself and it continued for months. I so desperately wanted to believe Adam when he said he wasn't doing drugs again.

In April 2016, Adam again said he needed to talk to his dad and me. He told us he had relapsed and was so upset with himself for going back to heroin. Adam said he knew he had to take it more seriously this time and do more than just detox. Once again, Adam made numerous calls trying to get help. I stayed with him for two days to help him through withdrawal until he could find a place. He finally got into a detox facility that had some rehabilitation classes, too.

Adam was released a week later and started outpatient classes the next day. He also went to group and individual counseling and attended Narcotics Anonymous meetings. Adam was given random weekly drug tests. He seemed to be doing well. He wasn't angry and he told me that it was up to him to stay clean and that was what he wanted. In July 2016, we went on our yearly trip to the beach. Adam was still attending an outpatient program, but we felt that this vacation time together, as a family, was important. We had the time of our lives! It was the best vacation ever! Adam was the Adam we had known and loved all his life. Three days after returning home, our worlds came crashing down.

On the afternoon of July 26, 2016, our daughter called her dad to tell him that Adam had not shown up for work and to check on him. My husband rushed home and found Adam's bedroom door locked. He broke down the door and found Adam on his bedroom floor. He wasn't breathing, but he was still alive. My husband started CPR immediately. He lives with the sights, sounds, and feelings of that moment each and every day. Narcan was also administered.

As soon as my husband called me, even though it was unexpected, I knew. How could this be happening? Adam was fine when I talked to him last! We were allowed to go back and see Adam after he was stabilized. The sight of him unconscious on the stretcher with tubes and monitors everywhere is seared in my brain. They needed to get Adam to the main hospital and admit him to the intensive care unit. We beat the ambulance to the hospital, and I still vividly remember the sight of my son being wheeled into the ICU.

We were told that Adam had been resuscitated six times and was alive but had sustained a great deal of brain damage and was in critical condition. We didn't leave his side. For eight hours, I stood next to him holding his hand, rubbing his head, kissing his cheek and talking to him in case he could hear my voice. I kept repeating over and over how much I loved him and how sorry I was for all he was going through. Adam's heart stopped beating again and even though the doctors were able to revive him, they said he couldn't take anymore. We had to make a decision about his care. Try to imagine a mother and father having to make the decision to end their son's life support.

My son was pronounced dead at 4:44 a.m. on July 27, 2016, with my husband, my daughter, and I by his side. It was so hard to turn away and walk out of his room. It took me two hours to leave.

An autopsy revealed that carfentanyl, an elephant tranquilizer, was found in Adam's system. It was disguised as heroin, yet contained no heroin. An amount the size of a poppy seed is deadly.

I have learned so much about drugs since Adam's passing. I wish I had known more before so that I would have understood his addiction. Addiction is a brain disease. It takes over your entire body. I deeply wish that people who knew he was doing drugs would have told someone and gotten him help. Adam's recovery folder told us how much he hated being under the grasp of the heroin addiction, how much he hated leading a double life, how much he hated making excuses, and how badly he wanted to be clean.

No parent should have their child die before they do, nor should any parent ever have to read their child's autopsy report or carry their child's casket. I carried Adam inside me for nine months when I was pregnant, and I was going to carry him out.

There are no words to adequately describe how much I miss and love Adam, how very sorry I am that he had to endure such a struggle, and how proud I am of his strength. Adam fought so very hard each and every day. He won many battles, but in the end he lost the war.

I will never be the same. There is a hole in my heart that can never be mended. I find it difficult to have a picture of my family taken because Adam is missing from the picture. The Carlyon name will never be passed on through the generations because Adam was the only grandson. I sleep on a pillow made from Adam's shirts, under a blanket made from his T-shirts, and holding one of his shirts...hoping that I can smell my son's scent.

I touch what Adam might have touched and use his chapstick. All my jewelry—a necklace, bracelet, earrings, and ring—are filled with Adam's ashes, because besides memories, this is all I have left of my Adam. And the rest of his ashes? We spread them at our favorite family beach on the one-year anniversary of his death, with our hearts breaking and tears streaming down our faces. It has been a little over three years since Adam passed away and my heart remains shattered. Nothing will ever be the same.

*

MARYBETH CICHOCKI
MaryBeth's 37-year-old son Matthew died
from a Percocet overdose in 2015

Have you ever met a guy whose smile could light up a room? Who made you feel like you had found a long-lost friend? The kind of guy who would give you the shirt off his back, and made every stray dog a family member? That was my son, Matt. He had that happy-go-lucky personality that drew people in and made them fall in love. Yet, Matt he never loved himself enough.

Matt experimented with marijuana in high school. He loved that high. He ended up in his first rehab while in high school. He spent thirty days as an inpatient in Newport News, Virginia. I foolishly thought that we beat his disease.

Matt went on to become an excellent mechanic. He moved to the beach, bought a home, and opened a business. His adult life appeared free of drugs. He was a successful adult. I took that deep breath and started to relax. Matt loved life and was living it to the fullest.

The beginning of his end began with a back injury. He was lifting an engine and felt a pop. The next day he could barely walk. He called to let me know he had been to his doctor and was given Percocet and told to take it easy. I remember a cold chill running up my spine. Call it mother's intuition or a flashback to his younger days. Being a nurse, I knew the dangers of any form of opioids and warned him to try to stay away. I knew his pain was real. I also knew his predisposition to become addicted.

Months passed and the signs were all there, yet I was in denial. Missing days at his office. Unpaid bills. Not returning my phone calls. Our close relationship was changing as the disease found him again. I felt like I was living the movie Groundhog Day, except this time Matt was an adult. My hands were tied.

Matt struggled with his addiction to Percocet for seven years. During that time, he lost everything he had worked so hard to gain. His business closed six months after his injury. He was abusing the pills and trying to continue working on cars. It was obvious to his steady customers that something was terribly wrong, and they took their business elsewhere. Mortgage payments were missed and Matt's beach house was repossessed by the bank. Everything he loved was gone. He came home to me.

Over those seven years, Matt was in and out of rehab. I referred to that time in our lives as the revolving doors of rehab. I felt like we were strapped to a rollercoaster, holding on for the ride of our lives. His insurance never permitted him to stay the length of time he needed to learn how to handle life without pills. He would come home clean and I'd look into clear eyes and thank God that Matt was back.

He was such a joy to be around. He never wanted to be that person who was tortured by cravings. Our life would just start to feel normal again but was always short-lived. Within weeks of returning home, he returned to his world of numbness and the cycle would begin again.

Matt had a horrible fear of needles. This gave me a false sense that I never had to worry about him graduating to heroin. Little did I realize that crushing Percocet and snorting it was just as deadly.

His last attempt to getting and staying clean took place at Bowling Green, a rehab close to home. After watching him struggle with the demons that plagued him most of his adult life, I was so proud and hopeful. Matt was coming back. His clear eyes and beautiful smile greeted me at each visit.

I remember us sitting together looking out over the water. Matt was headed to a recovery home in Florida. I was unsure about his decision, but every book I read had spoken of different people, places and things being the best choice for new sobriety.

Matt left for The Boca House on June 2, 2014. He wrapped me up in his big bearhug and told me he was so happy to have the monkey off his back. Little did I know that monkey would find him in Florida.

We spoke twice a day. I was going through withdrawals from him while he started a new life. Once again he was living by the sea, his happy place. He found a job and his self-esteem returned. I allowed myself to believe that this was his ah-ha moment, that finally he was in a good place in his life.

Our last words were spoken on a Friday night. My ears strained to pick up cues but found none.

"I love you, Mom."

"I love you, Matt."

For reasons my heart will never understand, Matt relapsed. He lost his battle on January 3, 2015.

Since Matt's death, I have been trying to pick up the pieces of my life. I started a support group for parents who, like me, have lost a piece of their hearts. I began writing letters to Matt and started a blog called Mothers Heart Break at mothersheartbreak.com. I share our story and educate others about the addictive properties of prescription opioids. I started a Facebook page, Breaking the Stigma of Addiction: Matt's Story. I post educational articles related to prescription drugs and their potential for abuse.

I would give anything for a do-over and to rewind time. Knowing what I know now, I would've held on tighter and never let him go.

*

KIM DELONG
Kim's 29-year-old son Tyler died
from a fentanyl overdose in 2017

Tyler was my firstborn son. I loved being his mother, and enjoyed watching him grow up. He brought a lot of joy and happiness to us all. His laughter and personality could light up a room.

Tyler had a wonderful sense of adventure and loved learning. He was an amazing young man, a free spirit. An honors student, he won many awards, received his black belt in karate, and learned to played guitar. He was a loving son, brother, grandson and nephew, and had lots of friends. Most of all, he was a good and kind person, and I was very proud of him for that.

Ty attended a few years of college and then dropped out. He got an apartment with roommates and had various jobs, working at UPS, gas stations and convenience stores. He started selling marijuana on the side and eventually quit his job. I tried to convince him to stop and get an honest job.

In August, we heard Tyler overdosed and had been saved with Narcan. He fully denied it, saying it must have been the person who stole his wallet during a robbery at his apartment several months prior. We were worried but had no reason to believe he was lying.

In November, I couldn't reach Tyler for several days. We usually spoke a few times a week and saw each other often, so it seemed odd. When I received a message asking if I would accept a call from the jail,

I thought it was spam. To my knowledge, Ty hadn't been in jail before, so we were shocked when we found out it was him.

We bailed him out on day five. Going through withdrawals, he looked awful. We asked what happened and he said, "I was giving my friend a ride and the police were following us and pulled us over. She had drugs on her and I didn't, but since I was driving, we were both charged with conspiracy to distribute drugs." Both were arrested and put in jail. They went to court a couple days later.

We brought Ty home to live with us so we could get him help. After being dope sick for almost two weeks, he started feeling better and looked so healthy. He told me he never wanted to ever feel that sick again. Tyler didn't want to die!

This was new to us and we didn't know where to begin. He went to some meetings and to an outpatient rehab program but checked himself out after the first day.

Ty had a heart of gold and was always helping friends, often to his detriment. When his friend AJ had nowhere to live, Tyler let him live in his apartment. After Ty passed, I found text messages between Ty and others stating that AJ was selling fentanyl from the apartment even though he knew Tyler was trying to get clean. His other roommates moved out on December 23, because of it.

Ty was going back to his apartment more frequently to pick up things. I was afraid he would be sucked back into the same old bad habits, and begged him not to go there. That was the last place Tyler went that night before he came home to my house.

The next day was Christmas Eve. While the rest of the world was getting ready to celebrate, I was wondering why Tyler was still sleeping. It was my mom's birthday and we yelled to him a few times that he needed to get up so we could go visit her.

When it got late and he didn't answer, we finally used the knob key to force our way into the bedroom. We found Tyler laying on his brother's bed. I reached out to wake him and he was so cold! He was gray and lifeless, and that's when I realized he was dead. I screamed and then kissed him on his head and said, "I love you Ty."

It's an image that haunts me. I couldn't believe it! I didn't want it to be true! Whenever I think of that day, I relive each horrific moment. My heart beats rapidly, I feel crushing pain in my chest and then the panic and anxiety take over. I want to scream at the world!

I have a hard time with trust now as I realize how Tyler's so-called friend was not a friend at all. The truth is that AJ was just another drug dealer trying to make a buck with absolutely no regard for Tyler's life or any other person's life, for that matter.

My heart aches constantly to hold Tyler, and to hear his voice, his laughter, and just one more of his stories. Every day I wake up, I immediately think about him and struggle to move forward with my day. I've cried myself to sleep so many times, as he's the last thought I have when I go to bed.

I often imagine what the future for Tyler would have been like, and it brings me to tears knowing his future is gone forever. I have trouble sleeping sometimes as my mind continues to replay the events of that horrific morning. The image of his cold, gray, stiff body lying there is forever burned in my mind.

I've had many nightmares where I wake up crying. I've replayed Ty's entire life so many times in my head. All the laughter, all the birthdays, all the school events, all the vacations, all the family time, and all the love and joy and memories spent with him over the years.

I feel guilty. Maybe I could've done something differently or done something that might have had a different result. I'm depressed and sad because Tyler was stolen from me. He'll never know the joy of being a husband, or a father, or an uncle.

My son Derek lost his only brother, his only sibling. His big brother Tyler wasn't there when he graduated from college last year. He won't be there when Derek starts his own family one day. Tyler will never share stories with Derek ever again. He won't ever laugh with him or give him brotherly advice.

My son is gone forever! I'll never again hear him laugh, feel his hugs, or see his smiling face looking at me. Mother's Day will always be bittersweet. I'll never hear him say, "I love you, Mom," ever again.

Christmas is a sad season for our family. It's a constant reminder of that unimaginable day when Tyler's life was snuffed out.

My son's sudden death has instilled in me a constant worry that something terrible will happen to my husband or other son. Whenever I hear parents talk about their children, I have difficulty being happy for them as it reminds me of the void of my very loved and missed son, and I have to remove myself either physically or mentally. Sometimes when I see parents with small boys, it brings me back to when Tyler was that age, and then panic sets in and I feel that awful pain again in my chest as I try to hold back the tears.

I've been to counseling, group meetings, and am currently on medication, but nothing ever takes the pain away. On the outside I might appear to be doing okay, but on the inside I'm dying. I've been sentenced to a lifetime of hell that no mother or parent should ever have to live.

After Tyler passed, I looked through his phone and learned a lot. Less than a year before he died, he met a young lady who was a heroin addict. He was so smitten with her that per his own admission, he soon started using just to be with her.

Although he sold marijuana, he had always been against hard drugs. We've had many conversations about it, and he was adamantly against it, so this was a huge surprise to us. I'll never know what made him use that first time.

It was six weeks from the day we learned of my son's addiction to the day he died. It went by so fast!

In May 2019, the friend who was living in Ty's apartment was sentenced to ten years in federal prison for his involvement in selling fentanyl for a major drug ring. Unfortunately, he could not be charged with my son's death because Tyler didn't have an autopsy.

*

ELAINE FAULKNER
Elaine's 25-year-old son Jacob died from
an overdose of opiates and Xanax in 2017

It was around the beginning of 2017. Jacob came over to our house to tell us he broke up with his girlfriend of two years. He said, "I want to make a fresh start."

He needed a place to live, and he learned that a basement apartment owned by some of our friends was available. He was so pleased to move into his own place, especially a place that was familiar to him. He was twenty-five years old and an adult, yet living in Pete and Delia's house would be like a second family for him. They have known Jacob since he was a baby.

Jacob got a job working construction on a new school building project. The contractor he worked for did not pay the crew their wages. Jacob was upset and angry, not just for himself, but for others on the crew who had families to support. He had emotional baggage from the painful end of the relationship with his ex-girlfriend, and now this violation of trust by his employer.

The silver lining was the unpaid crew were absorbed into a larger firm. The new employer was aware of the unpaid wages and gave them jobs. Jacob was able to continue supporting himself financially and was promoted as a leader on the crew.

We knew Jacob was struggling with anxiety and depression. He used substances to cope, along with drinking. Our anxieties about his use were quelled to some degree by his being employable and living in a safe and nurturing place. We kept the lines of communication open, and he would come home on Sundays to do his laundry.

When the construction job at the school site was completed, he decided to get a job as an electrician. It was his dream career. With the connections he made on the job, he was hired by an electrical company. He started working as a journeyman electrician and was excited to learn new skills.

He came over to do his laundry and announced, "I'm sober!" He told us he gave away all his marijuana pipes and stopped drinking. He seemed like his old self; one we hadn't seen in a while.

Two weeks later, he was back to his old habits. He lit up a pipe on our deck. I think he realized he was not able to stop using and gave up trying. He did not appreciate any offers to get counseling or professional help to stay clean. He left angry, and then sent me a string of angry text messages.

He did apologize for those texts later. It was typical of him when he was using. He was like Jekyll and Hyde. He had the sweetest heart, but when he was using, it was like being around a different person.

In the middle of spring, he came up with a new goal. He found a piece of land to buy and he wanted to build a "sweet" cabin on it. He texted, "I just want to know the feeling of standing on my own land and it would be all mine and not the banks."

He had the down payment saved from his construction job. The bank still turned him down for a loan. He had just started a new job and had no credit history. He was dispirited by this new turn of events. These were difficult lessons for him to learn. I received a text from him, "I just have to realize that life is a marathon, not a sprint."

His health began to suffer and he was sick a lot. He turned down invites to family events but kept in contact through text messages and an occasional visit. He was often tired. We observed that he was thin and pale. He hurt his back on the job. I was happy to hear that he was going to see a doctor. He talked about his depression and anxiety. He had a history of abusing pills, and I was uneasy about his use of medications, but at the same time I was hopeful that he would take care of himself and have medical supervision.

Ten days before he died, he got another prescription for Xanax, OxyContin, and medication for high blood pressure. In his last week of life, he flew in a small plane over the San Juan islands to work at a job site on Orcas Island every day. I can visualize him sitting in the window seat, loving the amazing view, and dreaming about his cabin. Sunday evening we got a call from Pete at the house where Jacob was living. Jacob had not responded to text messages from them asking him to join their family for fresh caught crab at dinnertime. It was unusual for Jacob to not respond to an invitation to eat. When Pete went to check on him, there was no reviving him, he was gone.

Multiple pill bottles were found by the police at the scene, the medical examiner ruled his death an accidental overdose.

*

SHANNIE JENKINS
Shannie's 31-year-old son Kyle died
from a heroin overdose in 2017

Kyle fought the battle of addiction for ten years at the time of his death. He had been through treatment three times.

Kyle was a fisherman in the Bering Sea, where he found his love for the sea. He stayed sober when at sea but fought the battle after returning home.

Kyle went to prison for a year in 2015, when he woke up to a place he knew he did not belong. He attended a rehab program while in prison. When he was released, He had Vivitrol implanted in his stomach. This medication stopped his brain from all the anxiety and triggers. After a year of being on the medication, he made the decision to get off it, which he did.

He was attending Bates Vocational School in the HVAC program and excelling in class. He worked on the weekends with his professor and loved the work. He was in a relationship and had fallen in love. Kyle became a daddy figure to his girlfriend's five-year-old son, and was soon to be a daddy himself. He was happier than he had ever been, and his life was falling into place.

Kyle ran into an old friend who suffered from addiction. Kyle smoked heroin and died instantly at his kitchen table. Brittany, his fiancée, came home and found him. She performed CPR until medics arrived, but Kyle had already passed.

The police called me at 10:30 p.m. that my son had passed away. My husband drove me to Kyle's apartment where I found Brittany sitting on the stairs in shock, with the police and coroner in Kyle's apartment. The coroner prepared his body so we could go in and say goodbye to our precious son.

Kyle was always open and honest about his disease, which allowed me to be open and honest, too. I always told him if this disease ever took him, I would not be quiet. I have been loud and speaking out about this epidemic killing so many of our beautiful young people.

Kyle was not only my son, he was also my best friend. His son, Knox Kyle Brinton, was born the following April. I had the pleasure of stepping into my son's shoes and being the support person for when his fiancée gave birth. Life will never be the same.

*

LORI LATIMER
Lori's 29-year-old son Greg died from
alcohol and fentanyl-laced cocaine in 2019

At 10:09 on Sunday, January 6, 2019, I received that call that no parent ever wants to get. My son Greg's girlfriend, Bethany, called and said Greg's roommate had called and told her that Greg was dead. I remember yelling into the phone, "What?"

I didn't burst into tears. I didn't fall on the floor. I went straight into shock and disbelief. I told Bethany I would drive up to the house Greg was living in so we could figure out what happened. She called me back a few minutes later and said that Greg wasn't at the house. Still in shock and disbelief, I asked her where he was. I thought maybe he's at the hospital. My mind simply could not process any of it. I still couldn't accept that my precious son was gone.

I called my older son, Steve, and my ex-husband to tell them what I'd been told. Then I headed out to find my child.

As I was driving toward his house, my cellphone rang again. A man asked for me, then he uttered words I will never forget.

"Ma'am, this is the Bartow County coroner."

I remember softly saying, "Noooo. Please, no."

That's when I knew what I didn't want to believe was true. In that instant, my entire life as I knew it had just been completely shattered.

I asked where Greg was and said I wanted to see him. The coroner was extremely kind but tried to talk me out of seeing him. I called my son Steve again, and he told me to come to his house.

Despite what the coroner advised, I had to see my son. I was there when he took his first breath, but I wasn't there when he took his last. I had to see him, and nothing on this earth was going to stop me. So Steve, their dad, and I went to the morgue.

The last place I saw my beautiful, precious son was in a morgue. I held him. I kissed him. I told him how much I loved him, and how very proud I was to be his mom. And I told him that my parents, his grandparents, were waiting for him in heaven and that it was okay for him to be with them. It was the hardest thing I've ever done, but it was the last act of love I could do for my child in this life.

Then came the questions. So many questions. I had just seen Greg the day before at a golf course to give him a bowl of clam dip I'd made. It was my dad's recipe and Greg loved it. He was fine! I hugged and kissed him and told him I loved him. He hugged me back and said he loved me. That was the last time I saw my son alive. What happened?

No one seemed to know what had happened. After playing golf that afternoon, Greg and his roommates had gone out to a local bar. Being responsible because they were drinking, they took an Uber to and from the bar. I later found the Uber charge on Greg's phone.

They got home around midnight and played video games. His two roommates went to bed around 2 a.m., but Greg stayed up. When his roommates got up Sunday morning, they found his lifeless body on the kitchen floor. He had a spoon in his hand. They thought he had choked. One of them tried to do CPR on him, but it was far too late.

Because Greg was young and in good health, his body was taken to the Georgia Bureau of Investigation for an autopsy. It took almost two months to get the final autopsy report. His official cause of death was mixed drug toxicity. Greg died of a lethal combination of alcohol and cocaine laced with fentanyl. I was heartbroken all over again.

Greg was working full time and attending college full time, earning straight As. He earned his associate degree and was just over a year away from earning his bachelor's. He consistently made the Dean's List. He was dating a lovely young lady who had two adorable little girls. They planned on moving in together later in the year and getting married the following year.

Greg loved life. He loved to travel. We took a trip to Italy in 2016. I remember the first afternoon we were there. He kept saying "Mom, I feel like I'm walking around in a painting."

He fell in love with red wine in Tuscany. He bought an Italian silk shirt and a pair of Italian loafers. He loved the beauty of the Amalfi coast. He and his girlfriend hiked and camped their way through northern California, northern Arizona, Utah, and Colorado. He and his friends traveled through Nevada and the southern California desert. He loved to look up at the stars at night. From the time Greg was a little boy, he was fearless. He grew up loving to have new adventures.

He adored his nephews, and they adored him. He loved watching them play sports. Sadly, he never met his youngest nephew, Hudson, who was only five weeks old when Greg died.

Greg had a passion for life, and was the life of the party. He loved summers in Georgia and floating down the river with his friends. He had a laugh that was infectious. And he loved his dog, Capone. He raised Capone from the time he was a puppy. Greg loved to take Capone hiking and to the lake. Sadly, Capone grieved Greg's death so much that he joined Greg in heaven just five months after Greg.

From the time Greg was a little boy, he wanted to play football. He played all the way through high school. He was named Defensive Player of the Year all four years of high school. Greg and I loved going to Atlanta Falcons football games and Atlanta Braves baseball games. Greg started doing jujitsu in his mid-twenties. He quickly earned his white belt and his blue belt. He watched what he ate and was very health conscious. Except...

Greg started drinking and smoking pot in high school. A year or two before his death, he told me he was doing mushrooms. I told him several times to be careful, and to be very careful about who he bought it from. I had no idea he was doing cocaine or heroin until after he died. From what I've learned since his death, Greg was a recreational drug user. He never used needles. The coroner said all his organs were normal for his age, so he had no organ damage from alcohol or drugs. He really was your average, all-American young man.

Greg cheated death three times, and those experiences had a profound effect on him. The last time was less than two months before his death. He was working and a man deliberately attempted to run over Greg and his coworkers, then pulled a gun on them. Greg was traumatized but wouldn't acknowledge it. I realize now that he turned to drugs in an accelerated way after that experience. His personality changed. I thought it was due to what happened at work, but I now realize it was also the drugs. Because I didn't have the slightest idea that he was using cocaine, I never had the chance to help him.

I had dinner with Greg three days before his death. He was sniffling and I asked if he was sick. It was a cold, rainy night. He said it was allergies and from working outside in the weather. I had no reason to doubt him. He was twenty-nine and didn't live at home. I saw him once a week or once every other week. It was easy for him to hide it from me. Looking back, I now see things from a much different vantage point.

I've never done drugs. My sons' father never did drugs. We were divorced, but they grew up in good, middle-class homes. We co-parented well together. If this can happen to my child, it can happen to anyone's child.

That one phone call on a beautiful Sunday morning in January, changed the trajectory of my entire life. It left a family shattered. It left me questioning everything I ever believed in. It brought me to tears and to my knees more than anything in my life ever had. If there's a hell worse than life after losing a child, I don't ever want to know what it is, let alone experience it.

*

AMANDA MARIE
Amanda's 30-year-old brother Cory
died from a heroin overdose in 2015

I wish I could fill this chapter with wonderful stories from our childhood, but I can't. Things weren't easy for either of us. Sometimes, that fact makes Cory's untimely death even more difficult because he didn't get much of a chance to have the life he so desperately wanted. He never went to college. He never got to marry or have children. He never got to travel. He never achieved any of the goals that he openly fantasized about so often.

Even though the good memories were few and far between, there were some, most of which occurred in the year before Cory died. I'm thankful for them all.

Cory's addiction may have turned him into someone who was difficult to like sometimes, there were also so many things about him to love. He was generous, and willing to give his last dollar to the man on the street. He was extroverted with a confidence I never seemed to gain, and could make friends with anyone wherever he went.

While Cory was a talker, he was also a listener which surely added to his charisma when "trying to find a wife," as he so succinctly put it. His sparkling smile didn't hurt either. He was silly in a way that would embarrass most people and loved to get a laugh. He was a hard worker and took pride in pointing at buildings, describing his participation in the project and gloating at his accomplishments.

Cory enjoyed fishing, and had no trouble at all getting up at the crack of dawn to sit in silence for hours waiting for a bite, just to throw whatever he caught back in the lake. He loved to be physically active and lift weights, play basketball and toss a football back and forth.

Although he wasn't very artistic, Cory loved to draw and write poetry, even though his spelling and grammar were poor. He wasn't musically inclined yet would make mixtapes, speaking his poems over instrumental melodies. He loved to read even though sometimes he would admit to not understanding the concept of the book. Although no one ever taught him how, he enjoyed cooking and the challenge of creating delicious meals on a tight budget.

Cory could see a future that didn't involve pain or addiction, and certainly not death. For a while, I could see it for him too.

*

DIANA MITCHELL
Diana's 18-year-old daughter Brooke died from
a mix of fentanyl, ecstasy, and cocaine in 2017

It was June 2015. I'll never forget it because the doorbell rang and it was really late; nobody comes to see us after 10 p.m. I opened the door and my daughter was standing in the walkway telling me she was a heroin addict.

Talk about having the rug pulled out from under your feet. You see, my daughter was always an honor roll student and never got in trouble one day of her life. She was a good kid.

First thing out of my mouth was, "Where in the world would you find heroin? And what would make you try it?"

"I was at a party and everybody was doing it."

I never thought she was a follower, but she was with a cute boy when she decided to try it. She became addicted immediately.

From the day she told me until the day I lost her was seventeen months. It was incredibly quick.

Where we live, we don't have a lot of help for seventeen and under. She was on the cusp of turning eighteen. So different programs wouldn't take her. I finally had to send her to a treatment center in Florida. She was there for forty-five days.

When she came home from drug rehab, she packed up and moved to Rome, New York. She was there for a couple months when she got sick and was put in the hospital. I brought her back home.

She was trying very hard to stay away from anyone who had anything to do with drugs, and we were blessed with a wonderful Christmas and Thanksgiving with her.

We spent the prior Thanksgiving in the emergency room because Brooke was detoxing. She was in so much pain yet was treated so badly by the emergency room personnel. The nurses and doctors looked at her as a drug addict, and of course they looked at me like I had done something wrong that caused my child to get into drugs. That's how society views you once your child makes such a decision.

The hospital staff came and talked to her about what her journey is going to be and what it's like. All I could think about was, oh, she's just seventeen and has no idea what she did to herself and what she's facing, but they don't understand that. After a heated discussion, I finally got them to listen and to treat her like she was a human being. I reminded them that she's a child who made a mistake. It wasn't like she was a forty-year-old who knew better.

After that Thanksgiving, we spent Christmas at home and then had New Year's Day dinner at my best friend's house. That evening when we got home, Brooke and I had some words when she decided to go out with her brother. She came into my room and said, "Mom, I'm going to Dylan's. I love you. I'll talk to you tomorrow."

Those were the last words I heard from my child.

She had just registered for college and gotten all her textbooks that morning. She was going to be a nurse and was so excited.

My son said Brooke got in the car with some people she had been avoiding. They went to buy what they thought was heroin. They did three lines and my daughter had a massive heart attack. They chose not to take her to the hospital and ran around with her for two hours, actually driving past our house a few times.

The police came to our door, and we went to the hospital for the longest walk of my life.

I knew that by Brooke making the choices she did, her likelihood of surviving wasn't good.

I prayed night after night to find something to help her with this addiction and let her overcome this huge demon, but none of us knew how, and the help wasn't really there unless you have a lot of money for the good type of help. Even though we had insurance, we still had a heck of a time getting treatment. In fact, we got a letter afterward from the insurance company stating that they were denying treatment for an addiction issue.

Brooke was dynamic. She was on the swim team and graduated with high honors. While in drug rehab, she was determined to beat this. I've since learned that she didn't have a chance because of the type of drugs on the streets.

Never in a million years would I have thought my daughter would try a drug like heroin.

*

WHITNEY O'BRIEN
Whitney's 23-year-old brother Michael died from
a heroin/cocaine/benzodiazepine overdose in 2016

I vividly remember the night I found out my brother was using heroin. It was in July 2014. It was miserably hot outside—typical for Arizona. I had just given birth to my first child two months earlier.

Around 1 a.m. I was jolted awake not by the cries of my newborn son, but by back-to-back calls from a number I didn't recognize. I ignored it three times before finally answering, afraid of what I might hear on the other end.

It was a police officer stating that he had pulled my brother over for driving under the influence.

"What was he under the influence of?" I asked.

"Ma'am, he will have to tell you that himself," he answered.

I went back and forth for a minute or two with the officer, trying to convince him this was all a misunderstanding. Michael had just started a new medication to treat his bipolar disorder and I explained that it made him extremely drowsy. The officer cut me off.

"Ma'am, you can either come pick him up or he's going to sit in jail for a very long time."

I got dressed, checked on the baby, and assured my husband I would be home as soon as possible and before our son's next feeding.

When I pulled up to the station, the police officer met me outside. He asked me for identification, I signed a few papers, and Michael was released. Without muttering a word, he got in my car and I drove him home to our parents' where he still lived. They were out of town for the weekend, or they likely would have been on the receiving end of that call. Several minutes passed before I broke the silence and asked Michael what he was under the influence of.

"Heroin," he said.

It took everything I had to conceal the panic pulsing through me. I looked over at my brother. He was leaning against the passenger door with his elbow propped on the arm rest. He looked defeated; his eyes wouldn't meet mine. He was clearly not proud of his answer yet also seemed relieved, as if a weight had been lifted off his shoulders when that word escaped his mouth. I asked if he was using intravenously.

"No, no, no. God no. I just smoke it. But I only use it every now and then," he said.

I was naïve enough to believe him. I knew nothing of the perils of addiction. Especially opiate addiction. Honestly, I didn't even know heroin was opioid even though I'm a nurse.

It was no secret my brother had experimented with drugs over the years. However, the occasional experimentation had progressed into a daily habit, then an addiction, and now a disease.

I always struggled to understand his addiction. It wasn't until after Michael's death that I finally was able to piece together life events that led to his demise.

My brother was born in the early hours of January 11, 1993. I'm told it was a cold and bizarrely foggy morning for Phoenix. I was a month shy of my fifth birthday, and his arrival completely changed life as I knew it. I marched into my mother's hospital room, plopped myself down in the recliner and with outstretched arms announced, "I'm ready for my baby now!" I took my role as big sister very seriously, considering myself less of a sister and more of a second mother.

Since that day, an instinctual need to protect him has governed me, and I maintained a watchful eye over his every move for the course of his entirely too short life.

With Michael's arrival came the earliest memories of my life. I remember my parents taking me to my aunt and uncle's house in the middle of the night on their way to the hospital. I recall my dad spraying No More Tangles in my hair and attempting to gently comb through the mess before taking me to meet my new brother.

I even remember what I was wearing the first time I held Michael; bright pink sweatpants with a white collared shirt, paired with white sneakers and scrunchy 90s style socks. I always remember what I'm wearing during momentous times, which is why I'll never forget the dress I wore to Michael's funeral twenty-three years later.

In the months leading up to his birth, before my parents knew the gender of my new sibling, I would confidently declare, "It's a boy!"

"But how do you know?" asked my mother.

"Because that's what I want. A brother."

So then, we were a family of four.

As a child, Michael was a smart, temperamental boy with thick, beautiful auburn hair. It was such a unique color of red, my mother was once asked by a woman if she had dyed it—Michael was three.

Curiosity over the red color was fed not just by the rarity, but also because neither Mom nor Dad had red hair, yet both their children did. Not privy to the rare shade of chestnut that was granted my brother, my color was often referred to as strawberry blonde which faded to mostly brown with time, hidden under years of coloring and heat damage, which Michael's hair only got better with age.

For many years, Michael bore a clean-shaven, militaresque flat top, a look influenced by our grandfather. After months of relentless coaxing, I finally convinced him to grow it out. As it grew, it curled and spiraled into the most striking male head of hair I've ever seen. Michael's hair was a regular cause for conversation and unsolicited attention throughout his life. Once, while riding the ski lift to the top of Big Bear mountain in California, a group of gawking teenagers mistook him for Shaun White. It wouldn't be the only time he was confused for the famous Olympian. Women, especially, marveled at his locks, and longed for such a color they could never get from a box of dye. Michael's hair would become a huge part of who he was.

Around the time he began walking and talking, I thought of him less affectionately and more as a nuisance who was constantly vying for my attention. Much to my chagrin, you could always find him hovering, following, or chasing me around. It was maddening.

We had a knack for instigating each other. If Michael was sitting in the beloved recliner in our living room, I would stake him out, waiting for an opportunity to swoop in and steal the chair. This became such a problem that each time we stood to leave, our mother had us start announcing, "I get here when I get back!" If we failed to recite said mantra, the chair was fair game for the other to claim.

Although we pranked each other most of the time, occasionally we joined forces and became allies against our parents, something we enjoyed doing well into our adult years. As kids, when sitting in the backseat of our mother's Honda Accord, we took turns smacking our hands together as loudly as possible followed by a howling yelp or cry, as if we'd just been slapped by the other. Infuriated and fed up with our fighting, our parents would threaten us from the front seat, which sent us into fits of giggles, laughing so hard we gasped for air.

We grew up in a cul-de-sac of an up-and-coming neighborhood with several other young families. We rode bicycles and scooters. We took turns driving around the block in the go-cart we received from Santa one year and were expected to share. We played outside until the sun went down. We escaped the miserable Phoenix summers by heading north where it was cooler. We camped in the woods and built forts and treehouses, caught critters, and slept bunkbed style in our family's camping trailer.

Michael loved fishing and hunting, a hobby he shared with our father. Their favorite place to fish was the Black River, which required intense hiking and a watchful eye for black bears. Michael was twenty-one when he shot his first bull elk—a proud moment for father and son after years of teaching and preparation.

It was an idyllic upbringing with fond memories and experiences. Although we certainly weren't poor, our parents worked hard to give us everything. We wanted for nothing. I look back on our childhood with nothing but wonderful, happy memories. We had a mom and dad who loved us and supported our every interest, dream, and desire. We grew up feeling safe and secure, just as all children should.

It wasn't until I was an adult when it occurred to me that perhaps my brother didn't feel the same way about our childhood. A year before his death, I learned that he had been molested around age five by our neighbor. It happened on more than one occasion. These acts were deliberate and calculated, and even though the perpetrator was a minor, he was old enough to know right from wrong. He ingratiated himself and took advantage of my brother's naivete and emotional vulnerability by grooming, luring, and controlling him.

Regretfully, we never had any inkling or suspicions. My brother did his best to bury and suppress his emotional trauma by never letting himself think, feel, or remember any of it. Try as he might, I'm not sure he was able to entirely bury the shame and pain. Learning of his abuse has helped me understand why Michael was so overwhelmed by his feelings all his life. He experienced emotions ten times what you or I might feel. He could be very irritable, angry, and introverted. But when he felt happy, he was euphoric. It wasn't until his early twenties when he was finally diagnosed with bipolar disorder—something I had suspected for years.

As he skated into his teen years, Michael's struggles became ever more present. He enjoyed alternative sports such as skateboarding, riding dirt bikes and BMX. His prized possession was a cobalt blue Fit bike. While out riding he once faceplanted onto a sewage grater, leaving his face a bloody, mangled mess. I accompanied him to the emergency room that night, as it was my unwavering sisterly duty to see to it that he be properly taken care of.

Hidden beneath those wavy copper-colored locks, Michael had started gauging his earlobes and would soon have holes the size of silver dollars. He also pierced and gauge his septum, which further perturbed our parents who were still trying to adjust to his expanding ear lobes. Some might call his gauging self-expression while others would argue it self-mutilation. He later divulged he had experimented with cutting while in high school. His risk-taking behavior was reaching a new high.

During his sophomore year of high school, I was cautiously optimistic when he began dating Erika. Anxious and shy until you got to know her, Erika was my brother's first real relationship. At times, I couldn't figure out why she was attracted to him. After all, she was bright, driven, kind, beautiful—so what was she doing dating my brother? Yet when he was around her, we saw a side of him we didn't get to see very often. He became tender and sensitive and was truly his best version of himself when he was with her. They were together on and off for the next four years. She was the love of his life.

As graduation neared it became apparent that Michael didn't necessarily have a career picked out or any plans for college. It was frustrating because he could have done anything. He had the intellect of an engineer. He once took apart the motor from his go-ped just to put it back together again. No one ever taught him how, he just knew. He understood the mechanics of engines and machines without ever having any formal training.

After graduation, he began working for my father's construction company. It was wonderful in that it gave him a sense of purpose and self-fulfillment, two things he desperately needed to thwart his self-doubt. He was driven by the prospects of impressing my father but their work relationship strained an already difficult personal relationship. They were two of a kind, and therefore clicked and clashed.

When they weren't at each other's throats, my brother worked admirably by my father's side. Because of their on and off relationship, he was especially close to my mother. As I watched her expend all her energy into my brother and his addiction, I often questioned their connection as co-dependent and dysfunctional. Regardless, I've never seen a mother-son relationship as devoted as theirs.

After I got married and started a family, it was important for Michael to be involved in my children's lives. Being an uncle was something he relished and took on wholeheartedly. It is not lost on me the amount of love and adoration my brother had for me. I always knew he looked up to me, but he truly put me on a pedestal. I wished he had the same amount of respect for himself that he had for me.

I couldn't have known it then, but the night I received that call to come pick up my brother was the start of his unraveling. I replayed that night in my head over and over again for several years.

What if I wouldn't have picked him up?

What if he would have sat in jail?

Maybe he would have gotten sober?

Maybe he would still be alive?

The what-ifs and should-haves never seem to end. His heroin use escalated out of his control. It was only a matter of time before he went from occasionally smoking heroin to injecting himself multiple times a day. I laid awake at night worried sick about him.

It's been three years and I'm still muddling through the aftermath of his passing. I struggle every day with the reality of his death. Often, I'm hit out of nowhere with this incredible feeling of disbelief that he is no longer here. It still takes my breath away. It still does not seem real to me. Losing him has been the biggest tragedy of my life.

I want to be honest about the unpleasant realities of addiction. I've been torn between sharing too much and not sharing enough. It's important that I be as transparent and thorough as possible so that I don't leave blanks for others to fill with their own imagination.

My brother's story needs to be heard, and I have taken it upon myself to be his voice. I am my brother's keeper. I do this for myself in hopes of healing my broken heart, if that is even possible. I do this for my parents whom I am vehemently devoted to. I do this for others who are tortured by this brutal disease. But ultimately, I do this for Michael. Because he was meant to do so much more.

*

ALICE RICH
Alice's 42-year-old brother Gary
died from a fentanyl overdose in 2015

Let me start off by saying that you would not meet a more likable, funny, genuine guy than Gary. He never met a stranger and he had an unforgettable, infectious laugh that could be heard throughout the house. I will never forget that laugh; what I would give to hear that laugh again.

Gary was a good 'ole boy. He liked his beer and liked to drink with the boys. This is where heroin was introduced. A neighbor of his brought it to Gary's one night when he and the boys were drinking in his garage. We will never know what he was thinking, or why he would even try heroin in the first place. I like to think it was a drunken lack of judgment, a bad decision. It was all downhill after that.

Gary proceeded to use more frequently as heroin dug its ugly claws in deeper and deeper. He almost became unrecognizable. He began stealing from everyone, even family, to get drug money. He even stole gas to be able to go get the drugs. I don't know if he knew what was happening to him at this point, but he had lost all control. That's not all he lost: he lost his wife, his house, his truck, his job, and no one could trust him any longer. If he was going to be where we were, we hid all purses and valuables. Afraid for his life, we all hoped he would go to jail. At least there he would be safe. At what seemed to be his lowest point, that's exactly what happened—he got arrested. Sigh of relief.

Once he was released, it seemed that we had our Gary back, but in what felt like no time at all, he started using again. Now living with our parents, because he essentially owned nothing but a few clothes, they were pulled onto the rollercoaster, the tug-of-war between Gary and heroin.

Mom and Dad spent countless dollars on rehab, treatments, and medication to no avail. He was selling the drug he was supposed to be taking and used the money to buy heroin instead. Sadly, he had the desire to quit, to have his life back, but the drug was stronger. Heroin always had a pull on him. I always thought Gary was so strong, and he was, physically. I never imagined something as small as a drug could have so much control over him. That happened to other people.

The summer before he died, we all thought he was on the brink of recovery. He was functioning, he went to church a few times, he had a nice girlfriend, and he worked off and on. Most of all, he seemed happy. But he was still using. Deaths due to overdose were all over the news and seemed to be on the rise. Every time I saw Gary, I told him that I was afraid that it would be the last time. I told him I loved his laugh and how much I would miss it if he died. "I'm not going to die," he said, and laughed a big laugh like only he could.

He overdosed three times that summer that I know of, and was revived with Narcan. The fear we all felt was real, it was deep—the fear of the truth. The truth was that our son, brother, dad was a heroin addict and going to die.

I bore my soul to Gary. I spoke to him from my heart with all the sisterly love I had. I cried and held him as I told him I didn't want him to die. We talked for a long time, and he said he didn't want to be the way he was. He said that the last time he woke in the emergency room, he secretly wished he had died so he didn't have to fight the battle any longer. He was tired. I held him tight, afraid it would be the last.

Gary went to rehab at the VA hospital that fall. This was going to be the magic time, the miracle we were all praying for. He got out in time for Thanksgiving. We were supposed to all have dinner together at our parents' house. He did not show up (he did that during holidays and birthdays). He called me about a week later and we had a nice talk. I told him "I love you, Gary." He said he loved me, too.

A few days later he called Mom on a Tuesday night. He said he was just checking in because he knew she worried about him. He assured her he was okay, and again they told one another that they loved each other.

I got the call the next day at work. It was Wednesday. My dad was calling, which was odd for the middle of a Wednesday. He said my name, and I knew. He did not need to say any more.

He choked through it. "Alice...your brother."

I heard the words "E.R.," "overdose," and "braindead."

My whole body went numb and it was hard to think.

"Dad, did you call Angie?"

"I can't," he said.

I told him I would call her, and would be there as soon as I could. I was at work and there were kids to get situated. Don't panic, I told myself. But first I had to call Angie, our sister. Angela lived in Florida. Whenever something happened with Mom or Dad, I would call her and let her know. She would always ask, "Do I need to come home?"

SURVIVING LOSS BY OVERDOSE

I looked her name up on my phone's favorites list and tapped on her name. She answered, and I said, "You need to come home."

"Is it Gary?" she asked. I said yes and tried to tell her the bits and pieces my brain held onto.

"I'll be right there," she told me.

I made it to the emergency room after what seemed like the longest drive. I walked in and immediately saw my parents there in the waiting room. I made a few calls for them as they asked me to. Gary's ex-wife and children arrived. We all had the same sad, puzzled look on our faces. Finally, we were allowed to see him.

The nurse took us to what looked like a trauma bay, and it looked as though they had been working hard on him. His face and body were so swollen, it almost didn't look like Gary. He was ventilated, meaning there was a tube down his throat to his lungs allowing a machine to breathe for him. His chest moved up and down with the sounds of the machine. Monitors were hooked up, lines were coming from different places, and he had a urinary catheter. There were ice packs around him. His hands were tied to the side of the cart. His heart was beating. He could still be okay, my brain said.

The doctor told us that Gary appeared to be braindead. They wanted to watch him for twenty-four hours and check again. I could see the hope on my mom's face. Don't get false hope, Mom, I thought.

Gary and all his lines, tubes, and machines were moved to the intensive care unit. More and more family began to appear, and we went back to be with him a few at a time. The rest of us just sat or paced, trying to make sense of it all. No one was thinking clearly, and it was apparent that we were all in varying states of shock.

Angie landed around 10:30 p.m., and Dad and I went to pick her up. It was a short drive to the airport from the hospital. We went back to the hospital, and Angie and I went back to see Gary. Seeing him like that for the first time was the hardest part. We held his hand and touched his face. We talked to him and even made a joke or two with him while simultaneously breaking down into tears. Eventually we all went home except for Gary's daughter, Kendall. She stayed the night with her dad.

We tried to piece together the events of Gary's day. Apparently, he was helping his girlfriend's mom and her daughter get Christmas decorations down and begin decorating for Christmas. He excused himself to use the bathroom and never came back.

The details are blurry, but I believe the little girl had to use the bathroom and could not get in. Gary was lying on the floor against the door, and the grandmother couldn't get it open on her own and ran to get a neighbor to help. It was only after they returned did she think to call 911. There was Narcan in the house but either she did not know about it or forgot in the moment.

The paramedics arrived and gave Gary more than one round of Narcan and CPR, transported him to the emergency room, but his brain had been without oxygen for too long. His strong heart survived but his brain could not.

About an hour later tests confirmed that Gary was braindead. There was no brain activity. The machines were keeping him alive. In the midst of that news, we were approached about Lifebanc. Gary would have given you the shirt off his back. Certainly, he would want this. My parents agreed and were off to do paperwork. I believe we went home for a night of fitful rest. Angie stayed with Gary that night.

During the night, Gary's nurse brought a new nurse in to show her what track marks look like. That's all well and good but not with his sister sitting right there. The nurses see a heroin addict, but we see our loved one. We see our brother, our father, our son, our baby.

The next night, Gary's ex-wife Belinda and I stayed with him. Belinda will always love Gary. "This is what I was trying to avoid, yet here I am," she said through tears.

The Lifebanc person came in to tell us that the last home for donation had fallen through. It was time to turn off the life support. This was almost worse news than finding out he had overdosed. The words landed in my head like a bomb. All the emotions that were inside me for the last two days began running out. I called Mom, Dad, and Angela to see if they wanted to come. Angela had taken something for sleep and could not come back. Mom and Dad said their goodbyes when they left earlier in the night. I called my husband Mark to come be with me. I was afraid of what was to come.

He arrived an hour later, and we told the nurse it was time. I was on Gary's right side and Belinda was on the left. Mark was behind me. "Do you want the monitor on?" they asked.

"I don't know. Do I? I've never done this before."

Mark said, "No," and the nurse turned it off. Better to not watch the flat line when his heart died. His strong healthy heart. I wish I could save that piece of him. We all wanted desperately for some part of Gary to live on, to help someone else. He could have made another family's Christmas wish come true.

The monitor went off, the IVs went off, and then the ventilator went off. Immediately his chest flattened out with the last breath of the machine and it never rose again.

"Breathe, Gary, breathe."

Nothing. He really was dead; this is really the end. My baby brother. He is so warm. Sobbing, I put my head on his chest to hear his heartbeat. It beat faster at first, maybe harder, too. I loved the sound of his heart—the piece of him that was still alive. Wait, is it suffering? Does a heart suffer as it dies? I opened my eyes to look at him. His lips and tips of his ears were turning bluish-purple. I did not want to see that. I looked at his hand, which was tight in mine. His nails were turning blue and his hand already began to feel cold. His heartbeat began to slow.

I am not sure how much time has passed. I can hear Belinda crying and feel Mark's hands on my back. Slower, slower, and slower still. Did it stop? Not yet.

Thump . . . thump . . . thump . . . thump . . thump . . thump . . . thump . . . thump. . . . . . . He was gone.

I sobbed with my head on his chest, still holding his hand. His hand was white. I did not want to see his face that color. Eyes closed, crying, I kissed his face, his head, and his big hand. I turned around and never looked back. Mark held me in the hall until Belinda came out. She needed time alone to say goodbye.

It was over.

*

CAROL WALL
Carol's 29-year-old son Jason died
from a heroin overdose in 2016.

How can I sum up my precious son's life in "what happened?" It was like a runaway train, it took on a life of its own and I feel when we stopped to catch our breath, Jason was gone. I feel he ran out of time, that is how quickly it felt to us.

My son Jay was the youngest of three. He grew up in a very loving, normal family. He had every opportunity presented to him through sports, travel, and education, and was deeply loved.

Jason lived to the extreme. He would try anything, drugs and alcohol included. To his detriment, nothing scared him. He was such a character! Very intelligent, very driven, very funny.

An accomplished athlete, Jay had traveled extensively, could play guitar and drums, and was a successful fifth year electrical apprentice. He owned his own home and was daddy to a precious little boy.

He had a lot of very close friends growing up, but, sadly, they didn't stick around when he needed them the most. This is what this drug does …. he had everything to lose by continuing to take it, but it didn't matter, the drug was stronger.

Looking back and learning so much about addiction in the last year and a half, the warning signs were there, though very subtle at first. When your child is outgoing, excels in school, and has lots of friends, you don't look closely for signs of masking problems. You are just happy your child is normal.

I don't know when things started to get out of hand. We were always honest in our family about the dangers of drugs. We didn't hide our heads in the sand. Jay entered adolescence doing the normal things teenagers did, though I can't believe that as a society, we think it is normal to have your first drunk experience at age twelve, thirteen or fourteen, as though this is a rite of passage. In retrospect, any drug is not normal for a child to experience, alcohol included, because it almost always starts with alcohol, it never starts with heroin.

It is so accepted, everyone does it—we are bombarded with ads that say so. But the young brain is forming and not fully developed until age twenty-five, especially in males. Most children survive, but there are those like Jason who have an addictive personality, or have alcoholism or drug abuse in the family genes; this is when the pattern is laid for future disaster.

If I could go back in time, I would have monitored Jay more, been stricter. Would it have helped or changed the future? Who knows. There is so much self-blame when your child dies under these circumstances.

When Jason was twenty-two, he found his cousin dead of an accidental overdose. This was a major trauma for Jason. He loved his cousin like a brother, a best friend. Jason's complicated grief was not addressed as completely as it should have been. He suffered from survivor's guilt and PTSD. We took him to counselors. He would go to one or two sessions and then say he was fine, he could handle it. He was a grown man and we had to respect his decision. This was a mitigating factor that led to Jason developing a substance use disorder.

In December 2014, Jason's life was spiraling out of control. He and his partner were fighting all the time. He was drinking and doing a lot of drugs. He thought he could still somewhat handle it, and was going to work, paying his mortgage, etc. but barely.

In January 2015, Jason reluctantly agreed to go to rehab. Through his union he went to a place called Donovo. I have nothing but praise for this place. He stayed there for thirty days and came home a changed man. But it didn't take long for him to relapse and slip into old habits. We supported him, but coming back to the same place, the same friends, and the same situation made it difficult to maintain sobriety.

By spring 2015, Jason and his common-law wife were splitting up. They had been together for over four years, but it had been tumultuous for at least the last two. The bond that kept them together was the love for their son. She moved out that July.

Even though Jason knew the relationship could not work unless things drastically changed, he was devastated that his son was taken from his daily life.

I could see him slipping before my eyes. He was drinking all the time, and now had no one he had to answer to. He had strange people at his house, and I had no idea who they were. He realized he needed to get a roommate to help with household expenses. Someone we didn't know moved in with two massive pit bulls.

Jason stopped caring for his home. We used to tell him, "Your home is your sanctuary, this is where you can find your peace. Respect it." The young man who moved in had lost his brother the summer before. The two of them drowning their sorrows together was not a good mix.

I was diagnosed with breast cancer that same spring. My husband and I were on high alert as far as Jason was concerned. We would get calls (always in the middle of the night) from police saying he had been pulled over, calls from him asking for money, calls from collection agencies, and calls from people we didn't know.

I was dealing with surgery, chemotherapy and radiation, but at the same time my heart was breaking for my child. My grown child who I wanted to protect was fading in front of my eyes.

He was missing work and getting so skinny, but never once did I think he had graduated to heroin. My brain was so muddled at this time. I was so sick. I was doing everything in my power to protect my son. I didn't want him to worry about me. I was driving around the drug neighborhoods at all hours of the night looking for him. My phone was beside me 24/7. If I called and he didn't answer, I would drive over to his house.

I read in one of his journals how he thought I didn't want to involve him in my treatments because I didn't trust him to help. I was only trying to protect him. I didn't want him to worry about me, as he was going through so much. My heart breaks when I realize that he thought he wasn't worthy enough for me to confide in.

CHAPTER TWO

when did the drugs start?

I think we need to educate our doctors
about addiction. ~MATTHEW PERRY

Every journey through substance use and abuse begins at the starting gate—the moment when curiosity, temptation, or a legal prescription led our loved one into a life nobody wanted. When did our bright, intelligent loved one begin to dance with the villain?

*

KIMBERLY CALAIS
Kim's 23-year-old daughter Emily died from a multiple drug overdose including heroin and methamphetamine in 2016

Emily's first year in high school is the year I associate as the bookmark of the time her painfully slow descent began. She was thirteen, and the change to high school meant the consolidation of other schools in our city. Her freshman class alone was more than three hundred students, and the high school student body was well over a thousand kids.

Emily always wanted to fit in and become one of the cool, popular kids. She was a very bright girl who had done very well in school, academically, and participated in sports, dance classes and competitive cheerleading. She was very creative and loved music, art and theater. She had a good group of friends as she entered high school, but that core base started to change with exposure to new people.

A few months into her freshman year, a new friend of hers called me to pick her up. When I arrived, I found her completely intoxicated and took her home. I was very upset by this but waited to discuss this with her the following morning. We talked and while she was somewhat apologetic, she also didn't understand why I was making such a big deal about this. I asked her more about these new friends, but she didn't volunteer too much.

A few months later, I found a note in her backpack where she was asking one of these new friends how she could get alcohol. I confronted Emily about this as well, not only for asking about alcohol, but for the response saying she could steal it from the local drug store. Warning bells went off in me about these new friends and I shared that with her. I asked her why she wasn't spending more time with her other (old) friends. She said she liked these girls and didn't understand why I was making such a big deal out of it.

I began meeting these girls when they came to the house. They were Emily's type in that they represented the crowd she always longed to fit in with. They were pretty, popular and had great social standing in her peer group—things that are seemingly very important to thirteen-year-old Emily—things that she didn't feel she was/had but desperately wanted.

I've learned that this age seems to be a common time when kids begin experimenting with alcohol and drugs. I had two daughters who were born two and a half years apart, who experienced the same things at home and school and each experimented. For whatever reason, the allure of drinking and using drugs was more attractive to Emily. She had been a risk-taker since she was a little girl, taking on any dare sent her way and always testing/pushing her boundaries. I often think back and wonder what I could have done differently that might have put Emily on a different path. The statement "hindsight is 20/20" is painfully accurate but the bottomless pit of what-ifs, could-haves, should-haves, although inevitable, serves no real purpose when it comes to trying to understand the heinous disease of addiction.

*

SUSAN CARLYON
Susan's 22-year-old son Adam died from
an overdose of carfentanyl in 2016

Adam was nineteen when he started using drugs. I don't have any facts; I am just guessing about how I believe his drug use started. Adam had very low self-esteem and he started hanging out with people who seemed to him to accept him as he was. I believe they started giving him prescription medicines and marijuana. Then at some point a neighbor boy who was Adam's age, gave him heroin and he was immediately addicted.

*

MARYBETH CICHOCKI
MaryBeth's 37-year-old son Matthew died
from a Percocet overdose in 2015

My son was about sixteen when I found out he was smoking marijuana and had started to experiment with pills. I really think he felt immense peer pressure to be cool. This was in the 90s when we didn't have the resources and education regarding how dangerous this period of experimentation could be or where it could lead.

I was shocked and so disappointed. I think the most important thing a parent can do is pay attention and don't be afraid to ask those questions regarding drug use. You might not like what you hear but if you keep the lines of communication open, the benefits are worth the struggle. Enable trust and keep talking with concern and compassion.

*

KIM DELONG
Kim's 29-year-old son Tyler died
from a fentanyl overdose in 2017

Looking back, I'm guessing that Tyler starting smoking weed about age fifteen to seventeen. He was an honor student and never had any issues in school. I didn't know he was smoking until he was about nineteen or so, when I started to smell it in his room. Since he was over eighteen, I just asked him not to smoke in the house.

I never had a problem with it because I know a lot of people who smoke and are respectable members of society, law-abiding citizens, and some of the nicest people you ever met.

Tyler was about twenty when I found out he was not only smoking marijuana, but also selling it. He had purchased a scale on the internet and when it came to the house, I asked him about it. At first, he claimed he needed it to weigh what he was buying. That's when red flags went up.

He stayed at home less and was always coming or going. His cell rang constantly, and he would get angry if we asked him to shut it off for family things. I finally confronted him about it, and he told me he was selling out of the house. We had a long talk, and I told him he could not do that in my house because it was not only illegal, but also too dangerous for him, his younger brother and myself. He agreed but as time went by, it became apparent he was still selling.

I found all sorts of paraphernalia in his room including a bong, which I destroyed. We had another talk and he again agreed to stop. I even asked his father, my ex, to talk to Tyler, but he wasn't helpful at all. I told my son this was his last warning. If he continued, I was going to report him to the authorities.

Finally, one night I smelled weed again in his room, very strongly. He was at work, so I decided to have a look around in his room. I found a few ounces of weed along with baggies and a scale. My youngest son was about fourteen at the time and he witnessed it.

We lived in a very small town with very low crime. I drove my youngest son and myself to the police station and told them what was happening, and asked for help. Their answer was to arrest Tyler the next morning at the house, which I went along with. It was one of the hardest things I have ever done, but I needed help and didn't know where to turn.

The next morning, they knocked on the door while Tyler was still asleep and they came in and arrested him. He was twenty-one. They searched his room, and took the weed along with his recently cashed paycheck and the money from his tax return, claiming it could have been from selling weed. They also found a small dark sticky tablet which they took for testing. They said it could be heroin but it turned out to be some type of natural incense.

Tyler was bailed out by one of his friends later that day, and he came home. He was furious with me. He had fines and court dates, and the detective never helped me with the problem. In fact, the police started to harass him, calling him all the time, asking him to rat out the bigger dealers and set people up. He refused to, so they made his life miserable, following him around, watching the house and always pulling him over.

I told Tyler he had to move out and get his own place if he was not to going to change his lifestyle. A few months later he got an apartment with some friends in the next town. He was about twenty-three by then. Our relationship improved and he stopped being angry with me. He seemed to enjoy having his own place. He continued to sell weed for several years and was never caught. I didn't agree with his lifestyle, but he was an adult. I couldn't do anything about it.

Tyler continued to hold small jobs. He worked at UPS, gas stations, convenience stores, and did electrical work. He was paying his bills, hanging out with friends, and had a nice girlfriend. He seemed happy. We saw him as much as we could, at Christmas, birthdays, and just to hang out or have him over for dinner or a barbecue. We talked about hard drugs every once in a while, and Ty always told me that he would never try them, that he only smoked weed because it was natural, and he thought it couldn't cause any harm.

Fast forward about six years, when I got a call from his father saying that he heard Tyler had gone to the emergency room for an overdose. He said our family doctor had told him. I immediately called my son and he denied it and acted very surprised. I questioned how the hospital had gotten his name and medical information. Tyler said it must have been the kid who robbed him of his wallet at his house a few months prior. His father and younger brother also asked him about it, and he denied ever using drugs to them as well.

I wish I knew the signs of using heroin and fentanyl at the time, and wish I had the right to see Tyler's medical records. Due to the HIPPA laws, I thought I had no right to contact the hospital to see whether it was true. Tyler was an adult and I had no choice but to believe his story.

Looking back, I should have seen the signs that summer. He no longer had a job. His apartment was very messy, he went through roommates, and didn't seem to care anymore. I constantly asked him if he needed anything, but he always said he was doing great.

About five months before he passed, he started to have serious money problems. He got an eviction notice and told me his rent was behind because of his roommates. I gave him the money but told him it was just that one time. I tried to have serious conversations with him about his finances but if he didn't like the direction it was going, he would hang up or say he had to go. He started to not answer my calls or messages right away, he became fidgety, forgot conversations we had, and he was always tired.

One time when I went to his apartment to bring him something, he was acting very odd. He seemed exhausted and looking back I think he was starting to nod. I had no idea what was happening at the time and neither did my husband. We witnessed it but just thought it was odd. I feel so stupid that I didn't recognize the signs. I never suspected he was using fentanyl.

*

ELAINE FAULKNER
Elaine's 25-year-old son Jacob died from
an overdose of opiates and Xanax in 2017

It started in childhood. Jacob had certain vulnerabilities which may have predisposed him to develop issues with substances. More than most children, he struggled with separation anxiety. He was tenderhearted. He responded to other's pain and didn't seem to have the armor of other children. He tried to rescue the bugs his sister was collecting for a science project; it upset him the bugs would die. He also had trouble reading and was diagnosed with dyslexia. He completed treatment for dyslexia and began to catch up to grade level. I think he was drawn to substances to cope.

Jacob first started smoking weed at about fourteen. We noticed changes in his attitudes and interests. He was concerned with wearing the right clothing brands and the right shoes. I believe his use began with a need to be accepted by his peers. He started spending time in his room playing RuneScape, a multi-player video game, and communicating with friends online.

Initially, we were concerned that Kyle might become dependent on video gaming. To our relief, he abruptly stopped playing his game of choice when he got his driver's license. With his driver's license, he had freedom to travel to see his friends. He could hang out with them in person rather than online.

At seventeen, he was binge drinking on the weekends, using marijuana daily, and started using ecstasy and other pills.

*

SHANNIE JENKINS
Shannie's 31-year-old son Kyle died
from a heroin overdose in 2017

Kyle's drug use started when he was around fifteen or sixteen. He started smoking pot. I knew he tried it, and of course talked to him about it. When he was seventeen, he got busted for weighing out pot in a parking lot. It was Christmas evening. I knew the cop who was busting him. They called me and I drove over to the parking lot.

I got in the back of the patrol car and told Kyle that he needs to be honest and tell them everything. I didn't realize that being honest for something like that was not in the best interest of the person.

That's when Kyle entered the court system. His charges were deferred as long as he didn't get into trouble before turning eighteen, and he would get his license back. Kyle ended up buying a moped that looked like a little Harley and he would ride down the side of the road to school. He took it in stride and rode that scooter also to his girlfriend's house and around town. I would always get worried if it was getting dark and tell him to start heading home. I was aware that he smoked pot here and there and drank beer at parties. In my view, it was as a normal teenager. I was very open and honest with both of my boys about things I tried when I was a teenager. I let them know that I didn't like what I tried. But later on, discovered in Kyle's eyes, he felt that since his mom tried things and she was okay that it would be safe. Kyle shared this at his first rehab. So, my sharing made him justify trying things. Of course, when you hear that, then the guilt creeps in.

I remember telling other parents, "Don't ever share anything you did in your past." Back then, when the police came to a party, the kids were breathalyzed and with zero tolerance, they would get a minor in possession. Back in our day, they just made you throw your beer out and go home. The kids who had any alcohol in their system would be charged and lose their license for a year per charge. I'm not saying that teenagers should drink and party, but so many generations do, and I was trying to be an understanding parent. Maybe I was more their friend then their disciplinarian? When I look back now, yes there is so much I would do different. If only we could...

*

LORI LATIMER
Lori's 29-year-old son Greg died from
alcohol and fentanyl-laced cocaine in 2019

Greg began smoking marijuana when he was in high school. My husband at the time (Greg's stepfather) smoked it, so Greg thought it was all right if he did it. Never having done drugs myself, I was naïve about it and didn't know he was doing it when it began. I left his stepfather when Greg was a senior in high school, and Greg and I moved out of the house we'd lived in during that marriage. While Greg was still living with me after he'd graduated from high school, I walked in one afternoon and the house smelled of marijuana. I told him that I didn't like him doing it and he was not to do it in my home again. I never smelled it in the house again.

A couple years before he died, Greg told me he was doing psychedelics. I'd talked to him about the dangers of drugs when he was growing up, and I reminded him that he was playing with fire. He brushed it off and said he was fine and knew what he was doing. I told him that's what everyone thinks, but he was an adult and didn't live at home, so other than having an adult conversation with him, I didn't feel there was much I could do. He was doing well at work and making straight As in college as a well, so there didn't seem to be a reason to worry. Every time I saw him, he was fine, happy and healthy, living and loving life.

Greg lived in a small town about an hour northwest of Atlanta, Georgia. It's the same town he went to high school in. Since his death,

I've learned that drugs are rampant in that county. It's one of the counties in Georgia listed by the U.S. government as HIDTA, a high intensity drug trafficking area, since at least 2010, and has been on the list continuously since then. This is just one more thing I've learned about since Greg's death, something I wish I'd never had to learn.

Greg was always adventurous and had a free spirit. He was also deeply spiritual and loved to engage in deep conversations. From what I've learned since his death, many people feel very connected spiritually when they use heroin, so in a way I can understand why he may have been drawn to that experience. I believe Greg knew his limits with drugs and didn't cross the line. Unfortunately, fentanyl changes the conversation completely. Greg chose to use cocaine and heroin at times. He never chose to use fentanyl.

*

AMANDA MARIE
Amanda's 30-year-old brother Cory
died from a heroin overdose in 2015

Cory began using alcohol and drugs when he was only nine years old. Like many others, he was self-medicating to drown out the internal noise and quiet the turmoil that arose from the pain of trauma. At some point, drinking and smoking weren't enough and he began using cocaine, which he would afford by selling crack.

Selling crack turned into smoking crack. Cory then attempted to mitigate those symptoms with prescription medication, downers. He started first with benzodiazepines like Xanax, Klonopin, Valium and Ativan and then opioids, abusing medications like Vicodin, Dilaudid, Oxy, and Fentanyl. When those stopped working, Cory tried heroin.

*

WHITNEY O'BRIEN
Whitney's 23-year-old brother Michael died from
a heroin/cocaine/benzodiazepine overdose in 2016

My brother's battles with drug use and addiction go back half his life (or more). I honestly have no idea exactly when his drug use started. It was a part of his life for so long that it's hard to remember when he wasn't using. I often wondered if I would even recognize him sober, as I had grown so acquainted with the Michael who was high all the time. If I had to guess, I would say that he began experimenting with marijuana around the age of twelve to thirteen. I'd like to think it began innocently and casually as a means to fit in. He likely found himself in a situation where it was being offered and he was curious and just went along with it. I think he found out quickly that he loved the way drugs made him feel. He was able to numb his erratic mood swings in a way that his prescribed medications couldn't. His emotional instability affected everything he did from school and work, to relationships with family and friends. Using drugs was probably a pretty satisfying way to cope, since nothing else really worked.

It's difficult to pinpoint the start of his substance use since he was simultaneously struggling with mental illness. For many years he went undiagnosed. His unstable mood, irritability, and lethargy were chalked up to side effects of his drug use. Like the old adage, what came first, the chicken or the egg?

I had a hard time untangling the mess of what came first: the drug use or the mental illness. When Michael was diagnosed with bipolar disorder in his early twenties, it brought our family some clarity. We now understood that his mental illness preceded his substance use. Many drugs he experimented with exacerbated his disorder, making him mentally, physically, and emotionally unstable. Depending on the drug he was using and whether it was a stimulant or a depressant, he could be thrown into a manic episode or a period of depression quite easily. I'm not sure he ever grasped how detrimental the substance use was on his wellbeing. It was painful to watch him self-destruct.

When I discovered he was using, I was very cavalier about it. My brother was a pothead, not a drug addict. It became obvious after he graduated high school that this was no longer just a casual pastime. He was a drug connoisseur, dabbling in whatever he could get his hands on. He was game for anything and nothing was off limits.

I wish I would have known how quickly and easily experimenting with drugs could lead to addiction, especially for those with mental illness. The majority who end up addicted say they started drinking, smoking or using drugs before their eighteenth birthday. It's easy to turn a blind eye, as I did. I held out hope that this was just a passing phase. By the time I realized it wasn't, he was already addicted and there was no turning back.

*

ALICE RICH
Alice's 42-year-old brother Gary
died from a fentanyl overdose in 2015

Gary began using recreational drugs at about age fifteen. Honestly, lots of people in our neighborhood smoked marijuana. Hell, half of the people at school smoked weed. I smoked weed from time to time if I was with a friend who smoked; my sister did, too. It wasn't that unusual. Nor was drinking.

Gary went into the Army a year or two after high school. He had been getting into some trouble and this was a way to get him away for a while. We were all so proud of him when he left, and he looked so handsome in his uniform.

He drank heavily while in the service; I hear a lot of guys do. He got married and had a baby while he was away. Then another baby a few years later, after they moved back home. Maybe he should've stayed away. Stayed away from the people around town. The bad influences. I'm not removing blame from him, but you can't tell me that if he had stayed away from those old friends, things would have turned out differently for him.

I really don't know when he started using heroin, 2009, I think. Sometimes I'm not sure of the year in which he died. It's like my brain gets jumbled up about some of that. I know how it started. He was having the guys over for a beer in the garage kind of night. His neighbor introduced him to heroin while he was drunk. He was hooked. He was snorting it at first but quickly moved to shooting up.

*

CAROL WALL
Carol's 29-year-old son Jason died
from a heroin overdose in 2016.

I believe he started using drugs in high school, recreationally, peer pressure? Not opioids by any means, marijuana.

CHAPTER THREE

The first red flags

These diseases are still not seen as real diseases.
People shy away from seeking help because it's
viewed as being somewhat morally off the path,
that they've lost their way. ~JIM IRSAY

Substance use comes with warning signs that raise red flags in our head but denial in our heart. Even when evidence is mounting, it's still hard to believe our kind, intelligent loved one can fall victim. What were the warning signs and when did you confront your loved one?

*

KIMBERLY CALAIS
Kim's 23-year-old daughter Emily died from a multiple drug
overdose including heroin and methamphetamine in 2016

I had always spoken openly with both of my daughters. We were very close, and I always let them know they could talk to me about anything without them being worried about my reaction. One of the first warning signs I noticed was that Emily started to withdraw. She spent more time in her room. She was less happy and moodier in her general demeanor. Her grades started to drop in school so as a response, I withdrew some privileges and she was grounded until she got her schoolwork done.

Her physical appearance also started to change. She began to wear more makeup and wanted to order clothes that were more suggestive and, in my opinion, not appropriate for a young teenager. The dynamics in our house were changing. She was becoming more volatile in her behavior toward everyone in the house. I began noticing her glassy eyes when she'd come home from spending time with her friends. And she always smelled a little off. I surmised that she had started smoking marijuana.

I found myself in such conflict. I remember being her age and doing what she was now doing. I had grown up in the same little coastal city just south of San Francisco, and attended the same high school. I drank alcohol in high school and smoked marijuana as well. I never told my kids this, but it did factor into my reaction, a mindset that I now regret.

My personal experience with these same factors at a similar time of life convinced me that I didn't need to worry about it, other than from a disciplinary stance. While she was doing things that I certainly didn't approve of, I believed that it was also something that most high school students did and she would eventually grow out of it. I certainly did, as did my friends. I never dreamed that she was laying the foundation for the path that would ultimately cause the end of her life.

I confronted her about her activities not long after finding a pipe in her room. She at first lied and said it wasn't hers. She then became defensive and started yelling at me, telling me to quit violating her privacy and stay out of her room. She could go from anger to inconsolable tears within seconds.

Her anger scared me, another warning sign, as this impacted my response to her eventual increase in drug use and substance. I was emotionally afraid of her. Her sudden mood changes and volatility made me shut down as to not antagonize or prolong her outbursts. I just wanted to calm her down and restore peace.

I watched her slowly change in front of my eyes. Her friend base continued to grow. She became too old to continue with her competitive cheerleading team. She also decided she didn't want to go to her dance school anymore. She was going out more, usually followed by sleepovers at friends.

During one of these sleepover weekends, Emily went to her first rave. She was smitten. I didn't know much about what a rave was or what was involved in its culture. I read up on raves and then had a talk with her about my concerns of drug use. She assured me that, while there were other kids who might do drugs, she and her friends weren't like that and she liked going as she loved the music and the dancing, and she could be the creative soul she always was. Part of me was happy she was making other friends beyond her school friends. I met her rave friends and spoke to their parents and my concerns were assuaged. But I later found out that I was completely duped by my daughter. It was at this point that she started taking pills, including ecstasy. While I did notice she had more difficulty sleeping, I attributed that to the fact that sleeping had always been difficult for her, even as a baby. I had a habit of laying with her when she was a toddler to help her sleep. This practice continued throughout her life. She found comfort in having me near, and often called me to her room saying, "Lay with me, Mom."

It was becoming increasingly more difficult to get Emily to go to school. At the beginning of her sophomore year, her counselor told me that given her failing grades from her freshman year, she would not be on track to graduate unless she participated in summer school and passed all her classes for her sophomore, junior and senior years.

After discussing this with Emily, she said the school environment was too stressful to handle, and she often had panic attacks. One of her middle school friends was attending a different high school and doing independent study at home. Emily said that doing independent study would help her work and regain focus without the distractions that, in her mind, kept her from excelling like she had in grade and middle schools. She had big dreams about what she wanted to do in life, and was confident that this was what she needed for a fresh start.

I thought long and hard about this change, including speaking to her counselor. After delving into what would be necessary and with the guidance of school officials, Emily began independent study and no longer went to her high school. Quite honestly, I also believed that this change would relieve some of the peer pressure she felt.

I was wrong.

Independent study, in theory, is a very good idea for those who have the commitment to do the work. I believe Emily viewed it as an extended vacation.

I would often drop Emily off at a certain friend's house so they could study together. When Emily was in middle school, I got to know this friend, Mandy. She came from a strict household, was very polite, did well in school and was shy and soft-spoken. Since her move to a different high school, Mandy's parents divorced and she lived with her mother. She had also changed quite a bit. Emily said Mandy had gone "Emo" as she tried to fit in at her school.

Something inside me was very uncomfortable with Emily and Mandy's friendship, a feeling that never left throughout the remainder of Emily's life, and a feeling that proved to be tragically correct. This period also served as a bookmark for Emily's continued descent into the abyss of drug use.

*

SUSAN CARLYON
Susan's 22-year-old son Adam died from
an overdose of carfentanyl in 2016

My son seemed sick a lot and he was very moody, emotional, and angry. I never confronted him about drugs because that was so far off my radar. It never even occurred to me as a possibility. I knew something was wrong though. I took him to his medical doctor and to a counselor who he had talked to years before, trying to find out what was wrong with my son. Adam was the one who came to his dad and I and told us about his drug use.

*

MARYBETH CICHOCKI
MaryBeth's 37-year-old son Matthew died
from a Percocet overdose in 2015

My son's grades started to drop and his interest in sports began to fall apart. He went to a private Catholic school. I foolishly thought that was the last place drugs would be so prevalent. Like many other parents, I thought, "Not my child." Looking back, I realize just how naïve we all were. It seems the 1990s were just the beginning of the opioid crisis we live with today.

I confronted Matt when I came home from an early shift at the hospital and found him home smoking marijuana on our deck. I then found out he was experimenting with pills, and sent him to a thirty-day treatment program in Newport News, Virginia.

*

ELAINE FAULKNER
Elaine's 25-year-old son Jacob died from
an overdose of opiates and Xanax in 2017

There were indicators that his substance use could be developing into a serious issue. He was irritable and had hangovers. He was using marijuana and alcohol in increasing amounts as well as frequency. He lost interest in school. The moment I realized Jake (as he now called himself) would step outside the bounds of normal teenage use and behavior was when I spotted a sore on his arm. He explained that he had been drinking and the sore came from playing the "burning game." This involved taking a lit cigarette and pressing it to your friend's arm while your friend did the same to yours. The person who gave in first lost. From the wound on his arm, I doubted he had given in. It was a big red flag to us that he was binge drinking and willing to go to any lengths to prove himself to his friends.

I, along with his dad, had numerous discussions with him. We shared information on the risks of drinking and substance use. We tried to keep the lines of communication open and listened when he shared.

At times he shared information that was upsetting and caused us anxiety. We created rules and he broke them. He would be in trouble, and then would get back on track. We discovered a pipe out behind the garage. He was in his room when we confronted him with the evidence. We had a rule of no drug use on our property. He became very upset and told us that if we didn't accept him as he was, he would never talk to us again. That statement haunted me because from his perspective we were judging him and trying to control him.

His identity was being shaped by his use of marijuana, and he had no intention of seeing it as a problem. He was willing to distance himself from his family and planned to keep smoking weed, drinking, and using whatever substance he chose.

*

SHANNIE JENKINS
Shannie's 31-year-old son Kyle died
from a heroin overdose in 2017

I remember Kyle telling me that one friend got a prescription pill from his grandfather's medicine cabinet. He told Kyle how good it made him feel and said Kyle needed to try it. He got more pills and some of the friends tried them. Kyle told me about it. I remember sharing my concerns but Kyle justified it, saying it was safe because it was a prescription.

A week before Kyle turned eighteen, he and his girlfriend got into a fight. I got a call around 4 a.m. from a sheriff deputy saying that Kyle had been in an accident and was in the hospital. I asked who was driving, and he said Kyle was. I replied that Kyle didn't have a license. He was scheduled to get it back in just one week.

I jumped out of bed to look in the driveway where his new Jeep was supposed to be parked. The Jeep was gone. My heart sank.

I rushed to the hospital to find Kyle strapped to the bed and being held down. They had to administer three shots to calm him. I sat next to him while he slept for three hours or so. He woke up to the reality that he was in some serious trouble.

He said he came home from the party, got into his Jeep and drove to where his girlfriend was. He hadn't driven the Jeep before and didn't realize how quick it turned. He overturned on a corner and flipped. The police came and he was arrested for driving under the influence. He later told me he had done cocaine and went into a rage.

82

Why did we let him hang his keys in his bedroom? I trusted that he wouldn't take the Jeep being so close to him turning eighteen. He was under the influence and made a horrible decision.

Kyle was at a very low point, feeling like things would never turn around for him. It was very disappointing and concerning, but we tried to let him know that things can always turn around.

*

LORI LATIMER
Lori's 29-year-old son Greg died from
alcohol and fentanyl-laced cocaine in 2019

I never noticed any warning signs until after Greg died and I reflected back on the last couple months of his life. Greg moved out on his own when he was twenty. I saw him once a week or so, and never noticed anything. I think he knew not to come around when he had been using drugs.

From what I've learned, he only began using hard drugs the last couple years of his life, and mainly at home with his roommates. He knew I'd never done drugs. He used to joke with me, saying he couldn't believe I grew up in Los Angeles in the 1970s and never did drugs. But it was true—I never did.

The only warning I ever gave Greg was when I once asked him where he got the drugs he was taking, and told him to be very careful. Once again, he brushed it off and said he was fine.

There was an incident that I now realize I should have dug into much deeper. Greg and his girlfriend were arrested the night of his twenty-eighth birthday, fifteen months before he died. He had come to a family dinner for his birthday, then met up with her. They went out and got arrested for having pot in their possession. It was a relatively small amount, but still illegal in Georgia. He hired an attorney, went to court, and took responsibility for it. I thought that had been a wake-up call for him.

There was one other incident that I now realize was a huge red flag. Less than two months before he died, someone tried to run Greg and his coworkers down in a parking lot, and then pulled a gun on them. It really shook Greg up. In the following days, he lashed out at me and his older brother. I knew something was wrong, because that was totally out of character for Greg. I thought it was the result of being in shock over the incident. I begged his father to check on him and make sure he was all right.

Looking back, I now realize he likely increased his drug usage to cope with the shock, and that's why he lashed out at his brother and me. I had no idea he was using drugs, so I didn't know that was responsible for his personality change. Had I known about the drug usage, I would have taken much different steps to make sure he was all right and received the help he needed to cope with what had happened at work.

Greg and I did reconcile a couple weeks after he lashed out at me, but I never had any idea of the path he was on at that point.

*

AMANDA MARIE
Amanda's 30-year-old brother Cory
died from a heroin overdose in 2015

As adults, there was a long period of time when Cory and I had no contact. I moved out at age fifteen and left him behind. I became a mother at nineteen. At the point when his drug use and the byproduct of addiction put me and my children in danger, I had to break the bonds of family that tied us.

Cory became verbally abusive which eventually escalated into physical violence. He would steal from his family and beg for money. He would get arrested and end up in jail. I empathized, but I couldn't enable or participate. I carried much of the same baggage he did but I was trying to unpack mine. He was just dragging his around.

*

WHITNEY O'BRIEN
Whitney's 23-year-old brother Michael died from
a heroin/cocaine/benzodiazepine overdose in 2016

One of the many burdens I carry is my complacency in all this. I stayed distant and remained as uninvolved as possible, despite the danger I knew he was in. It was a defense mechanism purposefully in place as a means to protect myself. As a result, I intentionally ignored the warning signs that Michael's disease had unraveled.

Truth be told, I didn't want to know that he was so sick, it scared me. I was absorbed in my own life and my own problems, and I didn't have time for his.

For many years, I convinced myself that this was just a phase of Michael's life that we would look back on someday and feel relieved that it was over and aghast that it ever happened.

When Michael was deep into his addiction, he was very thin. The weight loss was slow, so it was easy to overlook. Over the course of six years, he lost around thirty pounds. That may not sound like much, but he was always very thin and trim. He stood at about five-feet nine-inches tall and weighed around 175 at his heaviest. Slowly, we watched him physically deteriorate in front of our eyes.

He lacked any concern for his physical appearance. Hygiene was no longer a priority. He had to be reminded to shower. The only thing that mattered was getting high, everything else fell to the wayside. He hadn't cut his hair in two years and usually wore a beanie year-round, even during the summer when it was scorching out. Most of his beanies had holes burned in the tops of them. After he would get high, he would doze off with his lighter still burning and nearly catch his head on fire.

One of the most obvious signs he was using was his tendency to fall asleep anywhere at any time. He once fell asleep in a crowded, noisy restaurant while we were out celebrating my mom's birthday. His somnolence had me fooled for a long time because he used to take a medication for his bipolar that also made him drowsy. He spent the majority of his time alone, sleeping. He never seemed to have an appetite anymore and whenever he did eat, he was frequently sick afterwards. It was not unusual to find him vomiting in the bathroom after meals. Although I ignored many signs, I was intentionally looking for others. I was always inspecting his arms for signs of track marks—proof that his disease had evolved from smoking heroin to injecting it. I never saw any, even when he was shooting up. He waltzed around the house without a shirt on quite regularly, so he wasn't hiding. I think his visibly large veins made the job easy and he didn't miss his mark much, if at all.

I chose to ignore warning signs in hopes that they would go away. But you can't wish this disease away, as I so desperately tried. Frankly, I thought the only person who could help Michael was Michael. I felt powerless and defenseless. I can't imagine how he must have felt.

*

ALICE RICH
Alice's 42-year-old brother Gary
died from a fentanyl overdose in 2015

Gary had a wife, kids, pets, a house, a truck, and a job. All was well. One of the biggest clues was stealing things from our parents and borrowing money. His personality changed. It was hard to believe that he could steal from our mom and dad, but he did. He seemed desperate and different. Things began spiraling downward for him quickly.

The warning signs were a change in his priorities and his personality. Lying, stealing, not going to work. He stole jewelry from our mom and pawned it. No one trusted him and if we were together somewhere, we hid our phones, purses, and valuables of any kind.

Our parents were the first to know and the first to confront him.

First, they confronted him about the jewelry, he lied and said he did not do it, but Dad found an item at the pawn shop and they said it was Gary who dropped it off. Once our parents knew, they told the rest of us. It was hard to believe that he was using the devil drug that was killing so many people. He stole anything and everything that he could get money for, including gas cans from garages to gas his truck so he could drive around looking for scrap.

Afraid that he was going to end up killing himself by overdose, my sister and I went to his house to try to talk to him. He ended up stealing my sister's phone right then and there and running with it.

Coincidentally the police showed up to pick him up and a foot chase ensued. It was horrible to see. It was horrible to see him in cuffs. But hey, when he was in jail, we didn't have to worry about him. It seemed the whole family relaxed while he was gone.

*

CAROL WALL
Carol's 29-year-old son Jason died
from a heroin overdose in 2016

Toward the end, Jason was missing work, was sleeping all day, and was up all night. My son owned a home of his own, so he did not live with me. I found pawn slips for items he had pawned. We were always very open. At first, it wasn't full-on confrontation, just pure, raw worry. I was very uneducated about opioids.

CHAPTER FOUR

Discovering the evidence

No one is immune from addiction; it afflicts people
of all ages, races, classes, and professions.
~ PATRICK J. KENNEDY

Unfamiliar pills, burnt spoons, powdery baggies, and hollowed pens. Drug paraphernalia comes in many creative forms, including common household items. Did you ever discover drugs or drug paraphernalia on or near your loved one?

*

KIMBERLY CALAIS
Kim's 23-year-old daughter Emily died from a multiple drug
overdose including heroin and methamphetamine in 2016

I often cleaned my kids' rooms when they weren't home to get things better organized. My intention was not to spy or invade their privacy. It was to create order and get rid of things that they no longer wore or used. As a small aside, I just read a list of things a parent should stop doing if they want their child to grow into a responsible adult.

Cleaning up after them one—as were other things I had done—leaving me to feel like such a failure as a mother and adding a new layer of it's all my fault to the cement of guilt I carry with me every minute.

I never found anything in either of their rooms that led me to believe there was any drug use beyond the pipe I had found in the back yard following one of Emily's sleepovers, keeping my false sense of security and/or denial at play.

That changed in 2011.

One night in January, there was a knock at my bedroom door. I looked at my clock and it was 3:30 a.m. I opened it to find Emily's then-boyfriend who told me there had been an accident. He said she was not hurt. Emily had come back to the house and, while I was asleep, had taken my car keys from my purse. Shortly thereafter, she crashed my car through the fence of a nearby house, the vehicle coming to rest just a few feet from the house itself. She called her boyfriend, who came and got her and moved the car to the QuikStop market down the street. He helped Emily into the house and brought her to her bedroom where she collapsed on the bed and immediately fell into a deep sleep. There were so many emotions that I couldn't begin to process. I woke up Emily's sister who went with me to look at the car.

My car was totaled. We looked inside and saw a baggie full of marijuana, as well as my checkbook.

When we returned home, I woke Emily up and asked her what happened. She was emotional and still altered in some yet-to-be-known way. She said she fell asleep at the wheel while driving home. She asked if I found anything in the car. I said I hadn't, since I had a feeling she was asking about the marijuana.

A few weeks later I found out that she had taken some benzos and drank wine at a party, passing out in the five-minute ride from the party to our house.

I looked at the damage she caused to the house. The idea that she could have been killed or killed someone in the house was too much to process. I told a friend what had happened, asking what I should do. She said she would accompany me to their house if I wanted to speak to them. They were an older couple in their retirement years. I feared that my contacting them might result in their contacting the police, leading to Emily's arrest and prosecution. I was so torn. My upbringing and personal moral code told me I needed to go to their house and tell them what happened. My new, albeit involuntary, role as Emily's chief enabler told me I needed to protect her from arrest or incarceration as that—in my foolish opinion—might cause her to go off the deep end.

Shamefully, I did not go to their house. Instead, I chose the cowardly route...I put a cash-filled envelope in their mailbox, to cover the expense of their fence repair. I shake my head in disgust toward myself in remembering and sharing this.

My car was gone. Their fence was gone. Emily did not experience any significant consequences for either. I often wonder what would have happened if I had followed my heart by either contacting the police myself or knocking on that couple's door? Would exposure to the criminal justice system been the detour that would have taken her off the path toward her ultimate demise? I asked myself, what kind of mother turns in her own child?

Approximately five months later, I had another experience of finding things in Emily's room. I sigh as I allow memories of this time to return. Emily had come into my bedroom in the early evening. She was upset about something and said she needed money. I told her I would not be giving her any money. Her mood escalated quickly, something that had happened frequently. She left momentarily and returned saying that she had just taken about fifty Benadryl tablets to kill herself.

This was not the first time she threatened to harm herself and I knew on some level that she did this—and told me about it—to manipulate me in some form. I calmly told her that if this was true, I would need to take her to the hospital so they could pump her stomach. She said she didn't care, so I took her to the hospital which was about a twenty-minute drive from our house. During this time, she was busy texting friends, telling them what she had done. I checked her in at the hospital and we waited for her name to be called. I knew what all this meant, as we had walked this road before.

The nurse told me they would treat her overdose and refer her for a psych evaluation, which meant a seventy-two-hour hold. I let her dad know, and was told it was best if I got some sleep and returned in the morning. They gave me her phone and other personal possessions and I went home. Once home, I started to look through her phone. I learned through text messages that she owed money to someone for drugs. Drugs? I once again went into her room, but this time it was not to clean.

My older daughter helped me sift through the chaos that was her room. We found a box containing marijuana, a white powdery substance and some pills, as well as snorting paraphernalia. I felt sick. And betrayed.

The next day, Emily's sister and I took this box to our city's police department, providing them with her name as well as the name of the person we believed sold her the drugs, a person who was known to them. I felt I had given her a chance with the car accident. I was not going to let this go, regardless of the resulting consequences.

She called me from the hospital later that day and said they were going to transfer her to a mental health facility for further evaluation and treatment. This would be an involuntary hold which I was ultimately happy about as it would allow us some breathing room to process what had happened and what to do going forward.

Emily was transferred to a hospital in the East Bay. While there she met a young man she took an immediately liking to who was also under evaluation due to a heroin overdose. This person, Nick, was the one who eventually introduced Emily to opiates and so much more.

I have come to liken the what-if, should-have, and could-haves to being in a carnival funhouse and looking at myself through the many mirrors. Each distorts the reality of what is, and none of them change the image I see. I cannot change anything that has happened, but this feeling of self-distortion continues to this day.

*

MARYBETH CICHOCKI
MaryBeth's 37-year-old son Matthew died
from a Percocet overdose in 2015

I found some marijuana rolled into joints in his room. I began to search his bedroom and backpack every day. I felt like a horrible mom, but I needed to keep on top of this. I was disappointed and knew this could be an ongoing problem. Matt got angry at me for invading his privacy but as I said, you have no privacy in our home if you are doing harmful behavior.

He eventually stopped experimenting and went to college. It all came crashing back when he suffered a work injury that led to surgery and the prescription for opioids.

*

ELAINE FAULKNER
Elaine's 25-year-old son Jacob died from
an overdose of opiates and Xanax in 2017

We found Jake's pipes on occasion and marijuana in his room. He would throw his beer cans in the trash. He would keep empties in his car. I did not know if he had boundaries with different substances, so I had anxiety about what would turn up. He moved out when he was eighteen and supported himself with a job as a pizza delivery driver.

Most of his use and party lifestyle went on outside of our home. He did not want to change what he was doing and resented any suggestion that he may develop a problem. He was angry and irritable, and when we did find evidence of use, he meant for us to find it.

*

SHANNIE JENKINS
Shannie's 31-year-old son Kyle died
from a heroin overdose in 2017

The drug use of OxyContin went from taking a pill to crushing it up and snorting it, then to smoking it on foil. I felt so naïve. Why would someone smoke a pill? But Kyle kept justifying that at least he wasn't smoking them, and then at least it was a pill and not heroin.

Kyle was about nineteen or so. He was in bed and said he was too sick to get up. He told me all he wanted to do was smoke a pill. What? I was clueless as to why he would feel that way. He told me his friend had Suboxone but Kyle would have to buy it from him. I had no idea what Suboxone was, but if that's what Kyle needed to get up and go to work, then call him. His friend came over and gave Kyle Suboxone.

I asked a lot of questions. One thing about Kyle was that he was very honest about his drug use and the things he tried. That was the start of really understanding that this wasn't about choosing to use, but his body was craving the drug and making him sick. I saw powder on the kitchen table, and found foil with burn marks, but at this point was still very naïve. I had no problem going in my sons' rooms and snooping around or looking in their backpacks.

95

One time when I was living in an apartment, I opened Kyle's backpack and found a bag of black stuff. I wasn't sure what it was, but assumed it was heroin. I had never seen nor touched heroin before, and felt sick. I tucked it inside my closet. Kyle called after he left the apartment, saying I didn't hide things well. He was such a little turd at times. I would never tell him that I didn't like him, but did tell him I didn't like who he became under the influence.

*

LORI LATIMER
Lori's 29-year-old son Greg died from
alcohol and fentanyl-laced cocaine in 2019

I never found any drugs or drug paraphernalia on or near Greg. I didn't rifle through his things when he lived with me—I let him have his privacy. The only thing I ever saw were lighters for the marijuana, and I only saw those a few times when he lived with me. Hindsight always leads to the what-ifs and a multitude of other questions, so I often wonder if I hadn't been so naïve and trusting, would it have changed anything?

The spiritual part of me knows our souls choose our paths, so in some ways nothing I could have done would have changed things. As a mom, that doesn't make this any easier and I'll live with a lot of regrets the rest of my life.

*

WHITNEY O'BRIEN
Whitney's 23-year-old brother Michael died from
a heroin/cocaine/benzodiazepine overdose in 2016

Michael lived at home with my parents. In the beginning, he didn't use at home. So, drugs and their corresponding equipment were hidden and out of sight. Evidence was removed and disposed of. But gradually my brother became careless and my parents eventually lost control of the situation, if they ever even had it.

Michael started using in the house and was no longer covert about it. I never actually found drugs anywhere, but I knew they were there, and chose not to go looking for them.

Michael's room was where the majority of his drug use took place. His room was cluttered with various drug paraphernalia. He had a large collection of pipes and bongs. A roll of aluminum foil could be found in his closet. In a drawer beneath his bed was a bag containing hundreds of empty gelatin capsules. He was a connoisseur of electronic cigarettes and his desk was littered with all the appurtenances of vaping—cylinders, atomizers, drip tips, valves, liquid containers, etc.

A particularly upsetting memory was during a weekend getaway to our family cabin. When Michael came, so did the drugs. We trained our son (as well as you can train a toddler) to always stay out of his room. But he adored Michael and would frequently knock on his door looking for him, or follow him into the room, only to be removed by myself or my husband. One afternoon he wandered into his room looking for Uncle Mikey. My brother had left the door to his room open while he went to the bathroom. A couple minutes later, my son walked out holding a glass bong. I was horrified. I quickly and gently removed it from his grasp. I was so rattled by the sight of my innocent two-year-old holding a bong. This was the last straw for me. Not long after the incident, I made the very difficult decision to stop allowing my children to go to my parents' house. This quite literally broke me, but it went on longer than it ever should have.

*

ALICE RICH
Alice's 42-year-old brother Gary
died from a fentanyl overdose in 2015

His wife left him even though she still loved him. It was killing her. We cleaned out his house while he was in prison and found needles and spoons hidden here and there. We also found that he had removed and sold all the copper from his house. The house was cleaned up and fixed up and sold (my dad was the actual owner who bought the house for Gary and his family). The house was gone, the wife was gone, the dogs were gone, and he was in prison.

*

CAROL WALL
Carol's 29-year-old son Jason died
from a heroin overdose in 2016.

Yes, I did discover drug paraphernalia. I was shocked, saddened yet uneducated. I didn't know what some things were. My son denied anything and was angry with me for looking through his belongings.

CHAPTER FIVE

Role of friends

Be very careful of who you share your problem with,
remember that not every friend who smiles at
you is your best friend. ~KEMMY NOLA

Can friends lead our loved one into the throes of substance use, or does the substance use—and the lifestyle that comes with it—attract bad friends? Describe your loved one's circle of friends at the time he or she died. How well did you know them? Do you feel they played a role in your loved one's use?

*

KIMBERLY CALAIS
Kim's 23-year-old daughter Emily died from a multiple drug
overdose including heroin and methamphetamine in 2016

For the most part, I liked the friends Emily had made during her life. As previously mentioned, a friend Emily had made in middle school caused me concern during her high school years. I refer to this person as Mandy.

Middle school brought students from three other elementary schools together for grades sixth through eighth. It was now that Emily met a group of girls who did cheerleading through the city's recreational football league. Emily wanted to be a part of this group and gradually pulled away from most of her elementary school friends.

I had no real issue with these girls (other than my dislike for their talking behind each other's backs as groups of girls are prone to do). Mandy was a shy girl, coming from a very strict household. She was like Emily in that she wanted to be part of this group. Emily was a strong personality and she would be tough on Mandy at times, but Mandy looked up to Emily and Emily ate that up.

They went to different high schools, and during this time Mandy's parents divorced and she resided with her mother, the more lenient of her parents. She turned "Emo" during this time to fit in the multi-cultural high school she attended. Her confidence and newly found independence were noticeable.

I remember a time when Emily asked if Mandy could stay at our house for a while. I noticed a change in Mandy and felt uncomfortable with her now. She had an air to her that put me off and I let Emily know this. I told her she couldn't stay at our house and suggested that Emily start spending time with other friends.

Emily followed Mandy's lead in leaving high school for an independent study curriculum. Their time together was not only counter-productive for their courses but seemed to accelerate Emily's drinking and marijuana use.

Emily's high school friends didn't care for Mandy. Unfortunately, Emily's change from high school to independent study caused strain and distance with these friends. Emily was slowly left to hang out with Mandy and other girls who were also not in high school for various reasons. While most of these girls seemed to have issues that I didn't care for, I was most wary of Mandy. I implored Emily not to spend time with her. I probably could have approached it differently, as Emily's desire to go against my wishes fueled their friendship that much more.

During July 2011, Emily was involuntarily detained in a mental health facility due to her attempted suicide with Benadryl tablets. During this time she met a young man who was there due to his overdose on heroin.

Given the volatility and events that preceded her hospitalization, neither Emily's father nor I were desirous of her returning to either of our homes. Emily had punched at least fifteen holes in her bedroom walls. She had stolen from both of us and broken most if not all rules I had set for her. We constantly walked on eggshells as to not ignite her temper. Her sister and I locked our bedroom doors so she couldn't get in and steal things.

Emily was diagnosed with borderline personality disorder. The doctors suggested continued treatment for her mental health issues, as well as her drug use, in a dual diagnosis facility for at least six months. Since she was an adult, she could not be simply placed in the facility. She would have to go in voluntarily. She would have none of that.

As an alternative, Emily had the ability to go into a sober living environment and go to school to pursue her education. Much of the cost of this program would be paid for by the State of California, and sounded ideal. Emily said no.

We were told that she could not be discharged from the hospital without having somewhere to go. I could not stomach the idea of her going to a homeless shelter, so she and I entered into a written agreement that set forth the grounds in which she would be allowed to return to my home, and any violation of those conditions would result in her having to leave. Within ten days of coming home, she had broken six of the conditions and she was told she had to leave.

Emily stayed with various friends but ultimately started spending time with the young man she met in treatment, Nick, who not only introduced her to opiates, but also apparently sold them. Emily later told me she started smoking OxyContin with him but when that got too expensive, she switched to smoking heroin. By her own admission, she was addicted to heroin and endured an abusive relationship with Nick.

A few months later, her sister reluctantly agreed to let Emily move in with her and her roommate in San Francisco. Mandy often came over when the roommates were at work. I was told that items consistent with smoking drugs were found in Emily's sister's car.

This was a time of great upheaval for Emily. She later told me she was addicted to smoking heroin but was able to quit, which made her quite proud. I encouraged her to stay away from Mandy as she was in active addiction, accordingly to Emily, and her boyfriend at the time was a drug dealer. She told me she thought Mandy was not a good person and she would keep her distance, something she assured me of as recently as two weeks before her death.

I went through Emily's phone immediately following her death. One of the numbers she called after she got off work that night was a number I didn't recognize. After reading one of Emily's journals a few days later, I noticed that she had jotted down this same number. It belonged to Mandy.

Emily's laptop had also been returned to us by the coroner. Since I knew her password, we could access her open pages including her Facebook account. She had sent a private message to Mandy asking for the phone number of a male that we've concluded was a drug dealer. It was Mandy who gave Emily the contact to get that last buy of heroin. While unsurprising to me, it still causes a burning rage inside at times. I absolutely hate that I knew there was something about their friendship that concerned me yet was unable to stop it.

Months after Emily's death, I read in her recovery journal that Mandy had introduced her to injecting heroin at a house in a bad part of San Francisco, during a time when Emily was in a pretty good place in her life. Emily later wrote that she believed Mandy deliberately tried to pull her down whenever she knew her life was on its way up.

My worst fears about Mandy were realized in the most heinous way possible. In my heart, I believe that were it not for Mandy and Nick, Emily would still be alive.

*

SUSAN CARLYON
Susan's 22-year-old son Adam died from
an overdose of carfentanyl in 2016

My son didn't seem to have a lot of friends. I felt that a couple seemed seedy or shady to me. I did not know them well at all.

*

MARYBETH CICHOCKI
MaryBeth's 37-year-old son Matthew died
from a Percocet overdose in 2015

Matt was an adult during his active addiction. Although a few of his childhood friends remained in his life, Matt gravitated toward those who felt his drug use was acceptable.

I did invite these friends to my home for holiday events and tried to keep an eye on who they were. They were shocked to be welcomed into our home. Many had heartbreaking stories of childhood abuse and neglect that caused them to turn to drugs for comfort and to find a place to fit in. That was the time when tough love was the mindset for dealing with an addicted family member. Many came to Matt's funeral. I still wonder today if they survived their disease. ♡

*

KIM DELONG
Kim's 29-year-old son Tyler died
from a fentanyl overdose in 2017

Tyler had a huge group of friends. I knew some of them, but many I had never heard of. He lived in his own apartment, so I really didn't get to see his friends like I did when he was still living at home. He told me about his new girlfriend in July and showed me a photo of her. I thought she looked very rough around the edges and I commented that she looked about forty. He was only twenty-nine so I though she looked too old for him. He got a little upset and disagreed with me.

I invited both to come over for dinner with us a couple times, but he always said they were busy so I never got to meet her. I also knew a few of his long-term friends, who I still keep in touch with and they share stories about Tyler with me.

*

ELAINE FAULKNER
Elaine's 25-year-old son Jacob died from
an overdose of opiates and Xanax in 2017

Jake, as he started calling himself in his late teens, had a wide variety of friends. He attracted many types of people into his life. Jake had charisma and people were drawn to him. He grew up with neighborhood friends and numerous cousins and became especially close to his cousin Richard when he was around fifteen. Jake got his driver's license and the two of them would go off on their adventures. Richard introduced Jake to his friends from another school, so Jake's circle grew. Jake gradually became friends with many people in his age group across all the schools in the county.

We accepted all Jake's friends, and made them feel welcome in our home. There were times when we felt a friend was not a good influence on him, but we tried not to judge. Many of the friends in his social circle died. Car accidents, suicides, overdoses. It seemed like every few months someone else was gone. The losses were difficult for Jake. He grieved the losses. He memorialized one friend's death by getting a tattoo on his arm. The losses were difficult for us as well.

Then came relationships. Jake picked girls he felt he could help; he was drawn to them. We embraced the girls he dated with open hearts and welcomed them into our home. The result of some of those relationships and the way they ended gave Jake some very deep pain.

The spring before he died, he started to isolate more and pulled away from family activities. He still had friends who he was in contact with. After he passed away, we heard stories of some of the activities he did with his friends. We enjoyed hearing from the people he helped about the impact Jake made on them. We were able to meet some friends who were new to us. We welcomed his friends and the door is still open to them.

*

SHANNIE JENKINS
Shannie's 31-year-old son Kyle died
from a heroin overdose in 2017

Kyle had pretty much the same group of friends throughout grade school and high school. I worked at his elementary school until he was in high school, and knew almost all his friends, especially those who went to the elementary school.

In middle school, he started hanging out with a few other friends, some of who I liked better than others. I knew some of the parents and was concerned about lack of supervision. Kyle got mad if I didn't let him stay over, hang out, or have the freedom some of his friends had.

Middle school was a hard time for both my boys. It was an age when it matters so much what others think of you and what you wear. There were some kids who I would try to get him to avoid, and I wanted him to do more things with others who he grew up with.

Kyle was into sports and did high school wrestling. He also was a good water skier, a passion both boys shared with their dad. I liked Kyle's friends and they were welcome in our home.

High school was when Kyle started partying and began hanging out with different people. When Kyle and his friends used OxyContin, it was the popular thing to do. In fact, many from his class of 2004, have dealt with this horrible disease.

Kyle went to parties and then the guys would fight. I'm not sure where he got the fighting thing from; it always seemed so stupid to me. There were a few situations when they got in a group fight and this started a huge war between groups of guys. And then, of course, there was always retaliation.

*

LORI LATIMER
Lori's 29-year-old son Greg died from
alcohol and fentanyl-laced cocaine in 2019

Greg had so many friends, mostly people he'd gone to high school with. They put together a dinner in his honor two nights after he died.

I walked into a restaurant that was filled with his friends and their parents who all loved my son very much.

I knew some of Greg's friends but not many, mainly because he was twenty-nine and hadn't lived at home for nine years. He now lived forty-five miles away. I knew his girlfriends and stayed close to some of them even after they broke up.

For several years Greg was doing shiftwork, working twelve hours at a time, both days and nights. The last four years of his life he was working full time and attending college full time, so he didn't have a lot of free time. Since Greg lived almost an hour away from me, I didn't see him with his friends. He would come to my house or we would go to an Atlanta Falcons football game or an Atlanta Braves baseball game. We'd go to a sports bar to watch the Georgia Bulldogs play football on Saturday afternoons in the fall. We'd go to my older son's house for holidays, and we'd go out to eat together as a family.

Since Greg's death, I've become close to many of his friends and wish I'd spent time with all of them when he was still alive. They're wonderful people and they miss him terribly. His death has affected each of them in very profound ways. Greg used to invite me to come up and do things with him and his friends. I always thought he was just being nice, and I didn't want to be the nuisance mom hanging around. He was grown and had a right to his own life.

I only met Greg's last girlfriend three months before he died. He brought her to dinner with us for his birthday. After he died, she told me that she had been strung out on meth when they met, and he'd told her that he wouldn't let her meet me while she was like that. She told me that early in their relationship, he took her on a trip to northern California. When they got back, he told her she could either have the life she'd been living (using drugs), or he could have the life he'd just shown her on their trip. He told her to choose, but that if she chose to keep living the life she'd been living using drugs, he wouldn't stay with her. The sad irony of him dying from drugs is that he helped her get clean. I pray she stays clean for her daughters' sake, and for Greg's memory.

However, he was living in what I now realize was basically a party house. The three men living there (Greg and two others) all had full-time jobs, owned trucks, jet skis, and kayaks. They paid their bills. They were responsible adults in many ways. But they all liked to have fun, and the three of them living in that house together was a very bad combination.

I blame all of them, and I blame none of them. They're all adults and made their own choices. I will always wonder though if Greg hadn't been living there, would he have been using heroin and cocaine? That question will haunt me forever.

*

DIANA MITCHELL
Diana's 18-year-old daughter Brooke died from
a mix of fentanyl, ecstasy, and cocaine in 2017

Brooke's friends were different from the friends she grew up with. I tried to figure out exactly where they came from. All were beautiful young women, and most of them did pretty well in school. The parents had nice homes. One was a doctor, another parent was a nurse. When Brooke revealed that she was an addict, I started finding out more. These homes, these parents would actually look at me and lie to my face as they were giving my child Xanax and alcohol. My gut kept telling me that they were the wrong people, they didn't feel right to me. Brooke made me feel like I was being judgmental and crazy. It turns out that I wasn't.

*

WHITNEY O'BRIEN
Whitney's 23-year-old brother Michael died from
a heroin/cocaine/benzodiazepine overdose in 2016

My brother never had a hard time making friends. He was funny, charismatic, easy to talk to, and genuinely interested in what you had to say. He always had a large circle of friends. We witnessed this firsthand at his funeral. Friends from all different parts of his life were there. Friends from growing up, from grade school and high school. Friends he made at work and throughout his adulthood. Even several of his old teachers and principals were there. Many of them have reached out to me since he died and that's given me a great deal of comfort. In a way, connecting with them helps me feel close to him. We are able to share stories and memories and keep his spirit alive, which is something I strive to do every day.

After graduation, several of his friends began to pull away as his drug use started to spiral out of control. I can't exactly fault them. Most people who don't use drugs don't hang around with people who do. So, it's no wonder we started to see less and less of them. He wanted badly to rekindle these relationships and bring positive, influential people back into his life. Unfortunately, he didn't get the opportunity.

Around the time of his death, I wasn't too familiar with who he was spending time with. I heard names but I didn't know faces. He lived at home so he didn't bring a lot of friends around; he would go to them usually. Sometimes a friend coming over really meant that he went outside and got into a parked car for an hour out front of my parents' house. We can all assume what was going on. There really wasn't anyone in particular that stood out to me. Quite honestly, he seemed rather isolated by his addiction. The majority of his time was spent alone in his room.

*

ALICE RICH
Alice's 42-year-old brother Gary
died from a fentanyl overdose in 2015

At the time he started using heroin, Gary was hanging out with some of our male cousins and a few friends from childhood. I already said that if it were not for the bad influences in his life, I believe that his life would have turned out differently. Those who wanted nothing to do with the devil drug made themselves distant. He had no circle of friends for some time. Just drug dealers and his family.

*

CAROL WALL
Carol's 29-year-old son Jason died
from a heroin overdose in 2016

A group of friends started hanging around my son who I didn't know. We were a very open family. I knew all my children's friends as they grew up and welcomed them into my home. These new people I did not know at all. Also, with living in his own home I was unaware of who was visiting his home. There are a couple people in particular that I cannot help but hold responsible, I will until I die. I have not been able to completely forgive them. Ultimately it was my son's decision, but a few directly contributed to his death.

CHAPTER SIX

A downward spiral

Heroin grabs ahold of you, and it won't let go.
It turned me into somebody I never thought
I would be. ~CHAD COLWELL

For some, it takes just one time, one dabble, for the power of addiction to grab hold. Others play with the fire of drug use for years before getting burned. At what point did your loved one's substance use begin to interfere with his or her personality and priorities?

*

KIMBERLY CALAIS
Kim's 23-year-old daughter Emily died from a multiple drug
overdose including heroin and methamphetamine in 2016

As I look back on Emily's life, I can see that her drug use greatly interfered with her ability to keep a job. She had no problem getting a job; it was, however, challenging for her to meet the expectations of her employers. As the co-dependent/enabler that I had become, I believed what she told me. If she said there was a problem at her job that brought about discipline or a termination, I supported her and told her she'd find something better. And she ultimately did.

I believe frequent changes in jobs is a red flag. In fact, all signs of erratic change should serve as warnings. I remember asking why her long-standing friends were no longer in touch with her. She brushed it off by saying that they were either busy or they were bitches. I later read in Emily's journals that she would "blow off my straight friends to hang out with my drug friends." I also learned that she'd borrow money from her good friends, telling them that she needed it for rent, and never repaying them. These friends pulled away from her.

The last time I saw Emily, she showed me scabs she had all over her body. She said she had a condition that caused her to pick at her skin and pull out her hair. I went to the drug store and got her Aveeno oatmeal bath to help her heal.

A month later, as I read her autopsy report, the doctor noted these scabs and gave them a medical name; I quickly Googled this term and learned it related to a condition common to those who use methamphetamine.

But I had believed what she told me. I also wanted to believe what she told me as I believed she had survived the worst of it. She was my warrior, so strong, so fearless, so beautiful, and destined for such greatness for having experienced such darkness.

When I listen to my friend talk about her daughter's addiction, I hear what she says with much more awareness. Things are seldom what your loved ones say they are. Their disease has a voice that sounds exactly like the voice of the person you love so much. But it's not. It's the voice of their drug. Their demon.

I considered myself well-prepared to deal with a drug addict. I worked in the courts for twenty years and had heard every possible excuse/explanation for terrible behavior and resulting crimes. I read all the reports about those who came in for the drug court cases. I considered myself skeptical of what people said and looked at what they did. I educated myself about those who suffer from borderline personality disorder and attended Nar-Anon meetings. Emily and I used to watch "Intervention" both prior, during and after her descent into addiction.

I **thought** I knew, and I **thought** I was armed to help her battle her demons. But I ignored so many things that now seem so apparent. While I can only wonder if any change of response by me might have changed Emily's path, I know that I loved (and still love) her with every fiber of my being, and I will continue to do so until my last breath.

*

SUSAN CARLYON
Susan's 22-year-old son Adam died from
an overdose of carfentanyl in 2016

The drug use began to interfere with Adam's life about six months after he started using drugs.

*

MARYBETH CICHOCKI
MaryBeth's 37-year-old son Matthew died
from a Percocet overdose in 2015

Matt's drug use made keeping a job impossible. He began hanging around the house. No ambition to look for employment. He neglected his chores I'd given him to do as I was a nurse and had to work. Those were the flags, though Matt had plenty of excuses for being tired throughout the day. He did have legitimate pain from the rods in his back after surgery that was the start of his addiction to pain pills. I would tell parents to be on the lookout for mood swings, changes in interest regarding things that were once important. Different people coming around the house. Physical changes such as itching, sweating, weight gain and just laziness.

*

KIM DELONG
Kim's 29-year-old son Tyler died
from a fentanyl overdose in 2017

I really started noticing he was having some issues at the end of July. He was visiting me when he got a call from his roommate telling him that they got an eviction notice. He made some excuses about his roommates not paying their share and asked us to make him a loan. I did and told him not to pay me back. That was the first time since he was on his own that he ever asked me for money.

About the same time I noticed that Tyler was not coming over to see us as much, he would answer my calls less frequently and I would make plans to come by his apartment to see him and he wouldn't be there when he knew I was supposed to meet him.

At the end of October, two months before he passed, I told him I was coming by with a care package, which I did from time to time. When I got there, he wasn't home. I texted him and he was at the store down the street. He didn't have his car so I offered to go pick him up and give him a ride home. He finally called and told me I was causing a scene, and got really angry and told me to just leave the package with his roommates.

I don't know how he thought there was any scene, as I was sitting in my car in front of his house. I told him, "No. I came to see you and I'm not giving this package to your roommates."

That's when I realized he didn't care much anymore. It was an ah-ha moment. Crying, I headed home and called my husband. I clearly remember saying something was wrong, because Ty doesn't care if I'm in his life anymore or not. Ty called me back and I turned around and met him at his house and gave him the package. That was about a week before he was arrested with another girl who was selling fentanyl, because he was driving the car when she made the sale. Looking back, I don't know how I could have missed the signs of drug use.

*

ELAINE FAULKNER
Elaine's 25-year-old son Jacob died from
an overdose of opiates and Xanax in 2017

Using substances interfered with Jake's ability to finish school.

Even though the use of marijuana, alcohol and pills affected his schooling, it did not seem to affect his ability to get a job. He eventually completed his education with a GED. He worked many different jobs in the construction industry and his last job was a journeyman electrician. Having a job did not stop his use of substances, however, and it began to interfere with his ability to cope with life. He began to have increased anxiety and depression. He went to a doctor and was prescribed medication for anxiety. That medication combined with other substances caused him to overdose.

*

SHANNIE JENKINS
Shannie's 31-year-old son Kyle died
from a heroin overdose in 2017

I could see Kyle's outgoing, loving personality really change at times. He wasn't enjoying school like he should be, and it was more about the partying on the weekends. Kyle was always a happy young man with a huge smile. He still was like that and loved all people. He started not doing as well in school, then not giving his best at work. Kyle's eyes always showed his soul and how he was feeling. He and his friend went from partying a little bit to huge partying. Drinking hard alcohol and the mission was to get really messed up. I always told my boys that addiction was on both sides of my parents' families and I was always afraid of who would get the addiction gene. Looking back now, I should have been a lot stricter as a parent. I allowed them to party in the back of the house. I was that parent who would rather they be home and have a beer than out driving. Would I do that again? No!

*

LORI LATIMER
Lori's 29-year-old son Greg died from
alcohol and fentanyl-laced cocaine in 2019

I don't believe Greg's drug use interfered with his daily activities until about a month and a half before he died. He had worked at one company for six or seven years, and then changed jobs three months before he died. The last company he worked for loved him. Several coworkers came to his celebration of life. They spoke very highly of him and talked about what a great worker he was.

At the time of his death, Greg was working full-time and in college full-time, making straight As. Greg used drugs recreationally when he wanted to relax and have fun.

I learned from texts on his phone that a month before he died, he missed a day of work because he was detoxing from too much heroin. Again, this was just a couple weeks after his close call with death at work when the drug usage increased. It breaks my heart to know my son was suffering and I had no idea.

Going through his phone after I got it from the police told me a whole different story. I saw photos of drugs. I read text messages about buying drugs, including one less than thirty-six hours before he died.

I went through his bank records and saw that he was having financial problems because he was spending money on drugs and trips. He never once asked me to borrow money or let me know he was having financial problems. I think he knew that if he did, I would have asked why he needed to borrow money since he was making good money at work and had relatively few bills. Looking through his phone and bank records, I learned that he was borrowing large sums of money from his father.

*

AMANDA MARIE
Amanda's 30-year-old brother Cory
died from a heroin overdose in 2015

The signs of relapse were there but I wanted Cory to feel like I trusted him, like I believed in him. Because I did.

Three days before his death, Cory went to a friend's house and claimed car trouble. He said he would be back the next day, but with another day came another excuse. He called some of his friends, some of my friends, and then he called me.

It was late at night and I was exhausted after a long, hard day of being everything to everyone, and had curled up in my youngest son's bed to read him a book. All Cory did was rant about some ridiculous idea he had for a business which equated to nothing more than selling homemade crap to people who didn't want it or need it. I used to call him an "entramanure," instead of an entrepreneur. His ideas were just that crappy. But these ideas were crappier. Cory was talking a mile a minute, words racing from his mouth and into the phone. I knew something wasn't right, but I never thought it would go as wrong as it did. That was the last time I heard his voice.

*

DIANA MITCHELL
Diana's 18-year-old daughter Brooke died from
a mix of fentanyl, ecstasy, and cocaine in 2017

Brooke never changed the things she did. She had mood swings and snapped at me, which was normal. There was never anything in particular that got my attention, and her good grades never dropped.

*

WHITNEY O'BRIEN
Whitney's 23-year-old brother Michael died from
a heroin/cocaine/benzodiazepine overdose in 2016

I've watched how exhausting, expensive, and demanding the life of an addict can be. It didn't take long for Michael's addiction to consume him. The drug use effectively ended his relationship with Erika, on more than one occasion. They tried to work it out, but Erika and drugs could not coexist. It had to be one or the other. It was a source of conflict in all his relationships with family and friends.

After his DUI, finding a job was next to impossible with a felony drug charge on his record. So, my dad hired him to work for his construction business. We all hoped this would give him a sense of purpose and self-fulfillment. Alas, I think all it did was put money in his pocket and feed his drug habit.

Eventually, my dad had to fire him. He wouldn't get out of bed in the morning because he couldn't. If he did, they were almost always running late. He would fall asleep in the truck. He would spend too much time in the bathroom. He would argue and fight with my dad.

Just like his on-again-off-again relationship with Erika, my dad fired and re-hired my brother, sometimes all in the same day.

His life had become a revolving door. Get money to buy drugs. Use drugs. Get more money. Use more drugs. All he could think about was his next fix. He became withdrawn and separated himself from the rest of the family, often cooped up in his room using or sleeping it off. When he did come out, he was often unpleasant and irritable.

We noticed his health decline. He lost a substantial amount of weight and would get physically ill anytime he went too long without using. He spent hours in the bathroom heaving and retching.

Michael's hygiene took a hit, and we all noticed. But that's the sad reality of addiction. It's not that you don't care about yourself, your appearance, your relationships or your job, it's because your physical needs for survival are completely skewed. The basic needs for humans to survive are air, water, and food. But when you're a heroin user, you just need heroin.

*

CAROL WALL
Carol's 29-year-old son Jason died
from a heroin overdose in 2016

Toward the end, maybe about six to nine months before he passed away, it was affecting his ability to go to work. He was an electrician and had a demanding job. He stopped playing rec hockey and lacrosse. I wish I had been more aware of the signs. I wish I had more patience. I've prayed for a time machine so I could go back to save him.

CHAPTER SEVEN

Tight grip of addiction

Opioids reach every part of society: blue collar,
white collar, everybody. It's nonstop. It's every day.
~WALTER BENDER, Ohio deputy sheriff

The distinctions between substance use, misuse, and abuse is often blurred, especially when substances such as prescription drugs and alcohol are legal and socially acceptable. No matter how it's defined, at some point it becomes problematic—and dangerous. When did your loved one's use escalate into addiction?

*

KIMBERLY CALAIS
Kim's 23-year-old daughter Emily died from a multiple drug
overdose including heroin and methamphetamine in 2016

Emily told me that while she started smoking heroin in August 2011, she was able to—in her words—walk away from it without too much problem. She also told me that once she began shooting heroin in July 2014, she was hooked quickly. She likened it to being held in the warmest embrace, immersed in love. It was the best feeling in the world to her, a feeling she chased each time she used.

Emily's life had many tumultuous times. It is baffling for me to know that the timing of her intravenous use coincided with relatively happy times in her life. She lived in a house that she liked. She had a job, a social life, and she had resumed important relationships that had been severed due to her past drug use. She was in a good place. I could easily look at other dark times in her life and be impressed that she got through them without drugs.

Since the worst part of her addiction took place between July-September 2014, all of us were clueless that she had started down this black road. She was very functional. But she was so skilled at keeping the dark side of her life secret.

It was her admission that she needed help in September 2014, that made us aware that she had a serious addiction. I am so grateful that she opened the door to her black Pandora's Box. That was probably one of the most frightening times of her life and it took great courage to reach out. I was proud of Emily many, many times during her life, but the moment she reached out to reclaim her life is one of the brightest moments of pride I've had for her.

Her last—and ultimately fatal—relapse occurred after she had a small heartbreak surrounding a boy issue, and lost two friends in separate car accidents. I believe she became overwhelmed with the sadness and disappointment and just wanted to numb out, as she had done before.

A few days after her death, I learned she had been communicating with a friend on the night of January 1, 2016. They were texting about the sudden death of their mutual friend. Emily's friend invited her over to hang out. Emily declined, saying that she couldn't as she was pet-sitting, but looked forward to hanging out with her the next day.

But that was a lie. Emily was not pet-sitting. She instead chose to use the array of drugs she had brought home with her over time spent talking and mourning her loss with one of her closest friends. Her social media post of that night indicated that she was numb by the news of yet another loss within one week.

And then she was gone.

*

MARYBETH CICHOCKI
MaryBeth's 37-year-old son Matthew died
from a Percocet overdose in 2015

Matt didn't experiment. He became addicted from opioids that were prescribed by a pain management practice. At first, he took them as directed. In my opinion, the prescription dose was too high and it came with an unending supply. His need progressed when he required more to get the same result. I found him crushing and snorting his pills one day. That was my slap of reality that we progressed to a full-blown addiction.

*

KIM DELONG
Kim's 29-year-old son Tyler died
from a fentanyl overdose in 2017

I didn't know Tyler was using until we got the call that he was in jail. I called his roommate to find out what happened, and had to pull the information out of him.

I asked Tyler how he started using drugs and he told me that his girlfriend, who had been an addict for five years, got him hooked at the beginning of the summer. I also found out that he had overdosed in August. His roommate found him and called 911, and they saved him. Tyler kept that a secret from us.

The whole process of his addiction was very quick, only about six months overall. He died that year in December.

*

ELAINE FAULKNER
Elaine's 25-year-old son Jacob died from
an overdose of opiates and Xanax in 2017

I believe he became addicted to substances quickly with marijuana as his first drug. He started to use weed daily and moved on to dabs, a highly concentrated form of THC that was very addictive. He would binge drink on the weekends and had blackouts by the time he turned eighteen. When Jake tried to cut down on drinking alcohol, his marijuana use would go up. He'd then try to cut down on marijuana, and his drinking would increase.

He started to use Xanax around age twenty-one and was very likely addicted to it. He would combine the Xanax with alcohol for greater effects. Like most parents, we could see the evidence of a serious problem, but at the same time he would hide his use from us. When he moved out, his use escalated and eventually he could not stop on his own.

*

SHANNIE JENKINS
Shannie's 31-year-old son Kyle died
from a heroin overdose in 2017

Kyle's use escalated when he started feeling like he needed the pills—it was no longer about having fun. The cost was around eighty dollars per pill. I wasn't aware of everything that was going on. I also didn't understand about opiates and the addiction behind them.

Kyle would go hang out at a friend's apartment quite a bit. He was living on the edge and I was very concerned. I didn't know how to fix his issue and wanted to save him.

My younger brother came down from Seattle and we were going to do an intervention. We went to his friend's apartment and sat in Kyle's car until he returned from dinner with his girlfriend. We saw him walk up to his apartment like the cool guy. When he looked over, he saw his mama sitting in his car looking out the open window. I said, "It's time for an intervention, Kyle." He took off running.

Little did I know that he took off because he still had some cocaine and wanted to make sure he used it before he went to rehab. An addict has to make sure they get that last high before they go into treatment. He came back to the apartment and agreed to get help.

We found a bed for him near Seattle and my brother drove Kyle and dropped him off. I knew my son was sick and really needed help. I had so much faith that Kyle would go in for thirty days and his life would be back on track. He did well in rehab, and a lot of my family went with me to his graduation celebration. He was always worried about his girlfriend, who did not do drugs. A lot of his energy was focused on her more than getting himself healthy.

*

LORI LATIMER
Lori's 29-year-old son Greg died from
alcohol and fentanyl-laced cocaine in 2019

Greg was a recreational drug user, and he died from fentanyl poisoning before he had the chance to become an addict. Knowing what I know now, had he not died when he did, I believe there was a very good chance that he would have become an addict. If Greg had been a drug addict, I would have absolutely no problem saying so. I make the distinction that he wasn't because I want others to understand that it isn't only the people we think of as drug addicts who die from drugs. Fentanyl has completely changed that. I was unaware of any of that until Greg died. Had I known sooner, I might have been able to change my son's outcome.

*

AMANDA MARIE
Amanda's 30-year-old brother Cory
died from a heroin overdose in 2015

When Cory was twenty-seven, he was arrested for stealing from an unlocked car at a gas station and sentenced to Sheridan Correctional Center, a prison that has one of the largest substance abuse treatment programs in the nation. Unfortunately, Cory never took part in the program, claiming it was never offered to him.

Cory stayed there for two years and then transitioned to a halfway house. He went from one to the next, and then took to living in his car, where he piled his belongings into a couple of boxes stuffed in his trunk. He then moved from his car to our mom's house a couple hours south. Eventually, he landed on my couch.

Cory found employment at a small pizzeria. He went to the public pool, the park, mall and the apple orchard. He would jog with my then five-year-old son in tow, toting jugs of water in each hand, bandanas on their heads and big dumb smiles on their faces. We watched movies together and made dinner. We stayed up late laughing and sometimes crying, comparing notes and scars. Sometimes we just stared into space, letting the silence speak for us. Then I would walk upstairs to my room while he settled on the couch. Cory had trouble sleeping. He would stay up late and fall asleep with the television on full blast. I would get irritated by the volume and the incessant opening and closing of kitchen cabinets. I miss those noises now.

We slowly rebuilt a friendship, one that felt less like strangers and more like brother and sister. Cory began acting like an uncle which was something my children had never experienced. I thought I had my brother back.

He relapsed a few months later. First, it was a social beer, then anxiety and pain medications. I'm not sure at what point Cory fell back into the black tar trap of heroin, but when he was found unresponsive in a McDonald's bathroom, he blamed it on food poisoning, which we all wanted so badly to believe.

Just before his probation ended, Cory was arrested for stealing a pocketknife from a home improvement store. They dropped the charges and let him walk. When the probation officer came to my home to give Cory a surprise drug urinalysis, Cory boldly told him not to waste his time—he had been smoking cannabis to quell his anxiety and would undoubtedly fail. That was the truth, but it wasn't the whole truth.

I used to wonder if Cory would still be alive had they sent him back to prison for violating his probation. It may have bought him more time, but it definitely wouldn't have helped him.

*

DIANA MITCHELL
Diana's 18-year-old daughter Brooke died from
a mix of fentanyl, ecstasy, and cocaine in 2017

Brooke came to us in July 2015, and said she had a drug problem. Her eyes were so dark that it was very hard to tell when she was high.

Her attitude wasn't any different than most teenage girls, but I kept saying to myself that her friends weren't right, something wasn't right. I should have listened to my gut.

*

WHITNEY O'BRIEN
Whitney's 23-year-old brother Michael died from
a heroin/cocaine/benzodiazepine overdose in 2016

Seventy-five percent of heroin users say they misused or abused prescription opioids first. This was the case for my brother.

On a whim, he began using oxycodone the summer after he graduated high school. Unlike most who obtain a prescription for painkillers after an injury or surgery, this was just another one of my brother's experiments. Another attempt to numb and suppress his emotions.

Whether he intended to or not, Michael slowly but surely built a tolerance and needed to take higher doses in order to feel the same effects. This triggered a domino effect. Swallowing the pills led to snorting them. Snorting them led to smoking them. And then, when they became too expensive and hard to come by, he turned to heroin—the cheaper alternative that was easier to access.

I don't think Michael realized how deep his addiction had become until he tried to stop. The first time he experienced withdrawals was when he took a trip to Six Flags with his girlfriend, Erika. He hadn't yet started using heroin, he was still using oxycodone. I don't know too much about the trip and how it went down, I just know that in an effort to hide his habit from Erika, he attempted to go on vacation without any drugs and got violently ill.

To my knowledge, Erika had no idea Michael was sick because he was going through withdrawals. Or maybe he confessed that to her amid the vomiting and agonizing. That's not really the point. The point is that his drug use escalated rather predictably for a heroin user.

No one starts taking painkillers thinking they will become addicted. It's true that my brother's intentions were to misuse the drug to get high. But did he choose to become addicted, overdose, and die? No. That was the heroin wrapping its sticky, disgusting hands around him and never letting go.

I'd like to sit here and list a bunch of warning signs for you or create some sort of how-to guide on identifying heroin use. But the fact of the matter is that I ignored the signs. I chose to brush off the seriousness of his drug use. I stopped communicating with him about his problems and limited our conversations to a slew of topics I rotated through. So, all I can offer you is a disclosure of what not to do.

*

ALICE RICH
Alice's 42-year-old brother Gary
died from a fentanyl overdose in 2015

Gary went downhill fast. He went straight to addiction. None of us really knew what exactly to do. We were all afraid he was going to overdose at any time. The only time we were at ease was when he was locked up. We wished for him to be locked up.

Gary was so sweet and charming that each time he was clean from being in jail, he had us believing that he was done with all that. I think he believed it. But each time he got out of jail, it wasn't long before he was using again.

A paycheck was his worst enemy. He had a hard time keeping a job after that first paycheck, and after a while, he had a hard time getting a job. I don't know if he thought just one more time or this time will be different, but he couldn't escape, no matter how much he wanted to. No matter how much we talked with him. No matter how many times my mom cried. No matter how much he loved his kids. Heroin always won him over.

*

CAROL WALL
Carol's 29-year-old son Jason died
from a heroin overdose in 2016

I describe the end of my son's life as a runaway train. I cannot pinpoint when the true addiction took over. The worst was from late summer until he passed away the following spring.

The addiction had been there a few years before, but he was able to stop. He did go to rehab for the first time about fourteen months before he died. But from Christmas, it completely consumed him. He went to rehab for a second time in January. He got out at the end of January and was gone March 17.

The mentality and behavior of drug addicts
and alcoholics is wholly irrational until you
understand that they are completely powerless
over their addiction and unless they have
structured help, they have no hope.

~ RUSSELL BRAND

CHAPTER EIGHT

The point of reckoning

Sometimes the transition from being in control
of your life to having absolutely no control is swift,
but other times it is so gradual that you wonder
exactly when it truly began. ~MICKEY ROONEY

The lies. The coverups. The arguments. The exhaustion, worry, and fear. Somewhere amid those landmines, the point comes when our head and heart agree that our loved one is in the terrifying grips of a terrible disease. It is then when we wave the white flag of reckoning. At what point did you realize your loved one was addicted?

*

KIMBERLY CALAIS
Kim's 23-year-old daughter Emily died from a multiple drug
overdose including heroin and methamphetamine in 2016

I have had such trouble—both then and now—distinguishing and defining the difference between drug usage and drug addiction. I know I found it somewhat easier to digest the concept of Emily as a drug user rather than a drug addict. They're just words yet convey such different images. Perhaps it was because the idea of an addict carried the stigmatized visual of someone who had no home and lived on the fringe of society. Emily always had a roof over her head, food in her stomach, clean clothes to wear, and a family who loved her.

I also think that the concept of addiction conveyed a slow death sentence. We had watched enough of the show "Intervention" to see the road that addicts walked and how often they relapsed—and worse—what awaited them. Addiction, for me, was the absence of hope, whereas usage meant that she would somehow get through it, a belief I held up to the very last day.

When Emily called me in September 2014, she used the word addicted and that was the first time I allowed myself to believe that she was in trouble, despite her penchant for over-dramatizing things in her life, usually for attention.

When the word heroin was the noun that followed, I felt a hot rush of fear run through my body. Hearing her answers to my follow-up questions about how she was using it felt like I was hearing the nails being hammered to her coffin. These were—and are—terrible conclusions to jump to and I had to remind myself that she was coming for help and that she wanted to change her life, a difference for those who had participated in interventions of any kind.

Since her dad and sister were the next ones to be informed, there was no disagreement that she indeed had a serious problem which frightened each of us in many ways. Emily's sister and I had seen her at her absolute best—and worst—during our years of living together.

In October 2011, Emily's sister had taken her into her home, despite her own reservations due to Emily's volatility, following her desire to leave her abusive relationship with her drug using/selling boyfriend, Nick. This included the time when she was smoking what we later found out to be heroin.

The ending of their cohabitation culminated in June 2012, when Emily came home clearly altered, becoming volatile, assaultive and destructive to the apartment they shared, requiring a call to the police. This caused a rift between my daughters that lasted about two years.

Emily was toxic to her sister's mental health and feeling of safety and it was necessary for her to detach from the relationship with Emily in order to survive. That rift was resolved in May 2014. Emily's phone call about her heroin addiction came in September 2014, a time when everything in Emily's life seemed so good and solid. Her admission came at a time that completely blindsided all of us.

Comfort was hard to find in the days and months that awaited us. I joined Nar-Anon which, in retrospect, did little to address the painful truth of my new reality. I read as much as I could about addiction as well as her previous diagnosis of borderline personality disorder, learning how those who suffer with this affliction participate in many of the things Emily had been doing. It's funny how the expression you can lead a horse to water, but you can't make them drink, applies to this and many other times of Emily's life. No matter how much you want them to get the help you know they need, you are helpless in getting it for them. I had taken Emily to therapists throughout her life.

I had led her to many resources of the water necessary to address her pain, only to watch her stand there and refuse to drink. She was a very headstrong and stubborn young woman, always feeling she knew best.

I found no comfort in religion, as I felt that a loving God (by any definition) would not wish this journey on those He loved. How could He? It was cruel and painful and a heinous example of contempt to me. I found no comfort in sharing any of this with family and friends as no one understood any of it and it only served to make me feel more alone while in the company of those who had known me for many years.

Then there were the experts. Try tough love. Don't alienate them. Kick them out. Bring them home. Detach with love. Hold their hand every step of the way. Cut her off. Don't give her money. Support her in any way you can. Create a network for her. Let her hit her rock bottom. Don't enable but love them unconditionally. That was a tough one. I loved—and love—Emily without condition, yet the line between love and enabling was constantly blurred for me.

*

SUSAN CARLYON
Susan's 22-year-old son Adam died from
an overdose of carfentanyl in 2016

I realized that Adam was addicted to heroin when he told us, and yet even then I had absolutely no idea how strong the addiction was or what an all-encompassing hold it had on him.

*

MARYBETH CICHOCKI
MaryBeth's 37-year-old son Matthew died
from a Percocet overdose in 2015

When Matt lost his business and then his home, I didn't confront him but did try to get him to understand how much he had lost due to his use of opioid pills. He was thirty at the time and became addicted to legally prescribed drugs after back surgery. There was nothing to confront. Being a nurse, I tried to educate him on how the addiction had taken so much from him.

The only comfort I found was connecting with other parents who were experiencing the same issue with their adult children.

*

KIM DELONG
Kim's 29-year-old son Tyler died
from a fentanyl overdose in 2017

I realized that Tyler was an addict when I found out that he was arrested and being held in the infirmary at the county jail. I reached out to his roommates to confirm it.

*

ELAINE FAULKNER
Elaine's 25-year-old son Jacob died from
an overdose of opiates and Xanax in 2017

We were concerned that Jake was addicted to using substances. He didn't look healthy. It was difficult to know how much trouble he was in because he wasn't homeless or unemployed.

Jake stopped on his own three to four months before his fatal overdose. He came over to tell us about quitting all substance use; he believed he was done. The fact that he was unable to stay stopped was clearly a marker of his addiction.

He became upset when confronted about not being able to keep his commitment to stay clean. He didn't want professional help. He was aware of the types of treatment that are available and how to access services. He gained this knowledge from the experience of supporting his girlfriend after she relapsed. He helped with the plan to get her into drug and alcohol inpatient treatment.

He may have minimized his problems with substances since they were just weed, pills, and alcohol. Being drug tested for work may have prevented him from using substances that would cost him his job. I was comforted that Jake was working and had goals and dreams. He wanted to buy land and build a cabin.

I had underlying anxiety about his using, however, and dealt with that confusion daily. Is he okay? Is he not okay? I would think about how to connect with him, and show love and support. I waited for the right moments when he would be willing to talk about his use.

I was comforted that he attended twelve-step meetings (AA and NA) with his girlfriend when she returned from inpatient treatment, and hoped he would get connected to the recovery community. I prayed. This provided enough comfort to keep my anxieties down so that I could function.

My worst fear was losing him and even though in my heart I knew it could happen, I never believed it would. I did not know he was close to the end of his life. I had my own form of denial. It's still hard for me to believe and accept that he is gone.

*

SHANNIE JENKINS
Shannie's 31-year-old son Kyle died
from a heroin overdose in 2017

The realization that this was a serious problem and Kyle needed intervention wasn't too long into his use of opiates. He was hanging out with a friend who had moved into an apartment. I went over there one afternoon and knocked on the door. I went inside and saw a group of guys Kyle had gone to school with sitting around the apartment. I pretty much came unglued and told them each to take a good look at themselves, that this was a problem and they needed to figure it out. Of course, this embarrassed Kyle, but I didn't care at that point.

When Kyle introduced me to a new friend, I would shake their hand and say, "Do you have a drug problem?" Kyle started hanging out with young people I didn't know. I tried my best to keep an eye on him and what he was doing.

It was very clear Kyle needed intervention. The first time he went into treatment was when my brother came and intervened. Of course, during the time in treatment, Kyle felt really good and was ready to start a new clean life. But it didn't take long for him to get back into town, into the same environment, and hang out with the same people.

*

LORI LATIMER
Lori's 29-year-old son Greg died from
alcohol and fentanyl-laced cocaine in 2019

Greg never became addicted in the typical sense. Only a handful of people even knew he was using heroin or cocaine. None of us in his family had any idea until after he died. Looking back, I realize that in a sense I was spared the heartbreak that many families go through when a loved one has an addiction. Had I known Greg was using drugs, and had he ever become an addict, I would have done anything and everything in my power to get him help. I never had the chance.

Greg had a friend from high school who was drafted by a Major League Baseball team. The young man was a pitcher. He suffered an arm injury early on in his major league career. He had surgery, was put on pain medications, and ultimately turned to cocaine and lost everything he had. Greg talked about him off and on for several years and was clearly affected by what happened to his friend. I believe that's one reason Greg was more careful about only using drugs recreationally. He never used needles. I'm not in any way excusing his drug use, but he knew the dangers and while he straddled the line, fentanyl killed him before he crossed it.

*

AMANDA MARIE
Amanda's 30-year-old brother Cory
died from a heroin overdose in 2015

Cory began to slowly fade into the background. Any semblance of who he once was eventually disappeared. His addiction took full control, and Cory's life revolved around his next fix. I hated who he had become. I resented him for not being a brother to me, and an uncle to my kids. I despised the way he treated our mother and grandmother.

I was tired from the emotional labor it took to comfort those he hurt, and bitter over the responsibility he put on my shoulders to clean up the mess he left behind.

*

WHITNEY O'BRIEN
Whitney's 23-year-old brother Michael died from
a heroin/cocaine/benzodiazepine overdose in 2016

The realization that Michael's use had spiraled into an addiction was the culmination of several events since that night I first heard the word heroin. It wasn't something I realized in a single moment. It happened gradually. I think I finally realized on my twenty-eight birthday that, wow, this is serious. This would turn out to be the last birthday of mine we would celebrate with Michael.

My husband and I had invited our families over for dinner. I had just found out I was pregnant with our second child a couple days prior. We hadn't told our family yet and we weren't planning to tell them that night, either. Our little secret had us feeling giddy and more excited than normal to see our families. As usual, I was worried about what kind of mood my brother would be in. Would he be social or withdrawn? Angry and irritable? Or happy and pleasant? You just never knew which Michael you were going to get.

The evening was going well until I noticed he was nowhere to be found. I asked my mother where he was and she let out an exasperated, "I don't know."

I started searching for Michael while everyone else was mingling and the kids were rowdily playing. Of course, he was missing in action. It was the perfect opportunity for him to slip away unnoticed. Except, he never went unnoticed in mine or my parents' suspicious eyes.

As I walked down the hallway leading to our guest suite, I realized the door was closed. I could see a faint light from the bedside lamp escaping the two-inch gap between the floor and the door. I reached for the handle; it was locked.

"Michael!" I called out. No answer. "Michael!" I said, growing increasingly annoyed.

"Yeah, I'll be right out!" He shouted back.

"What are you doing?" I asked, firmly.

"Just using the bathroom!"

Yeah, right. I knew better. Yet I never said a word when he finally reappeared. After everyone had left, I went to the bathroom where he presumably had used, and searched using all my senses for any sinister signs. I sniffed the air. I ran my hand along the counter. I looked high and low. Eventually I saw several tiny black flakes on the countertop. I brushed them into the sink and washed them down the drain. I was appalled that he would use drugs in MY house! In MY bathroom! With children innocently running around in the next room. How could he? Well, he will never do it again, I thought to myself.

The next day, as I described in horror the details of the previous night's debacle to my best friend, she responded, outraged, "So what did you say to him?"

Shamefully, I replied, "Nothing." I argued with myself (and her) that it was not the time nor place for an intervention. There were kids around, after all.

So why didn't I confront him that day, or any day for that matter? I still do not know. I had an inability to challenge my brother face-to-face and say the hard things that needed to be said.

If you live the excruciating and confusing life with an addicted loved one, I urge you to have those conversations. Be blunt. Let your loved one feel your emotions; expose your darkest thoughts and fears of their drug use to them. Because honestly, that's the hardest part, right? Saying those awful thoughts out loud sort of brings to life the possibility that they may happen. But it needs to be said and it needs to be heard. Your honesty will flood their conscience. Because if one day, God forbid, you don't get the opportunity to voice those feelings, you will regret it. Like me.

*

ALICE RICH
Alice's 42-year-old brother Gary
died from a fentanyl overdose in 2015

Gary was addicted by the time I found out he was using heroin. I pretty much found out at the same time the stealing started.

*

CAROL WALL
Carol's 29-year-old son Jason died
from a heroin overdose in 2016

As I said, I could not pinpoint it. It stared us in the face, and we could not possibly ignore it when he overdosed (the first time). Still, I could not believe it was opioids, I was so uneducated. Yes, we confronted him. We told him we were willing to do anything to get him help. We supported and loved him a hundred percent. Not a lot brought me comfort at this time, only the fact that my son was still alive... I had to believe that as a family we could beat this.

CHAPTER NINE

Impact on family

If your family member is struggling with addiction,
love them. Don't fight them, don't judge them. And
for the love of everything holy, pray for them.
~ANGELA DAVIS, Lily's Place, West Virginia

Substance use doesn't affect just the person who struggles with it. It impacts family dynamics in unexpected ways. For some, facing the journey as a family can strengthen bonds. For others, judgment and shame can bring about strain. How did your family react to the news of your loved one struggling with drugs?

*

KIMBERLY CALAIS
Kim's 23-year-old daughter Emily died from a multiple drug
overdose including heroin and methamphetamine in 2016

There was never a time when anyone in our immediate family who blinked an eye in accepting Emily after her admission of drug addiction. Despite our embittered history, Emily's dad and I were able to work together in getting her the help she needed and supporting her through the detox, treatment and recovery process. In sharing these memories, I recall Emily saying that she didn't want her sister to know, as she didn't want her sister to think less of her.

Emily and her sister referred to each other as built-in best friends. They were very close, and I know that Emily's choices in the past had hurt her sister, but she was and is one of the most loving and forgiving people I have ever known. She had nothing but love for Emily, yet I know she was so hurt and fearful of what she was doing to herself. Her sister had spent years in the shadows of Emily's dramatic and volatile rollercoaster. In so many ways, I feel that these events, and the ultimate tragic conclusion, hurt her more deeply than they did Emily's father and me. Every memory she had was shared with Emily.

Due to the nature of Emily's issues, other family members decided to distance themselves from her. Some members of my family are very religious and, although helpful with a rough patch that Emily had encountered months earlier, had detached from her in the following months. Her many phone calls and emails/texts to these relatives went unanswered and I know this hurt Emily greatly. In their eyes, Emily was a sinner who fell short of doing what was necessary to have them in her life which was, chiefly, active church participation.

While I was raised in a Christian household, attended church regularly and actively practiced my faith well into my forties, I found that the judgment, condescension and overall disdain for those sinners did not agree with what I believed God's love—or love in general—was intended to be. The expression "God is love" is often spoken, yet I found that those who wore their faith on their sleeves represented anything but love, not just to my daughter, but to all who were sinning due to sexual preference, marital status, and drug/alcohol usage, to name a few.

Comfort came sporadically through education and reading, but my heart was never at rest during much of Emily's life once drugs became the dark and silent shadow that changed my little girl moment by moment until it was her uninvited constant companion that devoured her brilliant and beautiful light.

*

SUSAN CARLYON
Susan's 22-year-old son Adam died from
an overdose of carfentanyl in 2016

We were all in total shock!! We were in disbelief, and very, very scared. Our daughter was also very angry with her brother.

*

MARYBETH CICHOCKI
MaryBeth's 37-year-old son Matthew died
from a Percocet overdose in 2015

It was never really discussed in our family. My mother is very black and white, old fashioned, and had no concept regarding it being a disease. She treated both of us with silence and sometimes ignorance. I was ashamed and rarely brought it up at family functions. My sister was supportive and gave me a sounding board to vent when I needed.

149

Matt's stepfather was incredible. I really don't know what I would have done without his support. He never stopped me from paying for treatment when it became available.

*

KIM DELONG
Kim's 29-year-old son Tyler died
from a fentanyl overdose in 2017

My family was very sad and upset, and almost couldn't believe it. I was divorced from Tyler's father, yet reached out to him for help. He gave no input and was of no help at all. My husband Mark was extremely supportive. We agreed that Tyler could come live with us while we he was getting clean and we tried to get him treatment.

We had many serious discussions with Tyler, and told him we would support him and try to help however we could. We just didn't have any idea how to help him. This was all so new to us.

*

ELAINE FAULKNER
Elaine's 25-year-old son Jacob died from
an overdose of opiates and Xanax in 2017

Our family did not consider Jake an addict. He was a person with problems like each of us. He was not set apart from the rest of us as the family member needing to be fixed. There was an awareness within the family that he was struggling with emotional and mental health problems. His substance use was not a secret. I believe it created stress in each of us, especially the feeling of not knowing what to do. I felt helpless as I observed the difficult things he was going through and wanted to help. Jake felt set apart from our family as his use started to spiral. Our response was to invite him to stop by, come out to dinner with us, or participate in a family event. He explained in a text that he just wanted to be able to go home after work and not see anybody or do anything. He started isolating.

I knew of inpatient and outpatient treatment services in my work as a drug and alcohol counselor, and longed to offer my experience and plan for his recovery. I still don't know if we should have tried a family intervention. It may have saved him, or he may have felt judged and retreated further into isolation. We will never know.

I do feel each of us in the family were supportive in our own ways. Jack met with Jake for lunch when he was working construction on a school near Jack's work. There were texts going back and forth offering love and encouragement.

I carry a burden of wishing I had done more, or we should have done this, that, or the other, but there is no way of knowing if any plan we could have put together would have worked. I will never know if he would have quit his job to go to inpatient treatment. It's easy, in retrospect, to form a plan or think about how the outcome could have been changed. That doesn't change our current reality. I believe each family member did all they could. He was loved and knew it.

*

SHANNIE JENKINS
Shannie's 31-year-old son Kyle died
from a heroin overdose in 2017

Kyle's dad and I were not together, but we raised the boys with a lot of communication. We didn't always agree on everything, but our boys were our main priority. Other people in the family who had issues felt it was never that bad because to their thinking, Kyle was so much worse.

One of my brothers had Kyle move to Oregon where he lived and had him working at his restaurant. Kyle seemed happy at first but felt lonely and ended up driving back to Olympia to hang out with friends. I wasn't aware of this until after he moved back to Olympia. Then Kyle decided he wanted to go to school in Santa Barbara. He had another friend, one who wasn't into drugs, who was going, too. They were going to move into a house.

We packed up Kyle's little truck and he headed to California. The first week there, he had a headlight go out, got pulled over, and got a DUI. It wasn't long before he quit school, came home, and got a job at a local restaurant that was opening. He somehow bought a new little car, moved in with a friend, and was feeling good about starting a life for himself. But the partying continued, and things seemed to get worse. This is about the time when we did the intervention and Kyle headed to treatment.

Later on, my younger brother offered Kyle a job on a fishing boat in Alaska. I was nervous but felt Kyle had to figure something out. It wasn't easy being a greenhorn on a fishing boat, but Kyle found a new love—the Bering Sea. He also found that he could come home with a lot of money.

*

LORI LATIMER
Lori's 29-year-old son Greg died from
alcohol and fentanyl-laced cocaine in 2019

Since we didn't know that Greg was using hard drugs, we were shocked when we learned he'd been using cocaine and heroin. Then to learn he died from fentanyl that was laced in the cocaine, combined with alcohol he drank that night, was devastating to all of us.

Since learning that Greg died from fentanyl, I have devoted countless hours to learning about this deadly drug. I tell people that if you choose to use any type of illegal/street drug these days, unless you grew the plant yourself, you're playing Russian Roulette with your life.

Fentanyl is being laced into everything: pot, heroin, cocaine, meth, and black-market pills such as Xanax and OxyContin. Fentanyl is used in hospitals, and for pain relief for things like cancer. But the illicit, synthetic fentanyl that's being laced into street drugs is deadly, and only a tiny amount kills people.

Fentanyl or its precursor ingredients are mainly manufactured in labs in China. It's then either shipped directly to the United States via the U.S. Mail or carriers like UPS or FedEx. It's also shipped to Mexico where the cartels lace it into other drugs which are then smuggled across the border into the United States. Because it's synthetic, it's cheap and quick to make, unlike waiting for an opium or marijuana plant to grow and harvest. The profit margin on it is astronomical, which makes it very attractive to the cartels and drug dealers.

*

AMANDA MARIE
Amanda's 30-year-old brother Cory
died from a heroin overdose in 2015

Our family was small, which left few options for intervention, support, or success. Most of our collective behavior operated under the misguided and guilt-free premise of the popular idiom: You can lead a horse to water, but you can't make it drink.

Most of our collective reactions were kneejerk and derived from the ego—from the personal hurt one feels watching someone they love slowly kill themselves, from the lack of control and the hopelessness that brings.

No one had ever been accountable to us as children, to the trauma we experienced, or the damage we suffered for it. There was no clean-up crew to speak of. Both our fathers were completely absent. Mom and Cory formed a toxically enmeshed, codependent relationship that churned like an undertow. If you got too close, it would suck you down into the deep, dark depths to drown. No one could afford life jackets. Everyone did the best they could with what they had.

Unfortunately, none of us had much.

*

WHITNEY O'BRIEN
Whitney's 23-year-old brother Michael died from
a heroin/cocaine/benzodiazepine overdose in 2016

A truth I persistently denied is that addiction is a family disease. You're all in it together, as much as I didn't want to be. In fact, I don't think I accepted this reality until after Michael died.

My brother's disease wreaked havoc on our family and twisted the ties that bound us. None of us ever truly understood the roots of his addiction, which caused friction and fueled fires that we were constantly trying to put out. I always felt in the middle; sandwiched in between my mother's compassion and my father's tough love. I skated back and forth, taking sides and defending one against the other. We were never all on the same page at the same time.

The perception that this disease is caused by a lack of support or morals or values shamefully kept us from sharing our deep, dark family secret. Which was very isolating. Not many people knew, and those who did know, did not know the severity of the situation.

Michael's disease inevitably took a toll on my parent's marriage, and I resented him for that. I hated watching them at odds over him. They constantly fought about what to do with him and how to handle him. Honestly, they fought over my brother for years, even before his addiction. Ultimately, my parents wanted the same thing for my brother—sobriety. We all just disagreed on how to get him there. I thought he should be kicked out. Really let him hit rock bottom. My parents did not. They were concerned for his safety and overall

155

wellbeing, but particularly his mental health. Kicking him out would not have solved his problems, it would have created more.

I didn't believe this at the time, but I do now. The topic of letting your addicted loved one live at home versus kicking them out to the streets is emotionally charged and the answer is different for everyone. We might have lost my brother a lot sooner than we did if he had been homeless.

The fear that my actions or words would enable his addiction hindered my involvement in his life. It's hard to find the perfect balance between support and enabling, and I rode that teeter-totter on the regular. I feel guilty that I was likely not someone my brother would have regarded as understanding, or even sympathetic. It's true, he knew I would do anything for him. But I know it broke him up when he knew he was disappointing me. He wanted me to believe in him and I just couldn't. His promises fell on deaf ears.

I remember after he completed his first stint in detox, he texted me and said, "I completed detox, Sis." And I just couldn't bring myself to write a reply.

I was angry at him. Before he went in, he had stolen money from my dad, a new low that he had never stooped to before.

I sobbed to my dad, "I wish he would just go away and stop ruining our lives!" I cringe just thinking that I could have ever said something so hurtful about my own flesh and blood.

A few hours later he said, "I hope you're happy."

I made some snide remark about how he should be doing it to make himself happy and not me, and that he had to understand my position and realize that at best I was cautiously optimistic. This only fed his despair. He was losing hope that anyone believed in him, even himself. I was not a good sister to him in his final year. In fact, I've probably been a better sister to him since he died. I've spent hours learning about the disease that killed him. I've helped spread awareness whenever I can. I love and support him now more than ever. But it's too late.

*

ALICE RICH
Alice's 42-year-old brother Gary
died from a fentanyl overdose in 2015

Gary was so out of control that I think the family was doing more damage control than trying to form a plan. He was stealing, and lying, and disappearing. I remember being angry and disappointed. He was always so strong, and proud of his strength, physical strength. It did not seem plausible that something could take control of him.

We were filled with disbelief, fear, anger, sadness, and panic. It's hard to come together in the midst of chaos and find order. Sometimes we were so happy to just see him that we did not talk about what was going on. My parents were very supportive and would have done anything to have their son back again and free from that awful drug.

Gary was addicted from the get-go. We knew it was bad when the stealing and lying started. Initially, his whole personality changed.

He was cunning and manipulative. The last year and a half of his life, he was more himself than he had been in a long time. I believe this was in part to him not having to steal or lie about what he was doing. Different people gave him money—he was charming. He had money to get the heroin and he was open about using. There was rehab here and there. That didn't work. My dad shelled out a good amount of money for doctors and other drugs designed to keep the addict off heroin. Gary took it for a while, and looked and acted quite normal when he did. Then for some reason he started selling it and using heroin again.

The nodding off and pinpoint pupils were always the telltale sign that he was back on the heroin. He nodded off when eating, smoking, Facebooking, and talking. It was a strange thing to see. Oh, he would say he didn't sleep well the night before, but we all knew. Besides, not sleeping doesn't do that to your pupils.

*

CAROL WALL
Carol's 29-year-old son Jason died
from a heroin overdose in 2016

I hate the way this question is worded. Jason's drug addiction did not define him. He had a substance use disorder. Our family was very supportive! This was our son, brother, grandson, uncle, and cousin. Everyone loved him and tried their hardest to be supportive. A lot did not understand the complexities of this disease. My parents were almost eighty, and this did not exist in their world.

Toward the end, a lot of his friends abandoned Jason. They did not understand why he couldn't just stop. Our immediate family were the most supportive, my husband, myself, his brother and sister. He was in a tumultuous relationship with the mother of his child, his drug use only added to the turmoil in an already disruptive relationship. Some people I did not involve at all. His coworkers were very supportive, and he had a very supportive union when it came to dealing with their members' issues.

Getting sober was one of three pivotal events in my
life, along with becoming an actor and having a child.
Of the three, finding my sobriety was the hardest.

~ ROBERT DOWNEY JR

CHAPTER TEN

Searching for help

Addiction is a very, very important thing that
has to be treated but has to be treated as a health
problem and not as a police problem.
~WAGNER MOURA

Medical intervention for substance use and abuse can be confusing and overwhelming. We'll try anything to save our loved one, and spend hours searching for help. Interventions, rehab, and halfway houses all hold promise for a future free of toxicity. What type of intervention or help did you seek for your loved one's addiction?

*

KIMBERLY CALAIS
Kim's 23-year-old daughter Emily died from a multiple drug
overdose including heroin and methamphetamine in 2016

Soon after Emily's admission of her addiction, her father found a facility for her within a short distance from his house. As the day came closer and her panic grew, Emily said she just wanted to go live with her father or me instead of treatment. I lived in Canada and she didn't have a passport, so that wasn't an option. Her father told her he wouldn't even consider it until she received the help she needed.

She continued to vacillate in her desire to get help. Her dad took her to the facility's intake where she met a street-smart intake worker, who was a recovered addict, and told him she didn't really have a problem. This man flat-out told her that she was an addict and that if she walked out that door there'd be someone else who would take that bed. He saw right through her and called her on her excuses. She thought about it for a bit and acquiesced. She would need to detox and then be kept in residential treatment.

In conversations with Emily's dad about post-treatment plans, we felt that a sober living environment would be best for her ultimate ability to succeed in sobriety. As this housing option was not covered by insurance, we would split the cost and give Emily the best possible start toward her new life.

After her admission into the treatment hospital, Emily called me saying how much she hated it and didn't want to stay. I told her she needed to stay, and needed to give it time. She didn't like this response and alternated between crying and yelling at me. As had been the case many times when dealing with her emotionality, I would freeze and remain quiet and calm, but my body shook in a mini-panic attack.

This would be the first of many phone calls while she was in treatment. During this time, it became clear that she didn't really want to be sober. I talked to her about sober living following treatment, and she said she wanted help to get past the heroin but still wanted to drink and smoke weed. I told her that wouldn't be acceptable for a sober living environment, and she became enraged that neither her father nor I would let her live with either of us. I attempted to deescalate her anger, but she told me she would just leave, buy drugs, and wander the streets since no one cared about her. She then hung up on me. This was not an unusual tactic of hers, so I took a deep breath and tried not to panic, but the reality of her threat caused my heart to race and I became sick to my stomach.

Emily's dad and I were in constant contact and we were both startled to learn that insurance would cover only a brief inpatient stay of two weeks or so. Two weeks to detox and commence rehabilitation and treatment for a condition that could take her life. Two weeks to give her the tools and resources to turn from years of using and abusing substances to deal with the pain she was feeling.

Two weeks to reboot and save her life.

I was shocked and angered by this news. Two weeks couldn't begin to address all that was necessary to give her the opportunity to fight for her life. It seemed destined to fail, and all I could think of was that if she suffered from any other type of affliction, illness or disease, insurance would likely cover every aspect of her recovery. But there was no way around it.

I even investigated private rehab facilities all over California that treated dual diagnoses of her borderline personality disorder and drug addiction, but Emily would have none of it. She was doing what she was told to do, and wasn't going to spend more time cooped up.

As was the case for most of her life, I was in panic response mode. I asked myself, what can I do to make sure she doesn't want to use drugs anymore? My answer at that time was to keep her calm and not make her upset.

I was also aware she would not voluntarily submit to any form of hospitalization, so I stopped looking at private facilities.

Much to my surprise, she did agree to housing in a sober living environment in San Francisco. She would be in a house with other adults in various stages of recovery, supervised by a recovered addict houseparent, with rules, regulations, chores, house meetings and random drug tests. She was required to find a sponsor, get a job, and work her twelve-step program.

For once, I felt a bit of relief that she would be in a safe place, protected from others including herself, and that the structure placed by strangers would be likely more acceptable to her than the structure I had in place for her throughout the years in my home. These were people who could see through her bullshit and not be subject to her manipulations. There would be no enablers or co-dependence. She truly had a shot at turning her life around.

Following her release from her inpatient program, Emily was also enrolled in the hospital's intensive outpatient program. She was required to go to sessions with her counselors and caseworkers, attend group meetings, and family counseling. Given my physical location, our family therapy session occurred by telephone conference. Our session did not go well which, while not a surprise, certainly caused me to feel like a failure as her mother, which didn't make sense to me, as I loved her more than life itself.

Emily and I had a very close and uniquely entangled relationship from the time she was a toddler. We were extremely close throughout her life. She would tell me everything—including things I wished I never heard—but I always showed unconditional love and acceptance. But we were codependents, and I was her unwitting enabler. While I truly believed that everything I did was borne from love, I look back and see how many things I would do differently if given the chance. I protected her from the consequences of her actions.

While I'll never know what, if any, difference not enabling her would have made, I do know everything I did for Emily came from a place of immense and unrelenting love, doing the very best I could at that moment in time. She was my precious little girl, a remarkable young woman capable of attaining any and every dream imaginable.

When I think of the time she spent in treatment and in sober living, I'm surprised that anyone succeeds. It is my belief that her sophistication in drug use grew because of her time spent with other addicts. She would tell me about listening to someone talk about a relapse and she would crave the high this person would share. Chasing the dragon, as they call it. She told me how others would tell her how she could use and avoid detection. One young man developed a personal/sexual relationship with his house parent, allowing him to break the rules on a regular basis. She would mention—and would also benefit from—a second houseparent's soft rule that if a relapse did occur, the person need not go to a formal detox for the required forty-eight hours. They would just need to stay out of the house and test clean upon return, whenever that may be.

The system that is currently in place to help treat people battling addiction and mental health issues is a disgrace. It is underfunded, understaffed, and seemingly under constant construction. The battle of an addict attempting to wade through the waters of this black abyss is akin to trying to climb out of a muddy walled well with unending rain. It is impossible.

We have addicts supervising addicts. We have doctors too willing to write prescriptions that result in addiction or pave the way for relapse. Our society glamorizes alcohol and the party scene while simultaneously denigrating and stigmatizing those who fall victim to the clutches of addiction, a society where people walk down a street, see someone overdose, and do absolutely nothing to help.

Insurance companies are multi-billion-dollar revenue machines, yet the dearth of services offered to those seeking help at the most painful and vulnerable time in their lives speaks volumes for the (un)importance that the citizens of the most powerful country in the world deem adequate. It's an embarrassment. It's shameful. It's disgusting. It's **unacceptable**.

The conversation needs to change about what constitutes rehab. I have read no report or statistic that suggests that anything under six months of residential treatment could begin to change the way a person suffering from a substance use disorder can confront their disease. I have met so many people who walk the road that I am now forced to walk. We are people with insurance, with an income and most importantly an unrelenting desire to help our children, spouses, friends, and parents get the help they need to save their lives.

Insurance coverage reform is the first step in addressing this epidemic. We need more beds in facilities. And we need more facilities in every city. We need to strip away the stigma that robs our loved ones of their dignity, both in life and death, from a society who has no problem saying that drug addicts get what they deserve because they choose to live this way when they could just stop. I've read the phrase "culling the herd" too many times to count, and each time it makes my stomach turn.

When deaths from AIDS first started in the 1980s, those suffering were also tried and convicted by the moral majority jury. They were ostracized and stigmatized, as it was God's way of getting rid of the sinners. Due to the passionate movement of medical professionals and the outrage of families who watched their loved one die painful, lonely deaths, the conversation has changed.

It's now almost forty years later. Treatments have been developed and the death rates for AIDS sufferers have diminished greatly. We see AIDS awareness dates, fundraisers, AIDS walks, and most of all, a societal shift from disgust to compassion, from apathy to empathy. From hate to love.

The same needs to be done for this epidemic and it needs to be done **now**.

*
SUSAN CARLYON
Susan's 22-year-old son Adam died from
an overdose of carfentanyl in 2016

My son asked us to take him to the emergency room. He then checked himself into a five-day detox program.

*
MARYBETH CICHOCKI
MaryBeth's 37-year-old son Matthew died
from a Percocet overdose in 2015

Treatment in my state is horrible. There is nothing long term. It felt like a revolving door. Nothing was effective. Matt finally went out of state but the insurance company cut off his time in treatment.

Scientific research shows long-term, comprehensive treatment is essential for brain healing. We must get to the root of the problem. Matt never used heroin. It was all pills. The insurance industry must recognize parity and treat substance use disorder as they do any other chronic disease.

*
KIM DELONG
Kim's 29-year-old son Tyler died
from a fentanyl overdose in 2017

I tried to get him help but he had no medical insurance. We took him to a few NA meetings, brought him to his doctor for evaluation and got him into a day outpatient program. Tyler went to the NA meetings but soon started making excuses not to go. He went to the outpatient program and checked himself out the same day. He did manage to stay clean for forty-five days before his fatal overdose. I think addicts need to go to treatment for several months, six months or more, far away from their familiar surroundings and friends where the temptations are not present.

*

ELAINE FAULKNER
Elaine's 25-year-old son Jacob died from
an overdose of opiates and Xanax in 2017

When Jake was eighteen and still living at home, we were concerned about his drinking, marijuana and substance use. We set up an appointment for a drug and alcohol evaluation at a local outpatient clinic and Jake reluctantly agreed to follow the recommendations. My hope was that he would get counseling and treatment to address issues that were causing his use.

The evaluator had no recommendations for treatment services. I think Jake was honest during his evaluation, but outward appearances showed he was clean-cut, athletic, and appeared to have no problem. I was disappointed that Jake did not receive services. At the same time, I was hopeful that he might not have a serious problem. Our attempt to get him help escalated the tension in our home, and he started making plans to move out as soon as he could afford an apartment.

Eventually he returned home, and we were able to get him into counseling. He was in deep emotional pain from life choices and a difficult break up with a girlfriend. He had unresolved anger. He was twenty-two and trying to make a new start. He resisted all attempts to go to counseling until I showed him a picture of a counselor with tattoos on her arms holding a pit bull on her lap. I knew of her previous work experience as a counselor in a treatment agency working in a youth program. I felt confident that she could help him if he would be willing. When he saw her picture, he nodded his head, he was willing to go to see her for individual counseling sessions. The counseling lasted for five months until he decided he was done.

I know how difficult it can be to get a family member to accept help. Being willing is something that loved ones cannot do for them. If I am seeking help for my loved one, I should be willing to seek help for myself and demonstrate to that loved one my own willingness to go to counseling and attend meetings to address my own problems. I will be honest as I share my faults with my loved one.

We can't control all outcomes, some survive, others do not. We are not God; we don't have all power to change someone's addiction or their destiny. We try our best for our loved ones, we try our best for ourselves.

*

SHANNIE JENKINS
Shannie's 31-year-old son Kyle died
from a heroin overdose in 2017

Kyle did go willingly to treatment, and again when it was court-ordered. His dad and I kept feeling that the addiction was so connected to his thoughts and brain, and looked into doing adverse therapy at

Schick Shadel Hospital in Seattle, where they have you drink a lot of alcohol and then give you Antabuse to make you sick.

They had Kyle smoke an OxyContin pill on foil and then take Antabuse. He was so sick. They try to trick your brain into feeling sick just by the smell of alcohol or drugs. Then they do sessions with truth serum where they ask you questions, and you have no choice but to tell the truth.

Kyle did good and seemed to participate in a lot of the sessions. He met an attorney there who lived in our same city. Kyle connected with him, and the guy loved listening to Kyle share. Kyle had a gift of meeting people because he had such a huge heart.

The guy was released shortly before Kyle was. Less than a month later, Kyle heard the guy died by suicide. Because he was a successful attorney and grown man, it really upset Kyle. He attended the guy's memorial and introduced himself to the family. They had heard about Kyle at treatment.

Sometime after that, Kyle told me he was at a house where people were shooting up heroin. He said it made him sick to his stomach; he went outside and almost threw up. It shook Kyle up but not long after, he was with a friend who showed him how to shoot heroin. That was the beginning of a whole new nightmare.

*

LORI LATIMER
Lori's 29-year-old son Greg died from
alcohol and fentanyl-laced cocaine in 2019

None of us knew Greg was using cocaine or heroin, so we never had an opportunity to get him any help. I will always have to live with that "what if I had known" question. I know we would have done anything and everything in our power to help him. Unfortunately, fentanyl usually kills people before anyone has a chance to get them any help, and that's what happened to my son.

*

AMANDA MARIE
Amanda's 30-year-old brother Cory
died from a heroin overdose in 2015

There were many times when Cory wanted help and asked for it. While he was still living in the halfway house, I spent countless hours calling drug counselors, mental health therapists, treatment centers, support groups, in-patient, out-patient, community programs and any other social service I could to create a safe space for support and healing upon his return.

Either there were no spaces available, the waiting list was months long, they didn't accept patients without insurance, they cost more than anyone could afford, they only dealt with drug addiction or mental illness, but not both, they couldn't be utilized without a referral from a medical professional, they didn't accept patients who needed detox, or wouldn't accept them without proof they were clean.

When Cory left the halfway house, it was much of the same. He couldn't get an ID without proof of address, and he couldn't get a proof of address without bills in his name. He couldn't get bills in his name because he didn't have an actual residence, and he couldn't get an actual residence without an ID.

He couldn't cash his employment check without a bank, and he couldn't get an account without a valid ID. The homeless shelter couldn't give him a bed because he couldn't provide them with current identification, or a previous address proving he was really homeless. The Peace Corps couldn't accept him because he had a criminal history, and he wasn't permitted to volunteer based on his status according to any of the organizations I called. Who knows how many job opportunities Cory lost by having to check the felon box on job applications. All roads led to the same place: nowhere.

*

WHITNEY O'BRIEN
Whitney's 23-year-old brother Michael died from
a heroin/cocaine/benzodiazepine overdose in 2016

My brother's attempts at recovery were both voluntary and court ordered. He was opposed to many forms of treatment and open only to a select few. Sometimes it depended on the day of the week or the mood he was in. If he was suddenly motivated to pursue treatment, we had to scramble to find something that was immediately available before he succumbed to his next fix.

The main problem we had with getting Michael into treatment was his inability to totally submit himself to the process. There were always excuses and stipulations. He thought he knew exactly what he needed to do in order to get sober and could do it on his own. He completely underestimated the power of his disease.

As a fallout from his DUI, my brother was required to attend group counseling sessions and submit random drug tests. Should he fail to attend counseling and/or flunk a urine test, he would go to jail.

The first year he cheated his urine tests and sat uninterested and unengaged in therapy with no real intent to sober up. It wasn't until the last year of his life that he became serious about treatment and recovery. He started going to NA meetings as well as SMART Recovery meetings, which he enjoyed because they were non-twelve-step based and he had no ecclesiastical interests. He attended these meetings voluntarily in addition to his court-ordered counseling.

In September before he died, I was feeling incredibly helpless. Michael had relapsed within forty-eight hours of completing detox. Hoping to educate myself and possibly stage a family intervention, I binged watched episodes of "Intervention," a reality TV series where addicts are submitted by their friends and family to appear in a documentary, exposing the impact their drug use has on his or her life and the lives of their loved ones. At the show's conclusion, an intervention is arranged and they're given an ultimatum to seek treatment. After realizing I was ill-equipped to handle such a task on my own, I decided to submit Michael to the show.

I refused to let myself get excited or hopeful that anything would ever come of it. Three months after he died, I received an email saying that his submission had stood out and they wanted to proceed with the process of including Michael in the show. My jaw hit the floor. It was a huge setback in my grief process.

For the next several weeks, I let my imagination get the best of me. I constantly wondered what might have been had I submitted him sooner. I envisioned my family sitting in a room together rehearsing our intervention. I imagined our pleas for Michael to seek treatment, and be prepared for him to oppose, because he always did, but we would convince him to go. I pictured our reunion as he returned from treatment, sober. He would be heavier. His eyes would sparkle and be clear. We would embrace and my heart would pound with relief and pride because he finally did it! But this was just a dream. Something that could never be. And I would crumble all over again.

Recovery looks different for everyone. No two people are going to respond to the same treatment in the same ways at the same time. Part of our struggle was not knowing what recovery meant for my brother, because it can mean a lot of different things. For some, it means abstinence-based treatment; for others, it means medication-assisted treatment. I support whatever works as long as it's safe and effective. I believe it's important to not only treat the addiction, but to address underlying issues that may have predisposed that individual. There are many proven, effective modes of treatment for substance use disorder, and everyone has the right to evidence-based treatment.

*
ALICE RICH
Alice's 42-year-old brother Gary
died from a fentanyl overdose in 2015

I personally did not seek medical help for Gary. He was a grown man. He did not seek treatment at first and had to detox in a jail cell more than once. I would think, as horrid as it sounds to go through withdrawal, that once clean, a person would do anything to not ever feel that way again. That is a logical thought, but heroin thoughts take over all logical thought.

I don't know of any foolproof or proven treatment type to work. My parents did all they could for Gary. They wanted him to be safe; they didn't want their son to die. Money meant nothing if it meant they could have their son back. I offered to take him to meetings if that was what he wanted, but he just said thanks and smiled.

He was most like himself when taking Suboxone. He was working here and there, and had a nice girlfriend. He was able to go do things he hadn't done in years, like go to an amusement park. He was a huge help to my parents around the house. He seemed happy.

He took Suboxone best when he was given the daily doses. When he was given the whole bottle, he sold it to buy heroin.

I don't think Suboxone is a cure or the answer to saving the addicted, but it did keep Gary from overdosing on heroin and it did give him a chance at a normal life. Maybe Suboxone would be good temporarily, like until the addict could get hold of their life and break all ties from their previous life. If the drug dealer's number is still in their phone, they aren't quitting yet.

I believe there is some underlying problem, like depression or anxiety, that needs resolved. Heal the spirit and maybe the mind will follow. Hell, I don't know. If I did, I would have saved my brother.

*

CAROL WALL
Carol's 29-year-old son Jason died
from a heroin overdose in 2016

Jason went willingly to rehab the first time. He was very strong, and willing to change when he first came home. I wish he would have moved away at that time. "You cannot heal in the environment that made you ill." I firmly believe this . . . same people, same places. He should have made a fresh, new start. But that is a double-edged sword, as his support team, his family, was here.

Jason did go on Suboxone and it seemed to be working. He was going to Guatemala but wasn't allowed to travel with the full bottle needed for his entire trip, so he went off it. I am a firm believer in MAT. I also believe there are good rehabs out there. Just like there are good counselors, you have to find one that works for you. The best chance for survival is a combination of everything that works for you.

For every drug overdose that results in death, there
are many more nonfatal overdoses, each one with its
own emotional and economic toll. This fast-moving epidemic
does not distinguish among age, sex, or state or county lines.

~ CENTER FOR DISEASE CONTROL

CHAPTER ELEVEN

Close calls of prior overdoses

First responders including police, fire, and
paramedics are on the frontlines of the epidemic.
~ CENTER FOR DISEASE CONTROL

Our loved ones can't choose when and where an overdose will happen. Like a toxic game of Russian Roulette, each use runs the risk of an overdose—and a fatal end. Thus, we begin to live in fear of each phone call, each knock on the door. How many overdoses did your loved one live through before the one that took his or her life?

*

KIMBERLY CALAIS
Kim's 23-year-old daughter Emily died from a multiple drug
overdose including heroin and methamphetamine in 2016

There's so much coverage in the news of the ongoing epidemic of drug overdose. I have read and heard stories of people being revived multiple times following an overdose. I have also read of people dying following their first overdose.

In May 2015, Emily and I were watching her shows "Keeping Up with The Kardashian's" followed by "Intervention."

While watching "Intervention," Emily said out of the blue and very casually, "So, Mom. I overdosed last month at my drug dealer's house and almost died. He called 911 and they took me to the hospital. They gave me a paper that said I had to be brought back to life and everything. So, yeah, I almost died."

What did I just hear?!

Emily was residing in a sober living house, so the concept that she even used drugs was the first shock. As I allowed my mind to take in what I had just heard, I was dizzy from my brain spinning. I started to imagine what had happened. Then I wondered why she was telling me this now. Why not last month when it happened? Why did she tell me at all? Were we back to square one?

I asked her questions, which she answered. Her most significant response was that it scared her so much that she kept the discharge summary in her wallet to remind herself how close she came to dying.

I was proud of her for telling me about this yet scared to the bone at the same time. How did this occur while she was in sober living? To add a form of narcissistic injury to insult, after her death I found selfies she had taken following the overdose as she lay on the gurney at the hospital. Who does that?!

As my initial reaction subsided, I was comforted knowing that she just might have experienced her epiphany. Her rock bottom. She had survived that overdose for a reason. She was keeping that letter with her to stay focused and to remind herself of the danger of heroin. I exhaled a breath I had been holding. This was good. This was progress.

Eight months later while cleaning out her room, after the coroner granted us permission to break the door seal, I found that letter. It wasn't in her wallet anymore. It was under her bed amid used needles. The irony of that continually takes my breath away.

I put that letter back her in wallet which, along with many of her personal affects, now rests in my nightstand drawer.

*

MARYBETH CICHOCKI
MaryBeth's 37-year-old son Matthew died
from a Percocet overdose in 2015

He was with a friend when the overdose occurred. His friend started CPR and called 911. I really thought that after the experience of nearly dying, Matt would come to understand how serious his pill overuse had become.

Unfortunately, the disease tricks the user into thinking they are in control. I remember heated conversations with Matt where I would warn him that one day he was not going to remember how many pills he took and die. He would smile and say, "Ahh, Mom. I love you too much to hurt you like that."

On January 3, 2015, Matt overdosed in a Boca Raton motel. My life has been changed forever. ♡

*

KIM DELONG
Kim's 29-year-old son Tyler died
from a fentanyl overdose in 2017

I found out that my son had one overdose in August, four months before he passed. He never told me about it until he had been arrested, and we bailed him out of jail and brought him home to get clean. It didn't scare him at all. I got access to his medical records after he passed away and I found out that he told the medical staff at the hospital that he didn't want any help because he enjoyed using opioids. I wish he had taken the offer of help at the emergency room when he been brought there for the overdose.

*

ELAINE FAULKNER
Elaine's 25-year-old son Jacob died from
an overdose of opiates and Xanax in 2017

One night, Jake's friend Jesse brought him home at 2 a.m. Jesse came to the door asking for help. Jake was slumped over in the passenger seat of Jesse's truck. I woke up Jack and we went out to see what was going on. It was obvious they had both been drinking. Jake was unconscious and could not be roused. We knew immediately he had overdosed and needed to go to the hospital.

Jesse told us Jake had been drinking and taking Xanax. I told Jesse to go up to Jake's room and go to sleep, as he was in no condition to drive. Jesse took his dog and they stumbled upstairs to crash on Jake's bed. We wrestled Jake out of Jesse's truck and into our vehicle. At six-foot five-inches, he was not easy to maneuver. We made it to the hospital emergency entrance and a nurse came out to help wheel him into the hospital. Jake completely minimized this and called his passing out a "xani nap."

The hospital staff were reluctant to hold Jake against his will. They asked if he was suicidal. He said no. The staff explained to us that since he was an adult and declined services, he would not be treated. I hoped for a blood test; but it wasn't done. I hoped they would give him some information on seeking treatment. That did not happen. I felt the staff minimized our concerns, and we reluctantly took him home.

Jake passed out again and woke up the next day. He couldn't remember anything from the previous night. He did not remember going to the hospital at all. This escalated the tension between us, and he planned to move out as soon as he could. To me, it was a scary sign that he was mixing substances.

*

SHANNIE JENKINS
Shannie's 31-year-old son Kyle died
from a heroin overdose in 2017

Kyle overdosed I believe a total of nine times. The tenth time is the one that took his life. Most of the overdoses I was not aware of until Kyle got clean and shared with me.

There was an incident in our downstairs bathroom when Kyle was staying with us. My husband heard a noise and asked me what it was. I said, "Oh, it's just Kyle."

My husband had a weird feeling and went downstairs. He came back up and said the bathroom door was closed and Kyle wouldn't answer. I went downstairs and opened the door. It was hard to open because Kyle was laying on the floor with his feet against the door. He had a belt around his upper arm and there was a needle on the floor. I shook him screaming, and he came to. I'm not sure if that would be considered an overdose or he passed out. But whatever it was, it scared all of us. Kyle jumped up and started crying. He and I sat in the TV room all night and cried.

Another time, I got a call from his friend saying that Kyle was in the emergency room and had overdosed. I got to the hospital and went into the room where Kyle was. I knew the emergency room doctor on duty, and he knew Kyle since he was a young boy. I was very upset and also angry. I didn't understand a lot about addiction at that time and felt it was a choice. Kyle's demeanor was not good. I was not pleasant either and said my piece after I knew he was okay. I told his friends to give him a ride because I was going home.

Another time Kyle had returned home from fishing in the Bering Sea. He was at his brother's apartment with his girlfriend and her child. She went into the bathroom and when she returned to the bedroom, Kyle was passed out with a needle in his leg. She yelled for his brother, Ryan, and he ran in the bedroom. He tried to put Kyle in the shower to wake him up. The medics were called and responded to assist him. Ryan was so upset and I'm sure he still has that vision of his brother.

Another time I was aware of Kyle overdosing was two months before he died. His fiancée got home and found him. She did CPR until the medics got there. I met them at the hospital. Kyle had been clean for over two years, so we were all so surprised. When he woke up, he asked where he was. We told him he overdosed and Brittany revived him. He was very shook up and did not recall any of it. In fact, this overdose caused some brain damage and Kyle's short-term memory was affected.

He and Brittany and her son had gone to lunch together earlier in the day. Brittany then left to get some things from her grandmother's house. Everything had been going fine. Kyle remembered going to a local restaurant and visiting with a girl who worked there. I ended up calling the restaurant and asked them to look on their camera to see if they saw anything strange happen. The video showed Kyle at the restaurant and also showed him leaving in his car. Between there and his home a couple miles away, he got drugs, used them and overdosed.

Kyle was so upset about his brain, and often cried about the drug getting him again. He was on summer break from HVAC school and was scared he had forgotten everything he learned. He was worried he might not ever get his full memory back.

When school did start back up, Kyle still excelled and was one of the top students. He shared with me that even though he got a high score on tests, his brain didn't feel the same and it scared him.

Because of him being so shook up and scared, we thought he would never touch drugs again. If we only knew then what we know

now, we would have insisted that he go back on Vivitrol, an opiate blocker that stops the brain from being hijacked. I truly believe in this drug, and oh, how I wish he would have stayed on it, even if it was for the rest of his life. It is better than death.

*

LORI LATIMER
Lori's 29-year-old son Greg died from
alcohol and fentanyl-laced cocaine in 2019

Greg never overdosed prior to the night he died. I often wonder what might have happened if he'd been found before he died. If he'd been found and ended up on a respirator or in a vegetative state, I would have had the chance to say goodbye to him, to see him one last time before he died. But I feel that might have been harder on me, and I know it would have been harder on him if he'd had to suffer in any way. No parent ever wants their child to suffer in any way, and I most certainly would never have wanted that for him.

*

AMANDA MARIE
Amanda's 30-year-old brother Cory
died from a heroin overdose in 2015

Because I had distanced myself from my brother in order to protect my children, I had no idea he had been overdosing regularly for years. My mother carried Narcan in her purse and had filmed some of Cory's close calls, which she later made him watch in an attempt to get him to hit rock bottom.

186

In one of those videos, he tells my mother, "Don't show Sis. Please don't tell Amanda."

*

DIANA MITCHELL
Diana's 18-year-old daughter Brooke died from
a mix of fentanyl, ecstasy, and cocaine in 2017

Brooke overdosed twice before we lost her.

*

WHITNEY O'BRIEN
Whitney's 23-year-old brother Michael died from
a heroin/cocaine/benzodiazepine overdose in 2016

Michael outlived only one prior overdose just eleven days before the one that took his life. It was the week of Thanksgiving, and the entire month had been a rollercoaster of highs and lows. Our daughter was five weeks old and we were enjoying the climactic high of her arrival. But my brother's disease had hit an all-time low and it rippled through the family like waves.

By now, Michael had been in and out of detox a few times only to relapse within days or even hours. I was worried, but told myself there was only so much I could do. I had my own family to take care of, and besides, Michael had to help himself.

Thanksgiving was two days away and we had yet to hash out the final menu and details. I called my mom so we could settle on some specifics. I was surprised when it rang only twice before she, evidently, declined my call. Immediately I called back. This time she answered

187

and screamed frantically, "Whitney, I can't talk, I have to call 911!" and then abruptly hung up on me.

Without hesitation, I knew something was wrong with Michael. The panic I heard in my mother's voice had me overwhelmed with concern for her safety. My mind didn't even really consider that my brother could be overdosing. I thought she was in danger. Maybe a drug dealer had shown up to the house and things got violent?

I texted her and asked, "Are you safe?"

She responded, "Yes."

I then called my dad, hoping he knew what was going on. He had no idea what was happening, and we rushed off the phone so he could call my mom for answers. About fifteen minutes later my mom finally called to explain that Michael had overdosed, and she was following the ambulance to the hospital.

My brother had an appointment with his addiction doctor that day, and Mom had taken the morning off work to be with him. She was in her room getting ready when she heard a loud thud. She went to check on him and found my brother moaning on the floor of his room, foaming at the mouth.

She managed to somehow get him in his chair but when she tried to prop him up, he would slump forward. To keep him from falling, she had to hold him up. He was muttering something unintelligible and he couldn't hold his head up. She was screaming at him and demanding to know what he had taken. He was incoherent and it wasn't until she declared that she was calling 911 that he perked up a bit out of opposition.

When the paramedics arrived, rather than taking Michael to the nearest facility, they whisked him away to a hospital that specialized in behavioral health in hopes that he would receive more specialized care for his illness. Spoiler alert—that never happened.

Once they got to the emergency room, Mom was told by the doctor that Michael was gurgling and coughing a lot. They believed he was having trouble clearing his secretions, and planned to intubate him if he continued to have difficulty maintaining his airway. It wasn't long before they placed a tube down his throat and he ended up in the ICU for three days, missing Thanksgiving. He actually had no opiates in his system, he overdosed on Xanax and alcohol, which was shocking to us all, since my brother wasn't a huge drinker.

After Michael was moved to a medical unit, like all patients who are admitted with a mental health diagnosis, he was evaluated by a social worker. Her assessment would determine whether his overdose was accidental or intentional, which would determine his treatment course, influence his discharge plan, and most importantly, decide whether treatment would be voluntary or involuntary, and whether he was competent to make his own decisions. His overdose was deemed accidental in nature, and thus treatment was up to him.

My parents fought tooth and nail to keep him from coming home. They pleaded with him to go for inpatient treatment or to sober living. They told him he could not come home and keep living this way. His exact words were, "I know you don't trust me, and I don't blame you. But I would rather go live behind Fry's than go to treatment."

Michael said he knew what he needed to do to get sober—he needed Suboxone. He wasn't willing to completely submit himself to treatment. He wanted to be sober in his own way.

He came home the day after Thanksgiving. My parents cleaned out his room and threw away anything that looked suspicious. On Saturday, we finally celebrated Thanksgiving. My mom cooked dinner, and I came over with the kids. Unfortunately, my husband was out of town hunting. So, it was the original McCarty party of four, plus my two babies and grandma. Unbeknownst to me, it was the last day I would see my brother alive.

I remember walking out that night. My family followed me out to my car and helped load the kids, as they always do, and then we said our goodbyes while marveling at how full our bellies still were. I remember hugging my brother extra tight. Not because I had any clue that it would be our last hug, but because I was so relieved he was alive.

"I love you. You know that, right?" I sighed.

"I know. I love you too, Sis," he said.

*
ALICE RICH
Alice's 42-year-old brother Gary
died from a fentanyl overdose in 2015

Gary did live through prior overdoses. I'm not sure how many though. There were at least three others that I know about. My dad told me very matter-of-fact, "Your brother overdosed this week." Dad was trying to be strong but was crumbling on the inside. My heart sank. I didn't know the details. Details didn't matter. He was alive.

He was with his friend in the parking lot of Taco Bell. She overdosed and he called 911. He did CPR on her but ran when he heard the sirens approaching. He was on parole and couldn't get caught with the paraphernalia.

One would think that seeing something like that would scare a person straight, but no. Well, it did work for his friend. She has been clean and going to meetings for nearly two years last I heard.

He overdosed in the parking lot of a gas station and woke up in the hospital emergency room. They let him go. I don't know who he was with, if anyone, or who called 911, but someone did. He told me during one of our talks that he secretly wished he hadn't woken up, because he was tired and did not want to fight the battle anymore. "I don't want to be a junkie" he told me. "I'm not gonna lie, the high is like nothing else, but I don't want be an addict."

I cried and told him I was afraid he was going to die, and I would never see or talk to him again. I told him that I would miss his laugh and his big hugs. I hugged him a little tighter and a little longer each time we said goodbye, and I made sure he knew why—one of those times would be the last time. I would put my head on his chest and listen to his heartbeat, then get up on my tiptoes to give him a big kiss on the cheek or the top of his head.

*

CAROL WALL
Carol's 29-year-old son Jason died
from a heroin overdose in 2016

Jason overdosed twice. I know the first time it scared the hell out of him, out of all of us! I knew this was real. It was terrifying. I thought we were going to lose him. I thought we were lucky that he survived, that we would go on to beat this. I still didn't think it was real.

I thought this is something that happens to other people, not to our family. My love was always so strong for all my children, but my love was now all consuming for my child who needed me so badly. My worry had no boundaries—Jason was all I thought about day and night.

CHAPTER TWELVE

Handling societal judgment

There is no worse disease than ignorance.
-ANONYMOUS

Addiction often carries a stigma.that the overdose victim somehow brought it on themselves. Such a mark of disgrace creates societal attitudes and perceptions that produce tremendous obstacles for finding treatment. Even professionals who treat them can be calloused and judgmental. As a drug user, how do you feel your loved one was treated by medical personnel and social resources?

*

KIMBERLY CALAIS
Kim's 23-year-old daughter Emily died from a multiple drug overdose including heroin and methamphetamine in 2016

As a drug user, I believe medical professionals treated Emily with a modicum of respect, particularly those who dealt with addiction. As a whole, I do not think the profession has a great deal of respect for those who suffer from mental health and/or substance use disorders.

I remember Emily saying to me that she felt as if doctors and nurses viewed her as scum when she'd go in for treatment for unrelated issues. While I certainly don't agree that this is acceptable, I'm not at all surprised. People from every walk of life seem to have the opinion that addicts are just dirty losers, people with loose moral character who are a waste of space and air, and put normal people at risk by leaving their needles and such outside where their normal children might encounter them.

I can't help but think, my daughter was once just like your little girl. Your daughter isn't safe in a world who doesn't offer intervention and education about mental health issues and drug usage. Your daughter could be my daughter, and my daughter could be yours.

No child is safe in a world that does not see a growing problem. I've often wondered why this generation is getting hit so hard, right now. I think of how tenuous a teenager's emotional health is during puberty. I add the isolation that occurs because of the continued growth of technology, particularly with social media. Many parents have talk about how depressed their kids would become from time spent on social media, viewing the snapshot of the seemingly happy and successful lives of others as the barometer from which they then judge themselves as a loser. Conversations and time spent with friends is replaced by text.

Relationships are started with the swipe to the left or right. Emily had a very sensitive heart and I believe the coldness found in the light of the screen and the tapping of a keyboard fed her tendency to become depressed. She would often look at the Facebook accounts of her former friends, seeing how happy they all seemed and all the wonderful things they were doing together—things she wasn't part of. She'd sit in her room for days without any human interaction.

I have always felt that both of my children were tremendous gifts with limitless potential. Each of them was smart, loving, kind, sensitive, creative, humorous, generous and beautiful both inside and out. The manner in which Emily passed away seems to have cast a shadow, eclipsing all those wonderful traits, summing up her life to one of a drug addict.

I've seen the head-cock and tsk-tsk of many people when they learn the why of my daughter's death. The seeming lack of empathy or sympathy for the significance of such an incredible loss is relegated as predictable, given who she was and what she was doing. I wince just thinking of those people. I have no use for their opinions or presence in my world. I remember reading a comment that stated: When you lose a child, strangers become friends and friends become strangers. So very true.

My daughter was many things and she should not be defined by any of them. Instead she and every human being on this earth should be celebrated for the sum of their existence. The many lives they touched. The laughter they brought about. The love they shared with each person in their life. The tears they cried. The battles they won and lost. The dreams each had, and the beauty of the uniqueness that made them who they are.

While I could list so many traits that might describe Emily, none of them holds a candle to the brilliance of the light which is the result of the totality of all she was during her far too brief stay on this earth. Emily's life had a purpose and she mattered then, just as she matters now. The awareness of this knowledge is what allows me the strength to get out of bed each day. Emily's purpose, and all that she was, lives on in me. I read a quote once by Lao Tzu that perfectly sums up my thoughts about Emily's life.

"The flame that burns twice as bright burns half as long."

*

SUSAN CARLYON
Susan's 22-year-old son Adam died from
an overdose of carfentanyl in 2016

They all seemed very stern and harsh. There was no empathy, kindness, or support.

*

MARYBETH CICHOCKI
MaryBeth's 37-year-old son Matthew died
from a Percocet overdose in 2015

As an R.N., I was appalled at how Matt was treated, especially by medical personnel. We are not to pass judgment—we are to save lives. The stigma was alive in every detox and emergency room he was treated in. Matt was made to feel like it was his fault. No one ever blamed his overprescribing pain management doctor. No one ever treated Matt with dignity.

The social resources in Delaware were terribly lacking during Matt's struggle. Unfortunately, we still lack the long-term treatment proven to be necessary to for survival. I wish I knew then what I know now. I'm angry and completely disgusted that substance use disorder is still being treated as a moral failure rather than the brain disease scientific research has proven it to be.

*

KIM DELONG
Kim's 29-year-old son Tyler died
from a fentanyl overdose in 2017

I believe Tyler was treated all right when he overdosed. He was offered help and he refused it. Of course his life mattered! He was an awesome son and a person who had a profound effect on many people; he was kind and generous to everyone in his life. Tyler was often referred to as one of the most intelligent people around, he knew so much and was always sharing stories.

Since he didn't have active medical insurance, I didn't know how to get Tyler into treatment. I'm extremely frustrated because shortly after he passed, I started seeing help everywhere. Why wasn't that available for him?

*

ELAINE FAULKNER
Elaine's 25-year-old son Jacob died from
an overdose of opiates and Xanax in 2017

I believe that the professional people who interacted with Jake did not believe he was seriously addicted, and his life was in danger. He interacted well with adults and could talk his way out of his substance use issues. It may be that there was lack of understanding on the part of treatment and medical personnel about addiction to pills and the risk of mixing substances. It was frustrating to have concerns for our son and then have others minimize our concerns because they did not see what we did.

*

SHANNIE JENKINS
Shannie's 31-year-old son Kyle died
from a heroin overdose in 2017

When Kyle overdosed in August before his death, his fiancée and I sat beside him in the hospital. Kyle would fall asleep and then wake up and ask what happened. He did this probably twenty times. We would tell him what happened, and he would say, "It got me again, didn't it?"

Yet Kyle had a hard time believing us because he didn't recall anything. We told the doctor Kyle had been off Vivitrol for about a year or so. Kyle also looked so good, and the doctor could tell by looking at him and his veins that he was not a current user.

The doctor said they were going to run some tests on Kyle's heart along with blood and other tests because of him not remembering anything. So, we sat and waited a good while. The nurse then came in and started unhooking everything. We asked if he was going for the tests and she said, "No. He is being discharged."

Wait, what? What about the tests they were going to run? She said the doctor decided not to. I walked out of the waiting room and found the doctor. I asked him why he had decided not to run any tests. He mentioned Kyle was an addict and there was no need. I was shocked.

I walked with my son and his fiancée out of the emergency room and to the car. All I remember is wow, this is what it feels like to be shamed. I was experiencing it firsthand and was so shocked I couldn't even find the words to say anything to anyone.

Kyle and Brittany stayed at our house that night and Kyle asked Brittany every half hour or so what happened. The next day, Brittany took Kyle back to the emergency room. She said to them, "You treated my fiancée like an addict who didn't matter. How dare you."

They apologized and set up a call to make an urgent appointment for Kyle to see a neurologist. Brittany called place after place after place but could not find a doctor to see Kyle because he had state insurance. She finally got an appointment for him in March of the following year, seven months from then. Kyle died two months later.

*

LORI LATIMER
Lori's 29-year-old son Greg died from
alcohol and fentanyl-laced cocaine in 2019

I don't believe any medical personnel ever knew Greg used drugs until the day he died. He was a healthy young man who hadn't been sick or had to go to a doctor in years. I was sadly surprised to learn that most coroners (especially in rural counties) are not medical doctors and are very much unaware of the realities of fentanyl and drug overdoses. The county coroner where Greg died could not have been kinder. However, when he called to give me the toxicology findings, he told me that "Greg must have intentionally taken the fentanyl because fentanyl is only laced in heroin, not anything else."

This is absolutely false. I started researching and found so much information from government websites and other sources that told of the increasing issue with fentanyl and how it's being laced in heroin, cocaine, meth, marijuana, and black market pills such as Xanax and OxyContin. Taking any drugs you buy off the street or black market today is nothing short of playing Russian Roulette with your life. And one of the saddest things is that because there is so little awareness of fentanyl, people don't even know they're playing it. Greg didn't, and paid the ultimate price for it.

*

AMANDA MARIE
Amanda's 30-year-old brother Cory
died from a heroin overdose in 2015

After seven months of waiting, two days after he died, the local hospital psychiatric department called to offer Cory an appointment for a mental health evaluation. When I answered the phone, I told her "Sorry, but you just missed him. He died. Maybe had you called earlier, he wouldn't have." It wasn't her fault, but at that moment, I wanted her to feel like it was.

When the hospital chaplain came into the room where my brother lay dead, his feigned sympathy wasn't enough to forgive the inappropriately meddlesome barrage of questions.

"How old was he when he began using?"

"How did a child that young get drugs?!"

"Well, did you ever try to get him help?"

The police department didn't seem to care that we knew exactly where Cory bought his last dose, even though it was from a well-known dealer they had been "watching and waiting to bust for years." The coroner missed the tiny bag of heroin still in Cory's wallet, and transferred it along with the remainder of Cory's possessions to the funeral home who also managed to miss it. It was returned along with other items of Cory's to us in a paper bag. The detective didn't seem the least bit bothered when I demanded he make the forty-mile drive to my home to retrieve the tiny bag of smack my mother and I had been so unfortunate to find. I wanted to be able to look him in the eye when I told him he was, at the very least, the third person in that scenario not doing their job.

*

DIANA MITCHELL
Diana's 18-year-old daughter Brooke died from
a mix of fentanyl, ecstasy, and cocaine in 2017

Brooke was treated horribly. She was lectured, and we spent one Thanksgiving in the emergency room for twelve hours. I'm working very hard to try to get the stigma removed. She was a child, not an adult.

*

WHITNEY O'BRIEN
Whitney's 23-year-old brother Michael died from
a heroin/cocaine/benzodiazepine overdose in 2016

Anyone who has encountered the mental health care system, particularly in the state of Arizona, can vouch for their shortcomings. My brother's mental illness went undiagnosed for over a decade. In part, because of his refusal to seek care, but also due to insurance obstacles, lack of providers, delay and availability of care, and soaring treatment costs. Unless you're wealthy and can afford to self-pay or extremely poor and qualify for government assistance, availability of treatment is slim to none. Middle America is not unscathed by this epidemic, nor mental health issues, and yet accessing care is likened to pulling teeth.

After my brother's DUI, he was forced into drug court to avoid incarceration and felony drug conviction. He was assigned a probation officer who was not blatantly malicious, but her attitude toward my brother was understandably punitive. Mind you, my brother's crime was possession of substances with no prior history or record of crime. And yet, he found himself thrust into drug court, deemed a criminal, with a judge playing puppetmaster over what Michael's treatment and recovery should look like. No other disease in this country is managed by law enforcement or the justice system. So, why is addiction?

These hurdles created by our fragmented behavioral health system, coupled with the stigma against substance use in our country, certainly hindered my brother's recovery. At some point, Michael forgot that he was a valuable human being. He was slowly accepting this disease as his death sentence. He had written himself off—he couldn't be saved, nor was he worth the fight. The amount of self-loathing that he endured weighs heavy on my heart.

*

ALICE RICH
Alice's 42-year-old brother Gary
died from a fentanyl overdose in 2015

I cannot answer this question well since I wasn't there. I do know Gary was treated. I guess the paramedics could have not tried so hard to save an addict, but they did.

When he overdosed and was brought into the emergency room the final time, the staff were amazing to us. From the emergency room nurses and doctors, to the ICU nurses and doctors, to the Lifebanc people, everyone was empathetic, kind, and professional. One of us stayed with Gary the whole time he was in the hospital and to my knowledge, there were not any issues.

Being a medical professional myself, I do not treat an addicted person any differently than I do everyone else. Maybe that is because of Gary, maybe not. I'd like to think not.

*

CAROL WALL
Carol's 29-year-old son Jason died
from a heroin overdose in 2016

The first time my son overdosed, he was treated extremely well by the medical profession. They were caring, attentive and genuinely concerned for him. They could tell he was from a supportive, loving family. Also, it was obvious he was not a longtime drug user.

There is a clinic in Welland that offered the Suboxone program (www.segueclinic.com), where the staff was wonderful! They were warm, caring and supportive. That being said, we also saw the other side of the coin.

The second time he overdosed, Jason was treated so poorly by an emergency room nurse who actually rolled her eyes as she was caring for him. She had no time for my son and treated him so poorly until I said something to her.

Our own family doctor, who had been caring for my son since he was a child, was absolutely appalling. She had no compassion whatsoever. I quit her as my physician after my son passed away.

The final indignity was the treatment my son received at Addiction Canada, which has since closed. I believe they were a direct contributor in the death of my son. This was a private rehabilitation facility that we were paying for. We had no clue, we just wanted him healthy and thought we were doing what was best for our son by sending him there.

CHAPTER THIRTEEN

The day they died

Moments are fleeting. Memories are permanent.
Love is forever. -LYNDA CHELDELIN FELL

No matter how long our loved one lived with substance use and abuse, an overdose death is a traumatic death that results not just in grief, but also personal trauma. We're left with a sense of shock and disbelief, and when we reach for support we often find stigma instead. Here in this chapter, writers were given a safe place to describe the day their loved one died by overdose.

*

KIMBERLY CALAIS
Kim's 23-year-old daughter Emily died from a multiple drug
overdose including heroin and methamphetamine in 2016

Every so often it happens...the moment when I allow myself to relive the undeniably worst day of my life. And each time I revisit this day, I relive it with tremendous clarity as every moment of that day seems to have left its indelible imprint on my soul.

It had been a couple days since I had last spoken to Emily, which was not unusual. I had received her text message early in the morning on January 2, 2016, telling me that a friend of hers had died. I had responded to her by text right away, but she did not respond. Again, not unusual.

Early morning around 3 a.m. on January 5, I had awakened early and was unable to get back to sleep. After a few minutes, I got up thinking I might as well go downstairs to the gym and get a workout in. I grabbed my phone and went to the bathroom to get ready.

While walking to the bathroom, I saw a missed call a few hours earlier from Emily's dad. I also had a text message from him, asking me to call him on either his cell or home phone as soon as I received his message. I stopped in my tracks and my stomach lurched. I thought, uh oh, and feared something must have happened. I briefly contemplated not calling him back. What I didn't know wouldn't hurt me, right? I dismissed this thought and told myself it may not be so bad. Maybe it wasn't the worst possible news. I called him back.

He answered after two rings and I asked, "What's wrong?"

And then he said it. Those two words. The words that brought my life as I knew it to a screeching halt. The words that seemingly ripped my heart out of my body, shredding my soul, and sent my world into the deepest hell I could even imagine.

"Emily's gone."

"What?! What?!"

He repeated those two words.

I screamed. The sound was primal and didn't seem human. It was the sound of my own living death.

My husband, who was asleep in our bedroom, was awakened by the sound of my scream and rushed into the living room where I was sitting. The room was spinning. I could hear my ex-husband's words but could not comprehend what he was saying.

He told me that two police officers had come to his house around 11 p.m., waking him from his sleep. He said they came into the house, asked if he was Emily's father, and then told him that she had died from an apparent overdose. He gave me the number of the investigator from the coroner's office who was at the scene.

I couldn't breathe. I couldn't see. I was shivering although I wasn't cold. I felt waves of nausea. I wanted time to stop. I wanted my life to stop. I wanted the world to stop. I wanted my daughter back.

He told me she was found in her locked bedroom. Locked? Why was it locked? Was this intentional? He said they wouldn't know until they performed an autopsy.

An autopsy?

He gave me the investigator's number so I could talk to her. I asked him why he was telling me these lies. Why was he doing that?

I asked him if he had spoken to our older daughter. He said he had tried calling her but there was no answer. I told him I would get in touch with her. We hung up and I ran to the bathroom and vomited. I looked in the mirror and didn't recognize myself. I was distorted.

I called my daughter repeatedly, but she wasn't picking up, so I called her boyfriend's number. After a few rings she picked up, asking "Mom?"

I didn't have to say much. I repeated those two words to her. Her boyfriend took the phone from her as she sobbed, and I gave a few more details but asked to speak to her again. I told her I needed her to be with her dad, as I wanted them to support each other.

I called the coroner's investigator, a very kind woman whose tenderness during those impossible moments soothed me. She said a preliminary blood draw indicated the presence of multiple substances, and that paraphernalia in Emily's room was consistent with overdose by intravenous usage. She said Emily was found collapsed from a sitting position on her bed with a syringe in her arm. Her computer was open to her social media page as well as a news article about the friend she had mentioned in her last text message to me.

The investigator said she found no note or evidence to suggest that Emily's death was intentional, but the toxicology report would be more detailed in determining a cause of death. She said my daughter's body had been transferred to the county morgue.

Her body? The morgue?

Every word I heard was like acid burning and disfiguring me.

She asked me about Emily's state of mind and about her history with drugs. I told her what I knew. Rather, I told her what Emily had told me, which directly contradicted the reality of what had happened.

Emily's dad and I spoke about funeral arrangements later that day. We agreed that we would not do a funeral, but rather have a memorial service following her cremation.

Her cremation?

He told me his stepdaughter had met with a mortuary near him and preliminary arrangements had been made.

I planned to fly back home on January 7. I was told I would be able to see Emily prior to cremation as there would be a viewing for the family.

A viewing?

I packed my bags in a haze. I did not sleep. I could not stop crying. My head throbbed. My body ached. I called Emily and left her voice messages, asking why this had happened, telling her that I loved her. I sent her text messages. That's what we always did. But there were no responses. There would never be another response. Yet I continued to text. I still send her text messages to this day.

My husband would travel out to join me a few days later, giving me the opportunity to deal with all that awaited me. I felt like I was in stupor as I boarded that plane. As it began to taxi and build up speed for takeoff, I prayed for it to crash. I did the same as it landed in San Francisco.

I was met at the airport by my former husband and our surviving daughter who was now an only child. I found myself thinking, what do I say when someone asks how many children I have? Who thinks things like that at a time like this? What was wrong with me?! We hugged one another and cried.

Over the next few days we visited the mortuary where Emily's personal effects were returned to me in plastic bags. Her necklace with the "E" on it had blood on the chain. Her cellphone, which was pass coded. Her laptop. I asked if I could see the coroner photos. I needed to see what they saw. I could not accept the reality of this until I saw something. The coroner's investigator looked at the images on her computer and then excused herself to confer with her superiors. Upon her return, she told me she could not show me the photos. What? But I'm her mother. I need to see those photos!

She said that she couldn't allow that.

My mind spun again. I asked her to describe what position Emily was in, what she was wearing. Was her hair in a bun on the top of her head like always? I needed to see what my mind could not—and would not—accept. I left with only words to describe the final page in the book of my daughter's life.

Next, we went to the funeral home and planned for her viewing, cremation, and memorial service. I asked if I could see Emily before they conducted any previewing preparation of her. I was again told that I could not. The woman said that Emily had been found face down on her bed and that the bruising and blood collection in her face made her unrecognizable, and the image would be too disturbing for me to see. I insisted. Once again, I was told I couldn't.

I felt helpless. I needed to see her and hold her. I knew how scared she must be, and I needed to tell her it would be okay. That I was there. But I wasn't allowed.

I did finally get to see Emily on Friday, January 8, but it wasn't her. I was presented with an object that looked like my daughter, but her body was hard. Her arms crackled when I bent over them to kiss her. I was told the crackles came from an ice suit used to keep her body cold. I kissed her face and the paint came off and onto my lips. Her fingers were darkened by ink from the prints the coroner had taken. We were allowed ninety minutes with her. I held her. I laid my head on her. I sang her favorite songs to her. I reminisced with her. I tried to inhale every possible millimeter of her existence.

The woman who applies the makeup for such viewings came in and asked if we'd like to keep some of Emily's hair as a keepsake. That sounded like a good idea. I watched as she snipped portions of Emily's long hair for the three of us, the same hair I had just dyed two weeks ago at her request. It was then time to go. We each said our goodbyes and watched the door close.

Earlier that day we had gone to Emily's house to start the task of packing up the physical remainder of her life. I had just sat in her room with her two weeks prior, watching "A Christmas Story" and holding hands before I returned to Toronto.

We had to break the coroner's seal to enter. I lost my breath as we walked in. The room was more or less as I had just seen it.

More or less.

Her comforter was now stained with dried blood and urine. The blood stains had seeped through the thick comforter, through her sheets, blankets and mattress pad, resting in a large stain on her new memory foam bed that I had bought her ten days prior. I collapsed on her bed, the place where she had taken her last breath. And I sobbed. That blood represented her life and death. It was all that was left. Although we disposed of the bedding, I held on to that sheet. I couldn't let what represented the end of her life go. I kept the sheet and it is with me still.

The task of cleaning her room revealed many things. Used syringes were found on the floor and in her wastebasket, indicating to us that she had been using longer than one night. I found a container with white colored bar tablets. We learned from her laptop that she had bought fifty benzodiazepine 5 mg bars from a street dealer shortly after Christmas. Thirty-two of those bars remained. Eighteen were gone. Ninety milligrams had been ingested in less than one week.

What happened?!

I found a syringe with a brown liquid residue inside and a bent, bloody needle. I studied that syringe. I took a picture of it with my phone. I look at that photo from time to time and wonder so many things. But mostly I just wonder, why?

I was fortunate to have stayed with Emily's dad and his wife during this time. The support we could offer one another was critical for survival over the days that were yet to come. My husband joined me a few days later, and likewise was welcomed into their home. A new family was formed, one borne from tragedy, nourished with tears and pain, and woven together with strength, love and commitment as we honored our beloved Emily, not just then, but always.

*

SUSAN CARLYON
Susan's 22-year-old son Adam died from
an overdose of carfentanyl in 2016

Each and every moment of the day my son, Adam, overdosed is permanently seared into my brain. We had returned from a wonderful family vacation to the beach, and were all headed back to work that day. My son left the house before me because he had a drug outpatient class to attend. I left for work before he returned home. He and I texted each other later that afternoon. My daughter stopped home in the afternoon in between her two jobs. She and Adam were in their rooms bantering back and forth. They both worked at the same place, but my daughter had to start work an hour earlier, so she left before he did.

As the time came and went past my son's scheduled start time, my daughter started to worry. Her brother wasn't answering her calls or texts. She started to panic and called her dad to tell him to go home and check on Adam. She also called the next-door neighbor who was a dear friend and had a key to our house.

My husband rushed home and saw that Adam's car was in the garage. He ran up to Adam's bedroom, where he found the door locked. There was no response when he called out Adam's name or pounded on the door. He broke down the door and found Adam unconscious on his bedroom floor. He found that Adam wasn't breathing but had a very faint pulse. He started CPR and called 911.

The rescue squad and paramedics arrived and took over the CPR from my husband. Adam was administered two doses of Narcan but remained unconscious. He was transported by ambulance to the nearest emergency room. At that point my husband called me on my cellphone as I was driving to my second job of the day. I was in total shock and I kept screaming into the phone, "Is he still alive?!"

I was an hour away from home but quickly turned around and headed to the emergency room, not even remembering how I got there. When I arrived, the hospital personnel rushed me into a private waiting room where my husband and daughter were waiting along with all my neighbors who had seen the ambulance. The emergency room doctors were trying to stabilize Adam. We were not yet allowed to go and see him. Finally, a nurse came and said that my husband, daughter, and I were allowed to come back.

Adam was lying on a gurney with IVs and tubes going in and out of him. He was still unconscious and looked white and pasty. We were told that his heart had stopped a number of times, but because he was so young and otherwise healthy, they kept trying to revive him. They felt that he was finally stable enough to be transported by ambulance to the main hospital where a bed waited for him in intensive care. We were allowed a few minutes with him and were then told to follow the ambulance to the hospital. A neighbor drove us to the hospital. We actually beat the ambulance and were waiting outside intensive care as they wheeled Adam in. I felt sick to my stomach seeing my son like that, and was absolutely terrified.

Once again, we had to wait in a private waiting room as they got my son set up in his room. We were surrounded by friends, relatives, coworkers, and neighbors as we waited for news. A hospital chaplain came to talk to us along with a nurse and a representative from Lifebanc. I was trying to understand everything that I was being told.

After what seemed like an eternity, we were allowed to go back and see Adam. Once again, he had tubes and IVs everywhere, but this time he was also hooked up to life support. Was this really my son lying there?! How could this be?! He was so still, so quiet. The only noise was the machines keeping him alive. I so badly wanted Adam to hear my voice and know that I was there! I started talking and talking and talking. I told Adam how very much I loved him, how sorry I was for all his pain and suffering, and how proud I was of him. I held his hand and kissed his head and cheek.

Adam's friends, coworkers, relatives, and neighbors took turns going back to see him. We were told Adam was stable and holding his own, but tests were to be done in the morning to determine how much brain damage had been sustained. Everyone went home to get some rest except for me, my husband, and a very close friend-neighbor. We sat with Adam, talked to him and touched him, hoping he could hear us and feel us with him.

In the middle of the night, Adam once again went into cardiac arrest. We were quickly ushered into the hall as the doctors rushed into Adam's room. We waited outside his door, terrified, wondering if Adam could be saved. The doctors came out and said that they were able to revive him, but his body couldn't take anymore. We had to make a heartbreaking decision. I asked the doctor, "What would you do if this was your son?"

The doctor told me that Adam was in very bad shape and wasn't going to get better. I called my daughter to tell her to rush back to the hospital because we were going to take Adam off life support. She started screaming, and didn't understand why we would do that.

We called people back to the hospital. As soon as my daughter arrived, my husband and I took her into Adam's room to say our goodbyes. Tears were pouring from our eyes and our hearts. How do you say goodbye to someone whom you love more than life itself and who is being taken away from you so tragically?!

We told the nurse we were ready, but in actuality, we were never ready to have Adam leave us. My daughter asked if she could have some time alone with her brother. She was with him for quite some time, and then it was my turn. It took me two hours to leave my son's side. I had to leave before his body turned cold and hard. I wanted to remember him warm, soft, and alive. It was now time to start making the endless needed calls.

*

MARYBETH CICHOCKI
MaryBeth's 37-year-old son Matthew died
from a Percocet overdose in 2015

Matt overdosed in Boca Raton after relapsing at a so-called sober home. The owner took it upon himself to dump Matt at a motel rather than the emergency department or detox where Matt would have been treated by medical professionals. I had just spoken to him on a Friday night and he sounded fine.

I was working a twelve-hour shift in the neonatal ICU when my husband showed up at the hospital. A police officer had come to our house and gave my husband the news that Matt was dead. I remember seeing my husband's face and thinking his father had died. I never thought that it was Matt.

I remember feeling like I was dying. I remember screaming and feeling like I was leaving my body. My coworkers helped me out to my husband's car as I slipped into shock. I remember feeling disconnected from the world.

My husband and I planned Matt's memorial service. I wrote his obituary and spoke at his funeral. My mother requested that she and my father be omitted from Matt's obituary. That was a knife to my heart. She was too worried about what her friends would think about his addiction. She never called or came to my home after Matt's death. I felt abandoned and alone. To this day I have three friends who have stood by my side through my grieving.

I remember the cold, the snow, and the bitter wind. I remember Matt laying so still at our private viewing. I remember laying my head on his chest wanting to hear his heart beating. I wanted to wake up from the nightmare of saying goodbye to my heart.

*

KIM DELONG
Kim's 29-year-old son Tyler died
from a fentanyl overdose in 2017

It was the morning of Christmas Eve. Tyler was staying at my house, getting clean and trying to get his life in order. It was also my mother's birthday and we were all getting ready to head out to see her.

Tyler didn't answer when we knocked on the bedroom door, so we thought he was just trying to sleep a little late. About a half hour later, we knocked again and called his name. We finally forced our way into his room. He was laying on the bed and looked like he was sleeping. I reached out and touched his arm and said, "Hey, Ty, it's time to get up." I realized something was wrong; his arm was freezing cold and he was very gray. I screamed and my husband screamed, and we called 911. The dispatcher kept asking me if I thought it was too late. I was so upset and didn't know how to answer. How would I know whether it was too late or not? I'm not a doctor. The police and medics came, but it was too late. Tyler had been dead for about eight hours.

We made the arrangements and decided to have Tyler's body cremated. I felt very supported by my husband and my family. We were all very shocked. I will never forget what Tyler looked like, and think of it often, as it's imbedded in my brain. He looked very peaceful. He had a very small grin on his face, so I think he had no pain when he passed.

*

ELAINE FAULKNER
Elaine's 25-year-old son Jacob died from
an overdose of opiates and Xanax in 2017

I woke up that July morning with an uneasy feeling. Jake was on my mind; I couldn't stop thinking about him. It was a Sunday morning and I sat on the couch drinking coffee. I sent him a text and waited for a response. Sometimes he responded right away, and other times he would get back to me later. My anxiety built over the course of the day, but I reminded myself that sometimes Jake was slow to respond.

It was a beautiful sunny day. Maybe he was at the lake with some friends, I thought to myself. At 10 p.m. I went to bed and was just dozing off when I heard Jack take a phone call. I could tell by Jack's voice that something was wrong. The call was from Pete. Jake lived in Pete and Delia's basement apartment.

"That was Pete," Jack said. "Jacob's dead and we have to go there right away."

Those were the most agonizing words I have ever heard, and my heart broke in two. My worst fear was confirmed.

I immediately thought about our daughters. One lived nearby with her new husband, and our youngest daughter lived about an hour and a half away. I was especially concerned for her being alone when hearing the news. Jack called to tell them what happened. I was overwhelmed at how they would take such horrifying news.

We immediately got in the car and drove to Pete and Delia's house. I was devasted that this happened in their home. Pete and Delia had known Jacob since he was a baby, and loved him like a son.

When we pulled up to the house, the police were there and two officers were examining Jake's room for evidence. There was another officer out front. A volunteer came to emotionally support the family. I appreciated that a stranger would come out to help.

We sat on the front porch with Pete and Delia, and took turns consoling each other. I was in shock and tried to hold it together. I just could not think about what was happening and why we were there. It was just too monstrous to think of him passed away so close by.

The police said they found pills and believed it was an accidental overdose. They said there was no note or evidence to suggest Jake took his own life. They said staff from the medical examiner's office would arrive shortly, and we would be contacted by their office on Tuesday.

Two young men arrived in the medical examiner's van to take Jacob. I could imagine there would be some struggle getting his very tall frame up the narrow stairs from the basement. It seemed like a good moment to say goodbye and then leave to pick up our youngest daughter. I was anxious to comfort my daughters, and knew it was going to be a long road ahead.

It was dark and quiet on the highway. I don't remember if Jack and I talked much. I called my sister on the way. I asked her to let the rest of our family know in the morning.

*

SHANNIE JENKINS
Shannie's 31-year-old son Kyle died
from a heroin overdose in 2017

The day before, I was having a wellness retreat at my house with coworkers. We received a call that one of our coworkers, who was a dear friend to me, was given two weeks to live. He had been in the hospital for a couple days for his lungs. My coworkers locked up my house while I headed to the hospital.

I sat on Greg's bed and he said, "I need to marry Julie today."

Julie was his fiancée, and my dear friend. Our work family was incredible. We headed to the courthouse for a license, to the store for a cake, champagne, flowers, and to the Halloween store for a veil. We all met back at the hospital.

Julie asked if I would stand up with her. A male nurse grabbed his guitar and played while Julie walked through the door of his hospital room. It was crowded with friends and family. After celebrating, we all went home except for the close family.

Two hours later we got a call that Greg had passed. My husband and I rushed back to the hospital to say goodbye. We brought Julie home to stay with us. I promised her I would be her support person, and we would all get through this loss together.

The following afternoon, I took Julie to her car at the hospital and went back home. That evening, I was sitting on the couch by myself just thinking of the day before and how life can suddenly change.

Around 10 p.m. my cellphone rang. It was a police officer calling to say they were at my son's apartment and he had passed away. I yelled "Was it drug related?"

He said that it appeared to be. I told them to leave my son there, I was on my way. I screamed, and my husband ran upstairs as I tried to tell him Kyle died.

We got in the car and it seemed to take forever to go the five miles to Kyle's apartment. On the way, I called Kyle's dad to tell him Kyle died. My husband, Al, started to pass the driveway to the apartment where Kyle lived. I opened the door and jumped out.

There were several police cars with lights on. I ran toward the apartment and a policeman stopped me and told me it was a crime scene and I had to wait.

I looked over and saw Kyle's fiancée Brittany sitting on the steps in shock. She told me that Kyle went to an old friend's house the night before and when he came home, she could tell he had used. He smoked heroin with that person and was very sick all night. That afternoon, they were on their way to a wedding reception. Kyle was throwing up, felt horrible, and begged Brittany to turn around and take him home so he could sleep it off. She brought him home, they hugged each other for about twenty minutes, and she begged him to promise he wouldn't do anything while she was at the wedding reception.

Brittany said she and Kyle talked to each other throughout the afternoon and evening. When she was driving home, she called again, but Kyle didn't answer the phone. She felt it in her gut that something was wrong. When she pulled up to the apartment, she ran in and found Kyle slumped forward at the kitchen table. There was some heroin on foil and evidence that Kyle had smoked drugs.

She pulled him to the ground and proceeded to give him CPR. Thank goodness her son, Brody, was asleep and she left him in the car when she ran into the apartment. She continued CPR until the medics got there. She waited outside for the medics to come say they were going to transport Kyle to the hospital. Instead, the police came out and said, "I'm sorry."

She went into shock. She wasn't ready to be told Kyle was dead. I got Kyle's phone from Brittany and looked at his messages. The last person he spoke to was an addict Kyle grew up with. I called and told him Kyle was dead. The only response was "Why are you calling me?"

I said, "Because you are the last person on Kyle's phone who says you will be there in ten minutes."

I reached my arms as high as I could to the sky and talked to God. Al got Brody out of the car, saw me crying, and said he was taking Brody home. I thank him for that.

Some family arrived along with Kyle's dad Bruce and his fiancée Kelly. We all stood in the driveway waiting for the coroner to prepare our son's body. I told them that we needed to say goodbye to our son.

After probably a couple hours, they said Kyle was ready to see. Kyle's dad, Brittany and I walked into the apartment. He was laying on the gurney with a blanket up to his neck. He was beautiful! I touched him and said that he still felt warm. We cried and talked to Kyle, saying our goodbyes.

The coroner asked if we wanted anything off Kyle's body, and I asked for his earrings to give to Brittany. They covered Kyle and we walked behind the coroner as she pushed Kyle through the doorway and into the coroner van. All but one police officer had left.

As Kyle was loaded, a small white truck started up and slowly drove past us. We all looked at the truck and said, "Who is that?"

My niece said the person had been sitting there in the truck for a couple hours. To this day, I wonder who that person was. Did they walk out of the apartment and leave Kyle? It won't change the outcome, but who was it?

We called Kyle's brother, Ryan. It was horrible to have to tell him on the phone. He is a single dad, and his son was sleeping. Cousins ended up going to Ryan's to sit with him while all this sunk in. I took Brittany home with me. Brittany and I laid on the loveseat at my house for several days not wanting to be away from each other. We would sleep for a short bit and then wake up in a panic, realizing it was true— Kyle was dead. Brittany was three months pregnant with their child.

The following day, Bruce, Kelly, Brittany, Ryan, Al and I went to the funeral home and started the arrangements to have Kyle cremated.

We all came to our house for at least a week. We ate together, cried together, and talked about how we could honor Kyle.

A group of young people who knew Kyle asked if they could put together a candlelight vigil down at the waterfront. Of course, we felt honored. They had contacted a local TV station from Seattle that came and interviewed us. This was three days after Kyle passed.

The newsperson said it was rare to find a family who would share openly that their child died from an overdose. Because of the shame and stigma, most families do not share, and bury their child in secrecy. I wanted others who struggle to be at the vigil, along with parents of addicts. I wanted to speak to them about not being ashamed. It was clear that Kyle's death was going to have a purpose. We were ready to stand loud and proud for our son Kyle.

*

LORI LATIMER
Lori's 29-year-old son Greg died from
alcohol and fentanyl-laced cocaine in 2019

Sunday, January 6, 2019, was a beautiful, crystal-clear day. I got up early and was cleaning my house. I had just moved things off my coffee table to dust it when my cellphone rang. When I answered it, I had no idea it would be that call that people hear about, the one that no parent ever wants to receive.

It was my son's girlfriend, Bethany. I will never forget her words. "Lori, this is Bethany. Greg's roommate just called me. Greg is dead."

I remember my reaction. I didn't fall to the floor. I didn't break down in tears. It just wasn't in the realm of possibility for me. I think I shouted into the phone, "What?!"

She didn't have any other details, so she and I agreed to meet at the house Greg was living in. I thought there had to be some mistake, that he was all right and maybe just had been hurt somehow. I threw on some clothes and before I could run out the door, she called again. She said she'd spoken to Greg's roommate again, and he said that Greg wasn't at the house. I couldn't even process any of it. I had just seen him the afternoon before, and HE WAS FINE. I wondered where he could be and thought they must have taken him to a hospital to help him. It's really amazing what the human mind and body do to protect us in times of unimaginable pain and tragedy.

She and I agreed we would still meet at his house to figure out what was going on. As I drove, I called my older son, Steve. I called Greg's dad. I called a friend in California who suggested I call the local police. I did, and the woman said she'd see what she could find out and call me back. I will never forget my phone ringing a few minutes later as I was driving up the freeway. A man asked to speak with me and then said, "This is the Bartow County coroner."

I remember whispering "No. Please, no."

I knew I couldn't avoid the truth any longer. My beautiful son, my child, was no longer alive. My life was forever altered, and I was shattered in ways I couldn't yet begin to comprehend.

The coroner said he didn't yet know what had happened, but that Greg may have choked to death. He was found with a spoon in his hand and a plate of food on the counter. He told me Greg was in the morgue in the county he lived in. I told him I wanted to see Greg. He tried to talk me out of it. I then called my older son, got off at the next exit, and went to his house.

Walking into Steve's house and seeing his sons, my grandsons, broke my heart. Steve was beside himself. My eleven-year-old grandson was crying. My seven-year-old grandson was closed off. My youngest grandson was only five weeks old. It was only the sixth day of a brand new year.

I have no recollection of this, but my daughter-in-law recently told me that when I walked into the house, my older son, Steve, held onto me as I fell onto the dining room floor sobbing.

I called the coroner back and insisted on coming to see my son. Steve, my ex-husband (Steve and Greg's dad), and I did go to the morgue to see Greg. I had to. I gave birth to him. I was there when he took his first breath. I wasn't there when he took his last breath. And I needed to see my baby, my beautiful son, one more time.

When Greg was in high school, he got a tattoo. When he showed it to me, I was speechless. It was a rose over his heart, with my name tattooed above it. That was the connection Greg and I had. And when the coroner unzipped that awful bag on the gurney, that tattoo was the first thing I saw.

I held my child, my baby. I told him how much I loved him, how proud I was of him, and how proud I was to be his mom in this life. I told him I would miss him until I see him again. And I told him it was okay to go, that Granny and Grandpa (my mom and dad) were waiting for him in heaven and would take care of him for me. That was the last time I will ever see Greg's physical body, the body I grew inside of mine, the body that grew into the amazing man he became. Even as I write this now, several months later, it still doesn't seem real.

Then came the endless calls that had to be made. I called my younger brother in Arizona. I called my older brother and sister-in-law in northern Arizona. My best friend from junior high school in California called me. I talked to a dear friend in northern California. On the way to my son's house that morning, I called the attorney I've worked with for seventeen years. It was his birthday. I'm sure he thought I was calling to wish him a Happy Birthday, but that never even came up in our conversation. I don't remember who else I called.

Later that afternoon, Steve and I went to the house Greg had been living in, the house where he took his last breath. I mentally and emotionally disassociated from my body to be able to walk into that house. We went through some of Greg's belongings and took a few things with us. The police had his cellphone.

Steve then went with me to my house so I could get my dog and pack a suitcase for a couple days. I didn't know when I would return home. Everything felt surreal and like walking through dark, dense clouds that I just wanted to push away and walk back into my life where everything was right and normal. And where my child was still here, in this life.

I stayed at Steve's that night. The next day we made arrangements to have Greg cremated and to honor him by having a celebration of life. I was on autopilot and barely remember anything.

Four days later I was driving in the town he had lived in to meet someone who was putting together a photo montage for Greg's celebration of life. The sky was a perfect blue, with no clouds in sight. As I drove north, I noticed one cloud right in front of me out my front windshield. It was in the shape of a heart. I pulled over and took a picture of it. That cloud stayed in that heart shape until I reached the store I was going to. I took another picture of it before I went into the store. When I came out about fifteen minutes later, the cloud was gone. I knew that heart-shaped cloud was a sign from Greg that he was all right, and he was still with me.

*

AMANDA MARIE
Amanda's 30-year-old brother Cory
died from a heroin overdose in 2015

My phone rang at 12:08 a.m. No one ever called that late. I didn't recognize the number, so I didn't answer.

My teenage son and I were relaxing on the couch watching TV when my phone chimed with a voicemail.

"Help! I need you!"

It was my mother.

Her message came deep from her gut, out of her mouth and into a permanent recording I still have on my phone.

I called the number back without listening to more. I couldn't understand what she was saying. Her words were jumbled and broken, muffled by the sobs.

"Cory's dead . . . he died . . . hospital. Cory's dead, go to the hospital!"

I didn't believe her. My mom had a knack for dramatics, and I kept thinking maybe Cory was just in a car accident or got into a fight. Either way, I was going to save the day just like I always did, and Cory would be fine.

I hung up the phone and looked at my son. I tried to form words, but only grunts and groans spilled from my mouth. I didn't cry. I didn't explain. I just got in my car and drove.

I walked through the automatic emergency room doors under the buzzing fluorescent lights and up to the desk.

"Can I help you?" asked the receptionist.

"I think I am here to identify my brother's body," I stuttered.

Saying nothing and with her head hanging low, she stood up and gently led me to a room. She opened the door and I saw my mother, empty-eyed and stark white, sitting limply on a couch. A chaplain and one nurse with frowns carved deep into their cheeks stood in the corner of the room. The nurse, eyes swelling with tears said, "I'm sorry. We tried." I thanked her for trying.

The nurse asked if I was ready. Even though I wasn't, I nodded in agreement. She walked me to room seventeen and opened the door.

There Cory was, haphazardly stretched on a gurney in the exact position they left him when they called time of death—10:38 p.m.

His shirt was cut, his pants were down around his ankles, and his feet were shoeless. He had tubes in his mouth and blood on his face. His ears were purple, and his skin mottled yellow. Even though his body was still warm, rigor mortis had begun to set in. His hands were stiff enough that I had to pry them open to hold them in mine. Peeking open, his ocean-blue eyes had turned milky white.

Nobody had tried to reshape Cory's body into a more graceful pose, close his eyes, or cover him up with a sheet the way they do in movies. I remember softly muttering only one word with defeat. "Brother."

But he didn't respond.

Cory had been with so-called friends that night who claimed they tried to save him by administering CPR. They said they didn't wait to take him to the hospital. The truth was, they left him sitting dead in the passenger seat of a car for at least fifteen minutes.

At 8 p.m. that night, Cory went to score a bag from his dealer's house. From there he went to a pharmacy, and according to the receipt, purchased a box of needles at 8:10 p.m.

By 8:30 p.m., Cory was inside a dirty gas station's bathroom tying off and shooting up a fatal dose of fentanyl-laced heroin. He got in the car, leaned back into the passenger seat and pulled his baseball cap over his eyes, as he always did. At some point, while his friend drove the forty miles back, Cory took his last breath.

He was DOA—dead on arrival—when they threw him on the stretcher outside the emergency room. The hospital staff worked on him anyway. According to medical records, four doses of NARCAN was pumped into Cory's body and staff spent nearly an hour giving chest compressions. But none of it worked. He didn't come back.

After two years of sobriety, one year after leaving prison, and seven months after moving back home, it was over. Cory was gone.

The following Sunday, we went to the funeral home for our last goodbye. The funeral director tried to make Cory appear peaceful by curling his lips upward just a bit and securing them with glue. But he looked dead. He wasn't the strong, handsome, vibrant brother I knew. He was ice cold and stiff from laying in the dark mortuary freezer. He looked much thinner without all his bodily fluids and his baby blue eyes. The foam and plastic packing the undertaker used to reconstruct Cory's torso after the autopsy crunched under our hands. He always wore a hat, but this time he had to because his head had been cut open. Staples peeked out from under the brim and I nervously adjusted it, fearing my children would notice. We sat with Cory for so long that he began to thaw. Even though his chest caved in every time I laid on it, I struggled to lift my heavy head. I didn't want to leave him.

*

DIANA MITCHELL
Diana's 18-year-old daughter Brooke died from
a mix of fentanyl, ecstasy, and cocaine in 2017

It was January 2, a horrible day. I woke up to rain, and it just didn't feel right. I hadn't spoken to Brooke since she got angry with me the night before. When I called, she didn't answer the phone.

The police came at 7 p.m. to notify us that Brooke had overdosed and was in the emergency room. We were taken to a back room and I told my husband that this didn't look good. I was very scared. After two hours, I was finally allowed to see her. They told me she had suffered three heart attacks and been revived. When I walked in and saw her hooked up to all those machines, all I could say was, "What did you do? God, what did you do? Don't you understand how much we love you?"

The nurse said they were taking Brooke to the intensive care unit and asked me my plans if Brooke were to have another heart attack. Did she have a DNR? "She's eighteen. Nobody would ever think that she would have an end-of-life plan," I said.

Brooke was on life support for four days. We had to make a decision. I begged for her to stay, but she wasn't going to wake up, nor were we getting our daughter back. But I had to understand that this was her journey. I knew that if she stayed with us, it was just a matter of time before we would lose her. I remember the day she was born. I knew I was going to have to turn off the machines and watch her leave me. It still takes my breath away every day.

*

WHITNEY O'BRIEN
Whitney's 23-year-old brother Michael died from
a heroin/cocaine/benzodiazepine overdose in 2016

Saturday, December 3, 2016, was the worst day of my life. What makes it so poignant is that it started out perfectly normal. I was absorbed in my family and oblivious to the agony lurking my way.

We spent the morning lounging around in pajamas. We cooked breakfast and drank hot chocolate while watching Christmas movies. The tree was already up, and we camped out on the couch admiring the fruits of our labor. At twelve feet tall, the tree had taken us two days to assemble, fluff, and trim. With a toddler running amok and a newborn to tend to, decorating had to be done in stages, but it was finally complete and we relished the view. I remember looking at my husband and children and feeling overwhelmed with gratitude. We were together. We were healthy. We were happy.

The holidays were a welcoming distraction from the unspeakable scare we experienced the week prior when my brother overdosed the first time. It was a horrifying reminder of our most dreaded fear. But something seemed different in my brother, and for the first time I really believed he was serious about his recovery. Despite refusing to go to inpatient treatment, he had been seen by his addiction doctor and was given a prescription for Suboxone. We all focused on the road ahead, and eager to see his addiction fade in the rearview mirror.

Around 10 a.m. that day, I did FaceTime with my mom. I sat on the couch cradling my sleeping newborn while discussing Christmas plans and gift-giving ideas as my toddler bounced in and out of sight. Our conversation was lighthearted and filled with giggles and gags, per usual. In looking back, it seems bizarre that I had no foreboding sense of doom. I could not have been more carefree.

Just before 4 p.m. my dad called. My phone rang and then ended abruptly in the middle of the second ring. I turned to my husband and made a joke about Dad's technological inabilities. I figured he was fumbling around with his phone and didn't realize he was calling me. Less than thirty seconds later he called again. I answered, and will never forget his trembling voice. "Whit... Michael's dead."

Although muffled by sobs, his words were unmistakable and echo in my head to this day. I leaped from the couch as a flood of screams escaped me. There are simply no words in any language that can adequately describe the frenzy of emotions that ensued. I cried. I screamed. I shouted "No!" at the top of my lungs over and over again, until I crumbled to the ground.

I hysterically sobbed to my husband from the floor of our kitchen, "Michael's dead."

My father, who was still patiently waiting on the line, finally interjected to say, "You need to get here."

"I'm coming!" I shouted. We immediately sprang into action. I threw on the nearest clothes I could find while my husband called my best friend to come and stay with the kids. We were out the door and on our way to my parents' house within fifteen minutes.

On the drive over, I foolishly let myself believe that it might not be true. Maybe they had found him and his respirations were so slow and shallow that they couldn't tell he was, in fact, breathing. Maybe he still had a pulse and once the paramedics arrived, they could give him Narcan and reverse the overdose. Wasn't it possible they were wrong? This could potentially just be overdose number two. Maybe he would be alright. I was wrong.

When we rounded the corner to my parent's street, about five police cars were parked out front. I opened the car door and jumped out to run inside the house. My dad was sitting in his recliner and my mother was a few feet away on the couch. A police officer stood in front of them. Nobody was speaking. My mother stood as I walked over to her. I reached for her hands and begged, "Please. Please... are you sure?" She nodded her head before I had a chance to finish my plea.

My mother had found him. She went to check on him sometime after 2:30 p.m. to see if he wanted something to eat. She knocked on his door and after several seconds and no response, she unlocked the door and went in. Michael was sitting in his chair, slumped over his desk with a needle on the ground between his legs. He was already cold, already stiff, already gone.

My mother let out a bloodcurdling scream, a scream so loud that the neighbors heard and called 911 before my parents did. The second my dad heard her scream, he knew what it meant and began screaming himself. Because the only reason my mother would scream that way was because their worst nightmare had come true.

For the rest of the evening we all sat in the living room watching complete strangers go in and out of my brother's room. Police officers, the medical examiner and her assistant, and two workers from the fire department who were supposedly a crisis team but did nothing more than hover over us and uncomfortably offer us resources.

They wouldn't let me see him. My mom said I wouldn't want to. And then came time to remove his body from the room. Thankfully, the medical examiner prepared us for this and explained everything that would take place. I decided to excuse myself. I could not bear the sight of my brother's body in a bag, nor the sound of screeching wheels of the stretcher moving across the tile floor. If I had stayed, I knew I would never get the sight or sound out of my memory. I hid in the backyard with my husband.

After they took my brother away in a white van, it was time for the excruciating task of informing our family. We drove to my grandmother's house to tell her in person. My mother was worried about how my grandmother would react, and possibly need medical attention. I'll never forget my grandmother's excitement when she saw us standing on her porch. She should have known better. We never stopped by unannounced. I just shook my head.

"No grandma," I said, taking the lead so my parents wouldn't have to. "Michael died."

My mother then called her brother and sister. Hearing her relay details to both her siblings was literally torture. I relived the horrific reality every time I heard the story. After all, this had been our worst fear, a call I had prepared myself to receive but hoped I never would. We spent the next seven days planning Michael's funeral. Having never heard him express his desires regarding burial or cremation, we chose to bury him in the plot next to our grandfather, a place I feel he would be truly at peace, a place of comfort for him, finally.

Michael's body went from our house to the medical examiner for toxicology and was then released to the funeral home a few days later. The day before the open casket service, we arranged a private viewing for our family, in part so we could see him and be sure he looked presentable for the service the next day. We were especially concerned about his hair, of course.

They directed us to the room Michael was resting in, the same room where my grandfather's funeral was held. As we walked over, I clung to my husband, sobbing uncontrollably. I never imagined I would see my brother in a casket. I felt ill. My mother gasped, "He's beautiful!" And he truly was. We all embraced, holding one another up. We cried until we were breathless. The ability to see him, speak to him, and touch him was excruciating, but extremely necessary.

We chose to dress him in a charcoal long-sleeved button-down shirt, the same one he had worn two years prior in family pictures. I remember the day we had our pictures done in the cotton fields a few miles from my parents' house. It was the last time we had family pictures taken. He wore that shirt, tucked into his jeans with a belt. He looked great. He felt great.

"I wish I could dress like this every day," he said.

"You look so nice, brother," I told him. And then we playfully hugged, as we often did, and I rested my head on his shoulder while the photographer snapped away.

It felt fitting to put him in a shirt that he felt so confident in. We decided to dress him in his signature skinny Levi jeans and carefully tucked his knife into his front pocket, just as he always did. We also placed one of his beanies in the casket with him, as well as his coveted e-cig, his ragged old work gloves, a bobcat tail (a salute to our uncle), and his ring of keys so he would always have a house key.

I fully understood how dangerous his life had become and how sick he was, yet I thought he had more time. Nothing about me was prepared for him to die. I thought he would overdose at least a dozen more times before he would actually die. I couldn't understand why he didn't get more chances.

My family has had their share of turmoil these last few years, yet I would go through it all over again. As terrible as it was, it's still better than living without him. I would take it all back in a heartbeat. I'd take back all the torment and tears, the chaos and heartbreak. But I know that would mean my brother was still suffering. I try to remember that he is finally free from the tortures of his disease.

*

ALICE RICH
Alice's 42-year-old brother Gary
died from a fentanyl overdose in 2015

Describe the day Gary died. Was that the day he overdosed or the day they turned off his ventilator and his heart stopped beating? The day he overdosed was a Wednesday in December. I was at my desk at work when I got a call from my dad on my cell. As soon as I knew it was him calling, I got a sick feeling in my stomach. He could hardly talk. "Alice, it's your brother," he barely got the words out. I heard a few other words—overdosed, braindead, emergency room.

"Where is he, Dad?" I asked. "Don't let them do anything until I get there. Did you call Angie?" I asked him.

"I can't," was all he could say.

I called my sister Angie. She lives in Florida with her family. She answered and I said, "You need to come." She asked if it were mom and I said, "No. Gary. You need to come now."

"Is he dead?" she asked.

I said no, but he may be braindead. I said I was leaving for the hospital for more details. The thing about "you need to come" is that when I call her when mom or dad is sick, she always asks, "Do I need to come?"

She needed to come. She needed to be there, and I needed her there. I don't know if I'd ever felt this before, but I've felt it ever since. There were three of us: me, Angie, then Gary. I suddenly felt like they were a literal part of me, as if we were one person yet different people all at the same time. I needed Angie with me to feel whole, and I did feel complete when she arrived and the three of us were together. Even with the circumstances the way they were, I still felt whole.

After I talked to Dad and Angie, I walked into my boss's office and very calmly and matter-of-factly told her what had happened and told her I was leaving. I felt numb and emotionless, like a robot. I made my way to the hospital, and went in to see Gary, still feeling the same way. Numb. Calm. Eerily calm. But my brain wasn't calm, it was empty. It wasn't computing.

The next few days are a blur. I did make several phone calls for my parents so they wouldn't have to. We pretty much held vigil at the hospital waiting for some news. The doctors decided to wait a few days to see if any brain activity returned. I'm not sure why they did this, and it seemed to give the family false hope. I'm a nurse, and though I am not claiming to know everything there is about brain death, I know that Gary was down a long time without oxygen and his pupils were fixed and dilated when he arrived at the emergency room. He had no response to any stimuli at all. This never changed.

They were going to keep Gary iced to keep his body temp down, which apparently helps save brain tissue, but his body stayed cold on its own. Just another sign that it was trying to die.

Once the doctors finally announced him braindead, that was also called as time of death, yet Gary still had a heartbeat. Then Lifebanc came in. My mom and dad signed so many papers for this process, and it was hard for them. It gave me hope and some joy that parts of Gary would live on. It seemed wrong to let his big, strong body go to waste.

After a lengthy process and one disappointment after another, the Lifebanc lady came in and said that they had exhausted all avenues and the last piece of Gary, his heart, was not a match. That was the hardest news to take, and I broke down. My own heart felt as if it were ripped from my chest.

I had hope that some piece of Gary would be someone else's wish come true, an answered prayer for Christmas. Not only would he live on, but he would help another person also live. He would be an answer to a prayer, and that would give some meaning to this senseless death. He died for nothing and there was no prayer answered. I'm not mad at God, He did not take my brother away. Heroin killed Gary, not God.

Gary's nurse went to lunch. I waited with Gary's ex-wife for my husband to arrive. It was around 2 a.m. I touched Gary's face, held his hand, played with his hair and combed it back into place again with my fingers—he hated messy hair. I kissed his head and cheek so many times. His hands were so big. This can't be happening.

Once everyone had returned, I stood on one side of Gary and his ex-wife stood on his other side as they turned off the heart monitor screen and then the ventilator. He never breathed again. I watch his chest, waiting for his body to take over and take a breath, but nothing happened. The tips of Gary's ears, around his mouth, and his fingers began to turn a bluish color. His hand felt cooler. I could see his heart beating through his chest, so I put my head over his heart. I could hear it—it was alive, some part of him was alive.

I'm not sure how long it took. It seemed like forever and yet it was happening so fast. I lay there listening to his heart beat faster, then harder, then slower and slower, then slower still, until . . . nothing.

Silence. He was gone. I had listened to his heart die.

I could hear Gary's ex-wife crying and felt my husband's hands on my back. I looked at my brother, and he was so pale. I didn't want to remember him like that, that white color. I kissed him again, and with eyes closed turned and walked away. I never looked back.

Gary's ex-wife came out after a little while, she needed extra time with him. Like I said, she still loved him. There she was in the very position she had been trying to avoid, watching him die and grieving.

*

CAROL WALL
Carol's 29-year-old son Jason died
from a heroin overdose in 2016

Fall 2015, leading up to Christmas was a nightmare. I used to say we were living our own version of the Jerry Springer show. Jason was acting so irrational, the chemicals were causing their brain damage, he was like a stranger, not the Jason we knew. Our main job was to keep him alive. Every time the phone rang, we thought, this is it.

We somehow made it through Christmas and the New Year, but early January we knew something drastic had to be done. We planned an intervention with our family and two of Jason's closest childhood friends. I researched and investigated at least four rehabilitation facilities. We chose Addictions Canada because it had the least wait time. We did not have time to lose—Jason was going to die, it was that desperate.

They offered an interventionist, qualified nurses, psycho-therapists and doctors on staff. And if you relapse after your stay, you can check back in. Our family was desperate to save Jason's life, we would have done anything.

The interventionist came to our house and we ambushed Jason. It was nothing like you see on those television shows. The mediator (interventionist) was rude, swearing, and degraded my son, calling him a junkie. She was trying to shame him into going with her. I cannot believe I let her into my home. But we didn't know, and we were desperate. We gave her a check for twenty thousand dollars for a sixty-day stay. We convinced Jason to go, and he was voluntarily admitted on January 9, 2016.

We came to visit Jason on January 17. The disorganization and lack of professionalism was evident. We requested to speak with a counselor who told us Jason was supposed to meet one-on-one with a psychotherapist at least three times a week. That first week, Jason met with him only once.

When we asked if Jason had been attending group therapy, she said she wasn't sure as the attendance book had been lost for three days. Shortly after we arrived home the daily phone call progress reports started. I was contacted numerous times about behavior issues such as swearing, disrespecting counselors, being uncooperative, etc. Because of these infractions, Jason wasn't allowed his phone calls, not even to his son.

I do understand there has to be rules, but he was not in jail. We were paying for this care, to what we thought was a reputable facility. Of course, Jason was going to be uncooperative, he was going through withdrawal, and punishment does not work. You don't expect stigma from the facility that is supposed to be experts on this disease.

On January 20, Jason was moved to a second facility in Ontario. We had very little contact with him while he was there, his phone privileges were always being revoked. I had one phone call with Jason, and he had yet to see a psychotherapist. In his twenty-one-day stay, he saw a psychotherapist once out of the nine times he was supposed to.

On Saturday, January 30, it was prearranged that my husband, myself, our daughter and our other son to have a family visit. One of the counselors called me on Friday night to tell me we were to pick Jason up the next day and bring him home. He was being kicked out for testing positive for drugs on three occasions. I was dumbfounded! I asked how he could get drugs in a drug treatment center. I said, "You felt the need to call me every single day to complain about Jason's swearing, but you didn't think it important enough to call me about two previous positive drug tests?"

My husband and I drove there the next day. When we arrived, we were met by security and not allowed to go inside the building. The staff spoke to us through a crack in the door. Jason came out and we demanded to know what was going on. Jason said he had never taken any drugs whatsoever since entering treatment, and demanded they do a drug test right then and there in front of us. They refused.

We believed our son. Jason wouldn't have insisted if he had anything to hide. We drove him immediately to Huntsville Hospital. His identity was confirmed and at 2 p.m. he gave a urine and blood sample for complete alcohol and drug screening. Every single result came back negative.

Addiction Canada stated the test they gave him the day before was positive for barbiturate, benzodiazepine, cocaine, methadone and marijuana. We have a copy of their report. We then drove from the hospital to the police station in Huntsville to file a complaint.

The rules at Addiction Canada are, if you voluntarily leave before the full sixty days, you get a prorated refund. If you get kicked out for drug use, they are entitled to keep all your money, no refund. This place was just turning over beds! This sham of a treatment center has been charged with fraud, impersonating doctors and trafficking; www.cbc.ca/news/canada/toronto/addiction-canada-closing-claims.

We arrived home around dinner time and I wanted Jason to stay with us. He owned a home and wanted to go to his own house. He was twenty-nine and did not live with us. What could I do?

That night I was sitting on the front porch when he pulled in about 1 a.m. He had relapsed that night. He was crying and saying how proud he had been of himself for being clean for twenty-one days, and then Addictions Canada accusing him. He was emotionally fragile. It was so complicated.

The next two weeks got even worse. On Monday, February 15, Jason was charged with DUI. He slid through a stop sign into a ditch. He and the girl he was with walked away from his car. They were a few blocks away when a police car pulled over. They tazed him repeatedly. He spent the night in jail.

On Tuesday afternoon, Jason was attacked by his roommate's pit bulls, a pair of dogs that are father and son; neither one was neutered. My husband and I have both witnessed these two dogs go crazy fighting with each other. There is no way to break them apart. The father dog was in the living room and the son was in the bedroom. The father started acting weird and Jason decided to put him in his cage. He was backing him into his cage with Jason facing him when he went crazy! He started attacking Jason. His roommate who was holding back the son released him, and the father released Jason and went for his own son.

His roommate got Jason out on to the front lawn and called the ambulance, then called me. When we got there the police were there and I followed the ambulance to the hospital. The two dogs were in the house killing each other. We found out later when animal control got there that the father dog had killed the son, and animal control euthanized the father.

Jason ended up having twenty-six stitches and twelve staples. They didn't do a very good job in emergency and he had to spend the night. He had surgery scheduled for the next day to check for tendon damage and do intense cleaning of all the wounds while Jason was under anesthetic. The damage was extensive. His right and left biceps, his left leg, with most of the damage to his left hand, not counting all the puncture holes, bruises, etc. He even had a black eye.

We were all living a nightmare. Things like this happen in the movies. Everyone's lives, especially Jason's, was spiraling out of control. With Jason being injured, at least he conceded to coming to live at my house and letting me take care of him. He couldn't even move; couldn't shower he was totally convalescing. I was happy to care for him. I felt good taking care of him. I loved him so much, I felt I could help. I had finished my treatments, I felt I was getting healthier, I wanted so much to help my son. He did get better and he did get stronger, we felt like we were turning a corner.

On March 12, we spent the most beautiful day at the Toronto Zoo. Jason, myself, his son, his brother, my other grandson and my sister. It was one of the happiest days I remember! It was warm for March, we were a family, we were together, and my boy was coming back.

We got so many great pictures from that day. It would be the last time my boys would be together. Jason's brother is two years older than him. They are best friends! They went through the regular brother wars, but as they matured their bond was unbreakable. I cry for everything this disease has stolen from us. The long reaching devastation it has caused to every single one in our family.

On Monday, March 14, my cousin, Jason's godmother, invited me to her cottage up north for a couple days. She knew I needed a break and thought it would be good for me. I was very hesitant about leaving Jason, he was doing so well. Jason overheard me on the phone talking to my cousin and asked if he could come. She didn't even hesitate for a second . . . of course, he could come.

We were a very unlikely foursome: myself, my cousin, her friend, and Jason. We were only going for two days. It was wonderful! Jason was the old Jason. He brought his guitar and serenaded us. We went out for a great dinner and he helped my cousin and her friend (who is an interior decorator) decorate the cottage. Her cottage is a bit more like a condo and Jason coined the phrase "condage." We could not have had a better time.

On the drive home, Jason got a phone call. It was from a girl he had met in Addictions Canada who he had become close to. She called and said she had been released and was living at a house in a small town near Barrie. What were the chances that we would be traveling through this town in about ten minutes? She asked if we could pick her up and if she could spend the weekend at our house. I asked Jason to ask his aunt and she said okay. The planets were aligned. The timing could not have worked out if we planned it. Later, thinking back, I wish this never would have happened, it was as though fate was against us.

We picked her up and she came with us to our home. It was Tuesday night, March 15. This was the first time my husband and I had met her. We had heard about her, but there was no phone contact allowed while she was in Addictions Canada.

That first night home, we sat around, had a nice dinner and some conversation. We didn't really make any judgments about her, good or bad. The next day we got up and went to the local shopping mall. She needed some things, and Jason wanted to buy a gift for his friend who had just had a baby. We ran into my mother and my sister at the mall. Since Jason couldn't drive, he and his friend walked to Jason's friend's house and I drove home. Little did I know that they had been to the liquor store and were also drinking at the restaurant they went to for dinner.

They arrived back at our house in the evening. Jason was visibly high and so was she, but not as much. She brought back a bottle of wine for us. She was just out of rehab and was not supposed to drink. I was drinking that wine as fast as I could so there would be less for her. Again, the circumstances were as if they were planned.

My sister dropped them off and she forgot her cellphone in my sister's car. My husband and I went to bed and I thought at least they were safe in our home. I woke up about 2 a.m. because I thought I heard a car running. I came downstairs and they were both standing in the kitchen with their coats on and Jason had my car keys. I asked him if he was planning on taking my car. "No," he said, and threw me the keys.

I then heard a car in the driveway. I have no embarrassment or shame when it comes to protecting my children. I walked out the door, pulled open the car door and said, "Who the hell are you?"

It was a cab.

I walked back over and told them both to get back in the house. They refused. What was I going to do, lay in front of the cab? Again, they were adults. I was exhausted. But I never should've let them leave.

I tried to sleep. I phoned Jason's phone and talked to him about 4:30 a.m. He sounded drunk. He told me he was at his house and that his friend was sleeping. We talked for a while. I like to think I told him I loved him, I am almost sure I did. I told him that every time, but I can't remember for sure, and it is killing me. That is the last time I talked to my son.

At 9 a.m., I headed over to Jason's house. His mortgage term was coming due and we had an appointment at the bank to renew his mortgage. The plan was to sell his house. I was in my own car and my husband was following behind in the truck so they could get Jason's house ready to list.

When I got there, I went inside and the girl from rehab was asleep on the couch. I woke her up and said, "Where's Jason?"

She said she didn't know. I got back in my car and drove around the corner to a house where a known drug dealer lives. I looked inside the apartment foyer for Jason's bike. I didn't see anything and drove back to Jason's house.

When I got there, she was sitting on the front porch. I pushed past her into the house and said, "That's it. Get your bag. I am taking you home."

I came into the house as someone was coming in the back door. I thought it was Jason, but it was her. She said, "Jay's bike is here. He must have come home while you were gone."

I started yelling his name. I went down the stairs to the basement and my boy, my beautiful boy, my baby, my life, was laying on the floor. I knew he was gone.

I started screaming. I didn't run to him, instead I ran up the stairs, screaming for my husband. I will regret that for the rest of my life. Why didn't I run to Jason to hold him, to see if he was okay? Maybe because I knew he wasn't.

I ran right into my husband who was on his way downstairs. He said to call 911. My husband, my rock, my best friend, was left giving mouth-to-mouth resuscitation to his baby boy, cradling his grown son in his arms like he did the day our son was born.

My heart, our hearts, are so broken. The ambulance came and the paramedics were there for a long time. We followed the ambulance to the hospital, but we knew our boy was gone. My life ended that day. The cancer did not kill me, although I wish it had. I would gladly have given up my life for his.

We had the most beautiful service for our son. Our immediate family took care of all the arrangements. We were all very involved and took our own part in it. We picked out pictures and all wrote our own eulogy. Our son Jordan, Jason's brother, read a eulogy. Our daughter's husband read hers, and the officiator read what my husband and I had written. We had a million pictures!

So many people came to show us how great a person Jason was, and how much he was loved. One thing that really touched me was someone said if they didn't know who the service was for, they would have thought it was for a very old man because of everything Jason had accomplished, all the places he had been, everything he had done, and all the people who knew and loved him.

There were so many people at his celebration of life. What I remember from this day was that at one point they were showing a slide show of Jason's life, and I didn't even have the strength to lift my head. I thought to myself, raise up your head, look at this beautiful tribute to your son, look at all the people who are here who loved him. I raised up my head and looked around at all the love. I am glad I did. I remember his two-year-old son dancing to the music and saying, "Daddy," as he watched the screen.

The days, the weeks, and the months that followed are a blur. I remember not being able to lift up my head. Only being able to walk in a shuffle. We couldn't eat, we never knew what time or day it was. Crying every single minute of every single day.

Our lives are now divided by before and after. We are trying to live. We have two other children who are suffering as much as we are, and we have to go on living for them. Both my son and my daughter have had baby boys since Jay passed, and have honored their brother by giving the middle name Jay to both their baby boys.

Oh, Jay, I miss you so! I miss how you called me Mama Bear, how we would talk every single day. Your laugh, your sense of humor. The wonderment in your eyes as you gazed upon your own beautiful son. Everything about you.

I wish I could have saved you. You are forever in my thoughts from the time I wake up until the time I close my eyes. Sleep comes to me a bit easier these days, so does eating. I resent it! I don't want my life to go back to normal. I feel that means I am forgetting you. But you know, my boy, that is impossible. You live in my heart, where I will keep you safe.

Until we meet again, my darling, beautiful boy . . .

CHAPTER FOURTEEN

Grappling with guilt

The worst guilt is to accept an unearned guilt.
~AYN RAND

Guilt can be a component of many types of grief, but none more so than loss by overdose. Did we do enough? Could we have done more? Sensibility says we did everything we could, yet the guilt still haunts and taunts our hearts. Since the loss of your loved one, have you felt any guilt over his or her death?

*

KIMBERLY CALAIS
Kim's 23-year-old daughter Emily died from a multiple drug
overdose including heroin and methamphetamine in 2016

Guilt. Big inhale in, followed by a long exhaled sigh.

Before this journey began, I used to tell people that guilt is a choice. You or I cannot make anyone feel anything. It is up to the person to choose to feel it or not.

Since Emily's death, I have been drowning in a sea of guilt. The endless would-haves, could-haves, should-haves, if-onlys, the guilt associated with the endless analysis and review of what caused this to happen and how it could have been prevented.

I felt guilt over my divorce from Emily's father when she was four years old. Maybe that caused it. Or maybe when I let her leave high school to do independent study. That certainly was a pivotal time. Or perhaps protecting her from all the consequences of her poor choices, like when she crashed my car into that house, and I did nothing. Then there were the times I kicked her out of the house. And called the police on her. What kind of mother does that?

All that money I gave her over the years paved her way into addiction. Or maybe I didn't give her enough. If I gave her more, she could have used it in healthier ways, like buying all the material things she wanted. She had expensive taste, always asking me to take her to Nordstrom to shop. I didn't even shop for myself there. But maybe that would have helped her feel more at ease in her life.

If I had called her back after receiving her last text, instead of texting her back, I might have been able to stop her from shooting up that one last, fatal time. Even though I had no idea she was using again, I should have known…

The list is endless.

In 2011, I moved to Canada. Emily was living with Nick at the time and I was unaware of what she was really doing. Although we were still co-dependently close, her aggression and volatility had increased quite a bit during the preceding year. She had destroyed property, stolen from me and, at times, become physically aggressive toward me and her sister. She had been verbally abusive toward me for years. That was the norm. Despite the tremendous love we shared, our relationship had become quite toxic—to both of us.

During the months that followed, Emily seemed to have finally grown up and she was quite proud of her independence and accomplishments. The girl who called me for a ride from the shopping center one mile away was now navigating the San Francisco public transit system. This same girl, who never held a part-time job for more than a couple months, now had not one but two jobs that she held down successfully. She was buying her own clothes and food. She was going out with friends and she eventually started a relationship with a young man she had met at one of her jobs. She was—finally—happy in her life.

Despite all the personal accomplishments she achieved after I physically detached from her, the topic of my move to Canada caused me tremendous guilt. If I hadn't moved, I could have supervised her. If I had stayed, she would never had been isolated and alone in her room.

Every so often, usually when she was experiencing rough times, she'd ask me to move back and take care of her. She said she just needed to get on her feet. Stop working. Go back to school. Enjoy life without the responsibilities of adulthood. She'd tell me that I was her mother and that's a job for life. Memories like this and the guilt they ignite are like knives to my heart. The teeter-totter that bounces from pride that my departure brought about such happy independence to shame for allowing her to be on her own and not saving her from herself is relentless. The internal dialogue is constant, exhausting and emotionally debilitating.

Within days of my return to Canada following Emily's memorial service, my husband found a support group, as he knew I was in great despair and needed help that even he couldn't provide. The name of this group is GRASP (Grief Recovery After a Substance Passing). After speaking to the facilitator, I attended my first meeting on January 20, 2016, a little over two weeks since that life-changing phone call.

That first night I met other parents who were already walking the road I was now on. While the group is for any person who has lost someone to a substance-related passing, it just so happened that it was only parents at this meeting. I remember saying to them that I felt that I had been ripped from my former life, turned 180 degrees, and returned, only to learn that no one spoke my language anymore. No one understood me anymore. One of the mothers said, "We speak your language." And she was right. They speak it fluently.

I credit this group, as well as its online presence which, sadly, has more than nine thousand members, for saving my sanity and getting me through the darkest and most wretched days imaginable. It is also through this group that I learned a big lesson about the guilt I feel and all the coulda-woulda-shouldas we all have and will experience.

I have read/heard the stories of loss from parents with an intact marriage; parents who are divorced; single parents; families who were financially successful; families who were not; families of every ethnic background; families from every religious faith; families who were agnostic or atheists; families who used tough love; families who enabled; families whose loss occurred in their homes; families whose loss occurred somewhere else; families which were involved in every step of their loved one's journey; families who didn't know their loved one had a substance use disorder until it was too late.

The same can be said for victims of this disease. They are college graduates; they are high school dropouts; they are single; they are married; they lived alone; they lived with friends or family; they made a lot of money; they were on assistance; they had children; they had used drugs for years; they experimented this one time; they were found immediately; they weren't found for days or longer...

What everyone does have in common is that they all ended up losing their loved one to substance use. This is so powerful, and it has been the only revelation I've had that truly gives my guilt the battle it requires. Somebody, somewhere, has done whatever it is that we think we could have done to bring about a different outcome. Yet, it didn't.

The expression, "If love could have saved them, they'd all be alive," is so true and evident in sharing our stories and struggles.

Last year I saved a writing that I review when my resolve is low. It provides the important reminders which help keep me afloat in the turbulent and tranquil seas of my grief journey:

A LETTER FROM HEAVEN
BY LORELIE ROZZANO

Dear Mom and Dad,

Words can't begin to describe how sorry I am. I've put you in a position that no parent should ever face. I left—before you. It wasn't supposed to be this way. The natural order of things was skewed by my addiction. I can only imagine the agony you must be in. I know you're angry, despairing and sad, all at the same time. If only you could reach back in time and pluck me from the path I'd chosen, but you can't. You never could. God knows you tried. I wasn't completely oblivious to all you did for me. I always believed I had time and the truth is—I was too damned smart for my own good.

I underestimated the power of my disease.

I know you tried to tell me this. But I wouldn't listen. After I began using drugs I became desensitized. I thought I was immortal. I liked living on the edge. I felt so alive! Drugs filled a place in me that nothing else could. With them I was King. Without them, I was just, well me.

Maybe that was part of the problem.

I never did feel right, about being me. I always needed something more. I felt entitled to nice things. I wanted the best. I hated waiting for anything. When I wanted something, it was all I could think about—until I got it, and then I wanted something else. There were times I felt guilty for the stress I created in our family. But it was fleeting. The burning need inside of me was greater than anything else. This need had no conscience, integrity or morals.

This need—was my addiction.

I know I hurt you. I rejected your love. I rolled my eyes at you. I called you names. I stole from you. I lied to you. I avoided you and finally, I left you—for good.

I was so smug.

There wasn't anything you could have said, or done, to prevent this from happening. I thought I knew it all. Death by overdose was something that happened to other people. Foolish people—people who didn't know shit about using it. It wouldn't happen to me, no way, no how, not ever.

You begged me to stop. I tuned you out. Your words were like wasps in my ear. Although they stung, they were nothing more than an annoying buzz. When you cried, I cringed. When you put your arms around me, I wanted away from you.

And now, I want back.

But there is no back. There is only forward.

Please bring me forward.

Tell my story. Say my name. Have conversations with me. Include me in your celebrations. Rejoice in the time we had together. Cry, if you must, but not all the time. I know you're sad. I know you miss me. I know you love me. I know you did your best. But you were never stronger than the disease of addiction, and sadly, neither was I.

Please don't blame yourself, or me. It will only make things worse. We did the best we could. You must believe this. If you don't it will be like my dying all over again, each and every day. We will stay stuck and that would be a tragedy.

Take the love you have for me and put in into the rest of our family. Every time you want to hug me, grab one of them. Then it will be like I'm part of the hug. Give us a great big squeeze and I promise, I'll feel it—all the way up in heaven.

I hope you find peace in knowing I'm free in a way I never was before.

Up here there is no addiction. There is only love.

The kind of love that is greater than any of us will ever know, below.

You might tell yourself that I am gone. But you're wrong.

I'm right here.

I'm the wind on your face and the stars in the sky. I'm the raindrops, falling, outside your bedroom window. I'm the song of a bird and the dawn of each new morning. I'm the clouds and the sun and the waves in the ocean.

We will never truly be parted from one another. For love breathes life, even in death.

I am flesh of your flesh.

Stand still—and you will feel me.

Love always, your child.

*

SUSAN CARLYON
Susan's 22-year-old son Adam died from
an overdose of carfentanyl in 2016

Absolutely!! Should I have noticed something as my son was growing up? Could I have done more or handled it better? Was I a bad mom, therefore causing him to do drugs?

*

MARYBETH CICHOCKI
MaryBeth's 37-year-old son Matthew died
from a Percocet overdose in 2015

Every day. Now that I'm not so overwhelmed, I look back and wish I had handled things differently. Hindsight is a gift, unfortunately it's not available when you are dealing with the chaos of addiction. I wish for just one more chance to do things over knowing what I know now. Guilt and grief are both dancing in my brain. I feel guilty that I didn't fight harder to get him to stay in treatment. I feel guilty for the fighting when we should have had positive conversations. I feel guilty that he died because the system of care doesn't care. I feel guilty that he's not here to grow old with his brother.

*

KIM DELONG
Kim's 29-year-old son Tyler died
from a fentanyl overdose in 2017

Yes, I brought him home to stay with my husband and myself to get clean. I tried to get him into treatment, but because he had no current health insurance we had to wait. Once he got his health insurance, I brought him to his primary physician who referred Tyler to an outpatient program. He went and checked himself out the first day. He lied about it and told us they said he didn't belong there and had referred him to a counselor. He then claimed he tried to set up an appointment, but they never called him back. It was all lies.

I wish I had taken a leave at work and flew him across the country to an inpatient program far away from here. I didn't know about all the help available now. I searched for help from the Salvation Army on the web but all I found were donation sites. I thought I could nurse him back to health and fix him. I feel like I failed him as a mother. I try to remind myself that he was an adult with free will and the drug had the power over him. If he did go to rehab there was no guarantee it would have saved his life.

*

ELAINE FAULKNER
Elaine's 25-year-old son Jacob died from
an overdose of opiates and Xanax in 2017

I do not feel guilt. Guilt implies that I did something wrong, that I was culpable. I am not. I'm not all powerful, I could not control my loved one. I couldn't fix him. I couldn't cure his illness.

Jake was mentally, emotionally, physically, and spiritually ill. He was caught in a progressively destructive downward spiral as his use continued. I couldn't change him, how he responded to life, and the choices he made. He was a free spirit and lived his life with a wide-open heart. He loved adventures of all kinds. He took risks, he did not play it safe. I wouldn't want to change those things about him.

Do I have remorse? Yes.

Do I have regrets? Yes.

I do wish I had been more in tune with how he was feeling after a painful break up of a two-year relationship. I could have asked more questions. I wish I had not been so preoccupied with my new position at work and missed some moments of deeper contact during those last months. I have regrets about parenting mistakes I made.

It's painful to become a better person after this horrible loss, but that is all I can do now. I can only move forward with my life, as Jake would want me to, and remember the tender hugs from our gentle giant and the love we shared.

*

SHANNIE JENKINS
Shannie's 31-year-old son Kyle died
from a heroin overdose in 2017

Guilt is one of the main emotions we have as parents of addicts. Guilt and shame. My goal in life since Kyle's death is to speak out and help people take the shame out of the disease.

I felt so much guilt when Kyle struggled with addiction. His dad and I divorced when Kyle was around seven years old. That was the only thing we could figure out that was traumatic in his life. Although his dad and I remained friends and raised the boys the best we could together, divorce is always traumatic to all children. Guilt will eat you up inside. I remember times when I felt I never deserved to be happy because of my kids going through a divided family.

When Kyle went to rehab, the counselors had them dig into their lives and try to figure out what trauma they had. Kyle would tell me over and over that it was not the divorce, and he grew up in great homes. But still as a parent, we should always protect our children.

Kyle's fiancée, Brittany, carries a lot of guilt to this day. She can hardly talk about that day and night. Why did she leave him when he was struggling? What if she had come home twenty minutes earlier? What could she have done so he wouldn't have used? Why didn't she call me so I could have tried to save him? Brittany and I talk about the guilt, yet know we couldn't have done anything to save him.

The what-ifs overcome your mind. What did I miss? He was doing so well and was so happy. Did he try to tell me when we last visited? Could I have saved him? I honestly believe that if I didn't have my faith, I would not be able to live with the guilt. But I know that God's plan is bigger than ours, and He needed my Kyle as an angel. Why wouldn't He. Kyle was beautiful, loved everyone, and had the biggest heart and smile. What a beautiful angel I'm sure he is.

*

LORI LATIMER
Lori's 29-year-old son Greg died from
alcohol and fentanyl-laced cocaine in 2019

Guilt, shame, sadness, anxiety, anger, despair . . . the list is endless. So, guilt, yes. I have felt extreme guilt over Greg's death. I've felt guilty that I didn't know he was using hard drugs, and that I didn't spend more time with him. He used to ask me to come up and do things with him and his friends. I thought he was just being nice, and I didn't want to be the pesky mom hanging around. Since Greg died and I've spent a lot of time with his friends, I realize he was completely sincere. That's something I'll regret the rest of my life.

I have felt tremendous guilt that I woke up that Sunday morning and didn't know my son was dead. Isn't a mother supposed to know when something is wrong with one of her children?

Looking back, I realize I did know that something was going to happen. For several years I've had a ritual of sorts on New Year's Eve. I journal about the year that's ending, and I write my intentions for the upcoming new year. On New Year's Eve 2018, I didn't do any of that. I was anxious and felt off, but had no idea why.

A few weeks after Greg's death, after mentally beating myself up over not knowing he had died, I realized that I had known something was going to happen. I just had no idea what was coming or that it would shatter my world.

I have felt guilt and shame over many of the choices I made in my life that affected my children. If I had made different choices, would Greg have made different choices in his life? And yet, I truly believe that our souls make a plan before we're born. As his mom, I will never understand why Greg's soul chose to have a short life. And I will never understand why my soul chose to lose a child before I left this life.

In the end, I'm learning to transmute my feelings of guilt, shame, anxiety, and the rest into energy that moves me forward on this path in a way that will help others. One of my intentions in speaking out is bringing awareness to others, to try to end the stigma that often follows a drug-related death or drug addiction in general. I am not at all ashamed of my son or how he left this life, and I know he wouldn't want me to be either.

*

AMANDA MARIE
Amanda's 30-year-old brother Cory
died from a heroin overdose in 2015

Many people who suffer the loss of a loved one struggle with survivor's guilt, and I sometimes still do. But I can't apologize for being the one who did not die. Instead, I choose to remain grateful that I made it out alive even though he didn't. I choose to be thankful. I made it. Not always gracefully, or with integrity, or even with purpose, but I made it, and I will continue to. I am still proud of Cory for trying up until the very last moment.

There is no timeframe on the grief experienced from the loss of someone you loved so much. If my pain is a measure of the love I hold for my brother in my heart, it is a void that will never be filled; an unconditional and endless vastness.

I can't replace him, nor do I want to. Instead, I will hold that space as a memorial for him. I will fill it with pictures, messages, memories, laughter, and tears. The space in my heart will not make me jaded. It will not keep me from continuing to love and care so hard and so true, with every ounce of my intense soul. I will accomplish all the things Cory wasn't able to. I will do these things because I am strong, capable and worthy, and also to honor him. If he wasn't able to reach his full potential, I will make sure to reach mine.

*

DIANA MITCHELL
Diana's 18-year-old daughter Brooke died from
a mix of fentanyl, ecstasy, and cocaine in 2017

I have guilt about not being able to make Brooke understand what she was doing to herself.

*

WHITNEY O'BRIEN
Whitney's 23-year-old brother Michael died from
a heroin/cocaine/benzodiazepine overdose in 2016

My brother's death has sparked a guilt-fueled fire within me that I am unable to extinguish. I am constantly tortured by thoughts of remorse.

I wish I would have done more.

I should have tried harder.

I'm sorry I couldn't save you.

I don't blame myself, or anyone for that matter, but I know I could have done more. Perhaps that would have only delayed the inevitable, but I choose to believe that had he been given another chance, he could have been sober. But addiction doesn't always wait for you to hit rock bottom (I hate that term, by the way). It implies that only when a person has hit rock bottom will they be motivated to change, which is an erroneous and archaic point of view. Okay, I'll climb off my soapbox now.

269

What triggers the most guilt in me is feeling like I should have done more. As his big sister, and self-denoted second mother, I wanted to save him but didn't know how.

Ironically, since he died, I've spent hours reading and researching treatment and recovery options. It's become quite an obsession, actually. I didn't know much about heroin before he died. Now I am on a mission to know everything. This knowledge helps me understand his addiction and why it was so difficult for him to get sober. It has allowed me to realize that it was not a lack of strength or effort or desire on his part. But it has also forced me to question myself and ask why I didn't do this sooner? Why such a thirst for knowledge now? He's gone, remember?

The most unbearable emotion of all is the feeling of loss. You're supposed to get a lifetime with your siblings, and I only got a third. My brother had nothing when he died. No job, no spouse, no children. His life had not even started. The only grandchildren my parents will have are my children, and that devastates me. My kids will never have cousins, and I will never have nieces or nephews. Our family, small as it is, will grow only if my husband and I choose to have more children. But it will always be missing one person. I grieve the loss of the family we could have been. I don't get to watch him cultivate into the person he desperately wanted to be. He told me once that my husband and I, our relationship, was his muse. He wanted to build a life for himself, and then share it with someone. He had plans. He had dreams. And we will never know the great things he could have been.

*

ALICE RICH
Alice's 42-year-old brother Gary
died from a fentanyl overdose in 2015

I made sure Gary knew how much I loved him, and we talked frankly and openly about his addiction and my fears for his death, but I wish I had spent more time with him. He had invited my husband and I to go see a band with him and his girlfriend and we didn't go. We often have a full schedule between work and the kids, but that would have been my last time out with him. I should have made time. I should have called him more.

I miss him so much my heart hurts. I went from crying all day, to crying every day, to crying a few times a week. But my heart still hurts so much and there is this painful emptiness inside of me. I want to see him, to talk to him, to hear his laugh, and to hug him again.

When he died, a part of me went missing. It is that bond siblings have. I can FEEL he's gone. Angie can feel he's gone.

*

CAROL WALL
Carol's 29-year-old son Jason died
from a heroin overdose in 2016

I feel guilt every single day. A mother's job is to protect her children. I feel I failed. I wish I could go back. I wish I understood more. I can only imagine now the depth of pain Jason must have been feeling to think that drugs were the solution. I would have listened more. I wish I could have slowed things down.

271

My husband, my rock, tries to tell me every time I feel guilty that it was not my fault, that I—we—did everything we could, but I can't help feeling this way. Jason was my baby. I would have given up my life for his. The hardest emotion is the guilt. The hardest thing is just missing him, everything about him.

CHAPTER FIFTEEN

Shadow of anger

If someone shot 10 people, this community would be
in an uproar. There would be an army here trying to
stop it. That's exactly where we are with opioids.
But who's showing up to stop it?
~BRUCE LANGOS, Criminal Intelligence Center

Anger is common after loss by overdose. Anger at our loved one, our-selves, the drug cartels and dealers, pharmaceutical companies, and our government for not doing more to help. The list goes on. In relation to your loved one's death, what evokes the most anger in you?

*

KIMBERLY CALAIS
Kim's 23-year-old daughter Emily died from a multiple drug
overdose including heroin and methamphetamine in 2016

The emotions of my grief journey are all rhymes without reason as to expectation in any given circumstance. I can be driving, feeling calm, and then I will suddenly burst into tears and sob uncontrollably.

No build up. Just raw emotion. I give each of my emotions the space to just **be**, and I've learned not to hurry or bury them. They need to be recognized, understood and embraced for what they are and what they represent.

It's interesting. When people cry, others try to calm them or even do and/or say things to make it stop. We don't do that with smiling or laughter. We experience those emotions with them or let them be. We, as a society, seem to be uncomfortable with tears. For me, my tears are the outpouring of my heart. They may come from a place of pain. Or joy. Of sadness. Or appreciation. I don't need for anyone to soothe my tears away. I need and want to experience them, regardless of how uncomfortable that might make others.

Another emotion people have trouble accepting is anger. It seems as if anger has become my uninvited constant companion. An ever-present shadow. Like my tears, anger presents itself without notice. It feels dark and like venom in my veins. I dislike feeling anger since I've never been one to harbor the emotion for much more than a moment at a time.

I've come to know a volatility of my own, one in which I welcome a fight of any kind, even with perfect strangers. That is so very unlike my former self. I do not back down from any form of a slight, and feel like a danger to my own wellbeing quite often.

When I stop and let myself experience where it comes from, it almost always starts off with the anger I hold toward myself. How could I have let this happen? Why didn't I do something to stop it?

How could I have left her? Why am I still here? When will this pain ever subside? And so it goes.

I have anger toward others as well. The people I had thought of as friends or who are related to me by blood, people who now have no idea of how to be around me. This used to hurt my feelings. Now I fluctuate between being angry with them or not caring, the latter of which is a scary proposition as I know the opposite of love is not hate; rather, it is apathy, which is another emotion I've become close friends with. They either say the wrong things or say nothing at all. They are waiting for me to get over it and get back to normal. There is no getting over it and I will never be the person I was. How could I ever be that person again?

I also have great anger at society as a whole. A society that created and perpetuates the stigma about those who battle their addiction and judge the people who love them. A society that continues to turn a deaf ear and a blind eye to the growing epidemic that is taking our loved ones away in epic proportions.

Every day I see a news story or hear a report about another overdose in another town/city/state/province/country, and how each level seeks to call a state of emergency to deal with the heinous tentacles of the beast known as addiction. Yet the reports continue. Every single day hundreds are lost to a substance use passing, leaving families shattered yet invisible to the society of which they belong.

This society seems to default to the philosophy that it's their choice and therefore they deserve what they get. Who in their right mind would ever choose the existence of those who suffer from a substance use disorder and its addiction? NO ONE WOULD. Yet our spouses, children, parents and friends apparently don't deserve any help since they should just stop. I'm personally to the point where I can barely read anything on social media anymore. Each time I read a meme conveying the outrage of resuscitating an overdose with free naloxone and a cancer patient having to pay to receive chemotherapy, I truly want to scream. These people are uninformed, uneducated and unsympathetic to the circumstances that serve as the new framework of our lives.

Society would be well served to spend a moment in our shoes so it could experience the desolation that we experience as we try to help, support, treat and, sadly, grieve our loved ones. While it may be too late to educate the generations who have long since concluded that drug use is a choice made by a marginalized portion of society, those entering school have a chance to learn that substance use disorder is a disease and its victims should be embraced with compassion and treated with the dignity that all human beings deserve.

The one person I hold no anger toward is Emily. While there are so many emotions I feel in relation to her life and death, anger is not one of them. She suffered in so many ways, even when she seemed at her best. She lived with demons that I could not possibly understand, and she tried to care for herself the best way she could. She was a human being. She made mistakes as we all do. She was far from perfect. And she was and always will be my daughter, a casualty in a war on drugs that cannot clearly see that the opponent is not the drug user. They—and their families—are the collateral damage.

*

SUSAN CARLYON
Susan's 22-year-old son Adam died from
an overdose of carfentanyl in 2016

The extremely rude and hurtful comments made to us about our son make me angry. Drug addiction has a horrible and judgmental stigma attached to it.

*

MARYBETH CICHOCKI
MaryBeth's 37-year-old son Matthew died
from a Percocet overdose in 2015

I am angry at the shoddy treatment those suffering from addiction receive, and the fight with insurance companies who discriminate against people who suffer from substance use disorder. They ignore parity when it comes to treating substance use disorder as they do any other chronic disease.

Society must stop the stigma and start reading the research proving that SUD is a brain disease. Society must stop condemning and shaming people. They must stop denying Narcan and posting hate on social media sites. I cope by advocating in my state for laws that change how SUD is treated and bringing down pill pushing doctors. I honor my son by delivering "A Hug From Matt" bags to the homeless and those forgotten by society.

*
KIM DELONG
Kim's 29-year-old son Tyler died
from a fentanyl overdose in 2017

I'm angry that Tyler didn't ask me to help him after his first overdose, angry that he lied to me knowing I loved him and was always there for him and would do anything for him. I'm angry that his friends never contacted me to let me know wat was happening. I think it was partly society and the system. The younger generation accepts drug use behavior and the system is so expensive for private pay that those who need it most cannot afford it.

*
ELAINE FAULKNER
Elaine's 25-year-old son Jacob died from
an overdose of opiates and Xanax in 2017

I have felt anger surfacing and it has landed on various targets as I work through my grief. I've been angry at the doctor who prescribed the medications six days before Jake died. I've been angry at myself. I've been angry at his ex-girlfriends. I've been angry at God. I've been angry at Jake. I've been angry at how interventions could have happened but did not.

Today I recognize the anger for what it is, a way of deflecting my emotions to cope with the pain of loss. It's hard to let go of anger when it crops up, but there is no point in being angry. I will only hurt myself and cause more suffering. Pain is pain, but suffering is optional. I accept that it is over, I can't go back and change the outcome. If I accept myself and those around me, I set myself free. If I accept what can't be changed, I'm able to move on and not get stuck in an emotion that's not productive.

*

SHANNIE JENKINS
Shannie's 31-year-old son Kyle died
from a heroin overdose in 2017

I don't feel that the system failed Kyle. Kyle, along with so many others, dealt with a horrible brain disease. The only failure was that none of us knew the extent of this horrible disease. I wish I understood this addiction as I do now. We fought alongside Kyle the best we could and learned so much from him. I am thankful he was so honest about his battle and taught us so much.

Since Kyle went to prison, he was listed as a felon. It was hard to watch him be judged by others. For a felon to try to turn their life around, get a place to live, and find work is very hard. We encouraged him when he felt defeated, and God seemed to always open a new door for Kyle.

The only anger I feel is to see so many more people who are dying from overdose. They found a cure for HIV, and people are living with the disease. When will they find a cure for addiction? My heart breaks for all those who lose a loved one this way.

When someone reaches out and needs help for their loved one, I feel helpless. Trying to direct them to the services they need, where does a person start? They start to call each treatment center or detox facility only to be told no bed is available, or that the person needs an assessment which could take two weeks. When an addict reaches out for help, we have a twenty-four-hour window of opportunity to get them the help they need. The addiction is so strong that their body and mind will draw them back into the darkness of using. They have to—they have to use to stay well.

I see things changing and I don't have the answer. But my heart hurts knowing how many are dying every single day. Seeing the addiction, the homelessness, the mental illness. Whether it starts out with drugs and becomes a mental illness, or a person has a mental illness, in the end it is one and the same. These people need help. There are so many opinions on this issue, but again people are dying. There has to be an answer.

*

LORI LATIMER
Lori's 29-year-old son Greg died from
alcohol and fentanyl-laced cocaine in 2019

What makes me most angry about all this is that there is so little public awareness about fentanyl, the dangers of it, and the scope of its deadly effects—and that Greg didn't know and that I didn't know. I'm angry that it gets into our country so easily and is killing so many people every single day, yet there's no public outrage over it.

In 2017, approximately 192 people every single day died from drug-related causes. I'm angry that it took me losing my son for me to learn about all this. I'm angry that people are selling poison without telling their customers that what they're getting as a bonus in the illegal drug they're buying.

I'm very angry at whoever sold Greg the drugs. And yes, I've been angry at Greg at times for choosing to use illegal drugs simply to have fun.

Anger has led me to cut certain people out of my life who no longer deserve a place in it due to their hurtful actions and lack of compassion in the aftermath of what happened to Greg. My level of tolerance for certain things and people is at an all-time low. I simply do not have the energy for it.

The more research I do into the opioid issue, and the fentanyl issue in particular, the angrier it makes me. From the pharmaceutical companies that make the drugs, to the doctors who so freely prescribe them, to the people working in the labs in China, to the cartels in Mexico, to the United States government for not addressing this when they were first warned about it. I'm angry that we live in a society that shuns and stigmatizes people who struggle with mental health and drug issues. I'm angry at all of it.

I'm angry at some of the people who were the closest to Greg and should have known something was wrong but chose to ignore the warning signs, even when I begged them to when he lashed out at me.

I am also angry at myself for not knowing. Is that realistic? For me, it doesn't matter if it is or not. My child was crying out for help the last six weeks of his life, and I didn't know.

What I don't do is judge myself for my anger, or any of the other emotions I feel on a regular basis. I know that if I don't feel them, if I push them away or numb out on drugs or medication, they'll still be there, and I'll be faced with them in much more difficult ways later on. I allow myself to cry when the tears come, I write, I talk to people who loved Greg, and I connect with Greg in a different way, but I connect with him on a very real level. And I learn more about the opioid and fentanyl issue. I speak to people in our government in an effort to hold them accountable, and to parents and young people to bring awareness to an issue that is often swept under the rug because it's too uncomfortable to talk about, or carries with it too much stigma.

*

AMANDA MARIE
Amanda's 30-year-old brother Cory
died from a heroin overdose in 2015

I was angry. Angry at the system that failed him, angry at our parents and our family, angry at myself. Yet, I wasn't mad at him.

We were kindred spirits with joint experiences. I understood the relentless pain in his soul. I understood the need to make the mind quiet long enough to take a breath. I realize that the murky waters of restlessness and existential crises are so cripplingly deep that eventually you drown in them. I understood the passionate desire to feel nothing, if only for a moment.

I didn't blame him one bit. I wasn't mad, just disappointed.

*

DIANA MITCHELL
Diana's 18-year-old daughter Brooke died from
a mix of fentanyl, ecstasy, and cocaine in 2017

I'm angry that nobody told me.

*

WHITNEY O'BRIEN
Whitney's 23-year-old brother Michael died from
a heroin/cocaine/benzodiazepine overdose in 2016

I am not angry that my brother died. I spent the last two years being angry at him for using and not being able to get sober. His death has not aroused anger in my heart, it has shattered it. I feel completely and utterly defeated. Be that as it may, I hold not one person responsible for his death. Not the neighbor who molested him. Not the drug dealer who sold him his dope. Not the insurance company who put him and my family through the ringer every time he tried to get help. Not society who viewed him as a junkie. His death was an unfortunate culmination of all those occurrences.

What evokes anger out of me is the way addiction is viewed in our society. The stigma surrounding substance abuse is killing our loved ones and preventing them from getting treatment. In this country, we view drug addicts as criminals and regard jail time as treatment. Until we accept that addiction is a brain disease and start treating it like the public health crisis that it is, the death rate is going to continue to climb. An average of 142 Americans die every day from an opioid overdose. Which means you are likely to know someone in your lifetime who will die from addiction. This could be your brother, sister, parent, child, friend, spouse... So, who are you willing to live without?

The pace with which our country is moving toward change is too slow in comparison to the rate at which people are dying. We know what works, and yet we don't implement these strategies. The U.S. is lightyears behind Canada and Europe who have already implemented harm reduction methods such as needle exchange programs and safe injection facilities into their communities. Access to medication, such as methadone and Suboxone, and yes, even heroin, needs to be quick and affordable. But it's not.

It's time to accept that drugs are here to stay. Rather than fall for the delusion that drug cessation is the only definition of victory in the war on drugs, let's acknowledge that reducing harm is also a triumph. Instead of sitting here and letting my anger fester, I have chosen to become involved in this community and educate myself. This has helped me heal and to cope with not just the anger surrounding substance abuse in our society, but the heartbreak of losing my brother.

*

ALICE RICH
Alice's 42-year-old brother Gary
died from a fentanyl overdose in 2015

I'm angry that people continue to start using heroin, even though everyone knows that if you use, you die. It's no secret that people are dying in outrageous numbers. Just don't start using in the first place. I do not feel that my brother was failed by society. He honestly had plenty of chances and kept choosing to use and think, "Maybe I can control it this time."

I have way more sadness than anger, and that's how it has been since he died.

*

CAROL WALL
Carol's 29-year-old son Jason died
from a heroin overdose in 2016

The people who were involved at the end of his life. They didn't love him, they only used him up. The anger at the drug heroin! It stole my boy. The anger at this world we live in, that drugs that are out there that kill people. The anger that he is not here, that he is gone. My grief is often misdirected as anger, it ebbs and flows. I recognize it and sometimes I am angry for weeks at a time. Anger comes from helplessness. Helplessness that I couldn't save him. Anger at myself.

In 2015, the amount of opioids prescribed
was enough for every American to be
medicate around the clock for 3 weeks.

~ CENTER FOR DISEASE CONTROL

CHAPTER SIXTEEN

Fighting the darkness

The bereaved need more than just the space
to grieve the loss. They also need the space to
grieve the transition. -LYNDA CHELDELIN FELL

When we lose a loved one unexpectedly, the pain is overwhelming and crushing. We wonder if we can even go on. Experiencing suicidal thoughts in the aftermath isn't uncommon, yet few readily admit it for fear of being judged or condemned. Have you had thoughts of self-harm or suicide since losing your loved one?

*

KIMBERLY CALAIS
Kim's 23-year-old daughter Emily died from a multiple drug
overdose including heroin and methamphetamine in 2016

My grief has taken me many places I never dreamed imaginable. I have experienced some of the most horrific pain since that day in January. So many tears come from a place so deep inside me, drawn from a bottomless well.

My mind is constantly working to process this hideous existence. I am distracted most of the time. While it may appear that I am listening to you, I'm not. I can't. The echoes of the life that came before that day, and all the pain that has devoured me since, deafen me. I have little to no patience with small talk of any kind. I have little to no patience with much of anything.

My mind constantly spins as I see people caught up in the minutiae of living. Don't they know that everything can change in the blink of an eye? Don't they know how incredibly blessed they are to watch their child graduate, get married, have children? What an incredible blessing it is to be able to call their loved one on the phone, go out to lunch, hug and kiss them. Do they appreciate each and every opportunity they have to hear their loved one say, "I love you," and to tell them the same in return?

I've had many challenges in my life and have suffered my fair share of loss and death in my family. I lost my father to cancer when I was nineteen. I lost my sister to cancer when I was forty-two. I lost my mother to dementia and health complications when I was forty-nine. And now I've lost my daughter to an accidental overdose at age fifty-four.

Each loss was devastating, and I mourned each beloved family members. I was a very strong person. But no loss prior to my loss of Emily could prepare me or hold a candle to what I was about to experience. Every night while crying myself to sleep, I'd pray that I wouldn't wake up. The pain and heartache were impossible to carry.

Each morning I'd wake up, disappointed that I was still alive. As time passed, I gave thought to putting an end to my grief of my own volition. I live in a condominium and I'd often leave our bedroom and walk to the door, looking out, then stepping out, and wondered if the fall would kill me. Was it high enough? What if it didn't?

I'd think of the burden that I represented to those who loved me. My husband had to live with someone who would spend hours crying or not talking. Usually both. His love and unconditional acceptance of me in any and all forms throughout this journey humble me greatly. I self-excluded myself from life. I avoided having people over and avoided being around people.

More than once I said that if someone could offer me something that would take away even a small amount of the pain, I'd take it in a heartbeat. Then it dawned on me that this must have been what Emily felt like. This is what that pill, that buy, that baggie allowed her: peace within herself. An escape from the pain that was her mind. I now had a new understanding of my daughter, and am overwhelmed with compassion and empathy which touches me to the core.

Despite my overwhelming pain and despair, my thoughts turned to Emily's sister. She and I would talk about our loss in ways that only we could. We had walked so much of Emily's road together. We had front-row seats to the illness which destroyed her—and us. The selfishness of my thoughts made me cry. Here I am, so very blessed to have been the mother of these two incredible girls. Yes, one it now gone and that will forever and always cause me pain that I wouldn't wish on my very worst enemy. But one daughter remains. A daughter who still needs me, who does her best every day to make sure I know what I mean to her. A daughter who, like the phoenix, has risen from her sister's ashes and found a path out of the rubble life. A daughter who, like Emily, I love with the entirety of my heart and soul.

Time reflecting on my and Emily's life have also shown me that the truest tragedy would be to not honor the life and love that was Emily. In fact, one of my biggest fears is that Emily will be forgotten. So much of me died when she did, but I also remember what her dreams were and what she loved most about living. Her life was a gift to all that knew her, especially me. Although I am her mother, she taught me more about love, patience, strength and hope in her twenty-three years than all my other relationships combined. I look at those who suffer differently now. I seem to have endless compassion for those who are hurting, especially from mental health and substance issues, and know that they are someone's child. Their lives matter. They did not intend to end up where they stand, but they need not stand alone.

Having other children does not, in my opinion, make matters better or worse. Some might say—and have said—you have another daughter. True. But I only had one Emily. I still can celebrate holidays and special occasions, constantly reminded that someone is missing. Just as watching our loved one suffer with their addiction, it is very painful to watch your child or children suffer the loss of their sibling, especially when you're just trying to survive your own pain.

A mother who lost both her children to suicide once told us that prior to one son's death, her younger son told her, "At least you lived years before you had kids. I've never known life without my brother."

That hit home for me. The guidance and support we offered to our lost loved one needs now be given to their sibling, their partner, their children, their friends . . . any person who now survives them. These people all deserve to know what our loved one meant to us. We can share their dreams with them. All the stories of their lifetimes. It is this mandate that gives me purpose. It is this incredible love that gives me the strength to share Emily's story for this book. If anything I can share about Emily gives you even a moment of peace, acceptance, understanding, knowledge, relief or insight, then I know I am serving her memory well, providing a place for all the love I carry for her to continue to grow.

As was true during my pregnancy, my heart once again beats for two and I need to do my best to take precious care of the gift of her life which I will carry for the remainder of my own.

*

MARYBETH CICHOCKI
MaryBeth's 37-year-old son Matthew died
from a Percocet overdose in 2015

No. I want to use my time left to fight the broken system hoping no other mother will get that horrific phone call. I survive by helping people get into treatment. I advocate and use my voice to bring awareness to the disease of addiction.

291

*

KIM DELONG
Kim's 29-year-old son Tyler died
from a fentanyl overdose in 2017

I feel like a complete failure and I want to stop the excruciating pain I feel every day. I'm no longer afraid to die because I hope to see my son in heaven one day. I have another beautiful son and loving husband and family and friends. I have thought of driving my car into a tree, but I would never do it because I don't want to leave them or make them suffer with immense grief as I am. My biggest fear is that my son will be forgotten, and nobody will say his name anymore.

*

ELAINE FAULKNER
Elaine's 25-year-old son Jacob died from
an overdose of opiates and Xanax in 2017

I did wonder if I was going to make it. Surviving every day was a chore. I had to talk myself out of bed, and dreaded facing the day, facing the pain. The loss was a big black hole. I didn't know how to cope. I couldn't think. My brain didn't work. I was in a murky fog.

I worried about my daughters and Jack. I told Jack one day that I didn't know how I was going to be able to go on. It was a simple statement from my perspective, but from his, it seemed like a suicidal statement. I could see from his reaction that I was in a bad place emotionally. I promised him that if I felt worse, I would drive myself to the hospital and commit myself. I would not do anything to cause him or our family more pain.

It was bleak some days, having thoughts wearing me down while bearing the loss. Somehow, each day, I got what I needed. Somehow, I was able to connect to my loved ones, or a stranger's random act of kindness would lift me up.

I participated in every grief and loss group available. I read books. I went to weekly counseling sessions. Jack and I participated in the local group, The Compassionate Friends. I learned to accept my feelings and they have strengthened me. I know that I can go to deep places and I will survive. I continue to have irrational fears for my family and their safety. I'm afraid that some cruel twist of fate will wrench another loved one out of my arms. I understand that these feelings are natural and normal after loss. When others share their feelings and fears, it helps me understand my own.

*

SHANNIE JENKINS
Shannie's 31-year-old son Kyle died
from a heroin overdose in 2017

I have not felt thoughts of self-harm since Kyle's death. There were times when I just felt like I didn't care. But I have another son, and a husband, and kids and grandkids. I live for them and I know that God has and will continue to use me to help others. God has already blessed me to share Kyle's story with so many and speak loud and proud about my son. I will keep him alive. And his son, Knox, will know his daddy through his mommy, brother, and all our family. I know I am still in a fog and still in shock. I'm not sure when or if this will ever go away. But my heart is totally open to what God has planned for me. There was a reason He took Kyle home. Although I do not know His plan, I trust in whatever happens in my life.

My biggest fear is that I will forget it felt like to hug Kyle, I might forget the freckle on his nose, or his great laugh. It's been two years since he left. I look at his picture and find myself shaking my head in disbelief. The first year, I was so numb and in shock. To know that I will never hug my son here on earth is the worst feeling ever. But because of my belief, I know that I will be reunited with him in heaven.

I'm not afraid of dying, especially now. When my time comes, I want to be ready and I want God to be proud of what I have done for Him here on earth. There is a song "Well Done," by The Afters. When I heard that on the radio, I wept. I thought that is what I want Jesus to say to me when I am standing in front of Him. And I feel that is what He said to Kyle, also.

Another song I listen to almost every day is "Go Rest High on That Mountain," by Vince Gill. The words give me so much comfort that Kyle's work on earth was done and now he will rest with our Heavenly Father.

*

LORI LATIMER
Lori's 29-year-old son Greg died from
alcohol and fentanyl-laced cocaine in 2019

Before Greg died, I was afraid to die because I had an amazing family and wanted to spend as many years as possible with them.

When Greg died, that changed. I've never been suicidal or thought about hurting myself, but I'm not afraid of dying now because I know that when I do, I will see him again. I'm also in no rush to die. I still have a beautiful family, there's just a hole in it now that no one else can ever fill.

I believe my older son, Steve, deserves me to be the best mom I can for him. My grandchildren deserve for me to be the best grandma I can for them. I want them to have good memories of me when it is my time to leave. My youngest grandson was only five weeks old when Greg died, and I want him to know me and I want to make great memories with him like I have with my older grandchildren.

But the level of darkness and raw pain that I've experienced since Greg died is overwhelming at times. I've cried more than I ever thought humanly possible. I have felt hopeless and helpless. I have wondered what the point of life is. I wasn't prepared for the physical effects of such deep loss. I lost my dad when I was thirty-three and lost my mom when I was fifty-four, just four years before losing Greg.

I loved my parents very much and had a great childhood, and I was deeply sad when they died. But losing them wasn't anything close to losing my son. The brain fog, the inability to concentrate or focus, the panic attacks, the insomnia, the exhaustion on every level, and so much more—no one is prepared for any of that because until it happens to us, we don't seek out information about it.

I'm using my experience and pain and turning it into a new purpose. I've been blessed to have had a very successful career as a family law paralegal. Now I'm speaking out about things I never envisioned because I want to spare anyone else from ever having to learn these things in the way I've had to—through losing a child. Greg deserves for me to be his voice and his legacy. For whatever time I have left in this life, I will speak out and I will live my life. It isn't always easy; in fact, many days it's a struggle just to get out of bed. I'm still alive though, so there must be a reason. And I know Greg is beside me with each step I take.

*

AMANDA MARIE
Amanda's 30-year-old brother Cory
died from a heroin overdose in 2015

I've dealt with the trauma of losing Cory in many ways. Sometimes, those ways were not so healthy. I cried every day for months. I swam in the subterranean throes of torment. I suffered in profound, unidentifiable ways. As cognizant and conscious as I typically am, grief snuck violently into my foundation and broke apart my roots. From the storm's ruin sprouted a new version of me—an overachieving but self-destructive shell suspended in survival mode.

I spent a lot of time unstable and detached, oscillating between disassociation and presence, fully aware or completely removed. I earned a bachelor's and then a master's, worked two jobs and raised two children—alone. I developed an eating disorder and lost forty pounds in six months. I stopped sleeping. I could add up all the years of trauma after trauma, yet the sum does not total the devastation I felt the moment I called out Cory's name without reply.

Words cannot describe the pain, but sometimes I tried to make them. Sometimes it was sentimental letters or creative poems. Other times it was just pages and pages of rage. It was the only healthy way I knew to cope with the unimaginable loss and a broken heart, along with the guilt and shame.

*

DIANA MITCHELL
Diana's 18-year-old daughter Brooke died from
a mix of fentanyl, ecstasy, and cocaine in 2017

I don't know about suicide, but I did wonder why it wasn't me instead of her. Why did it have to be her? She had so much to live for, she had such big dreams.

*

WHITNEY O'BRIEN
Whitney's 23-year-old brother Michael died from
a heroin/cocaine/benzodiazepine overdose in 2016

When he died, I was six weeks postpartum and experiencing the usual hormonal changes and mood shifts many women experience after childbirth. Now add to that the devastation of losing my brother and most days I felt like my knees were going to buckle under me.

I've never considered harming myself or experienced thoughts of suicide, but there are times when I am so completely consumed by my grief it feels as though I'm suffocating. It's been the lowest time of my life, to say the least. I put my best face forward (most days) and I am able to mask my sorrow quite well, particularly on social media. I don't

297

think anyone knows just how deeply depressed I am. Maybe not even me. Michael's death has had an enormous impact on me—mind, body, and soul. It has completely changed everything about me. I look in the mirror and I don't even recognize the person I have morphed into.

Inevitably, with the amount of impact it's had on my personal wellbeing, it has affected my marriage also. But, by the grace of God, my husband has been at my side to walk with me through this journey through hell; taking the lead and lessening the blow in any way he physically can. I've been humbled by his ability to assume without any questions asked. He's picked me up off the shower floor, dressed me, cooked for me, given me space while still being fervently present. His love is steadfast and solid, his support unrelenting, and frankly I don't know how I would have survived those first few months without him.

Rather than take my own life, I feel obligated to stay alive and stay healthy—mostly for my parents' sake. If they had to bury another child, it would kill them. I have to be here for them. They need me and I need them. Through each other, we are all we have left of Michael. My biggest fear is losing someone again. I can't even let myself entertain the notion.

*

ALICE RICH
Alice's 42-year-old brother Gary
died from a fentanyl overdose in 2015

I had the thought once that I can't wait to get to heaven so I don't have to feel this hole in my heart any longer, but didn't intend on taking the fast track there. I shared this thought with my sister and had to clarify that I was more than willing for the good Lord to take me in His time, but I know there will be joy where sadness now lives.

*

CAROL WALL
Carol's 29-year-old son Jason died
from a heroin overdose in 2016

Yes, I have had dark thoughts, but I won't. The reason I won't is that I could not put my husband, daughter, son or family through the sadness of losing someone else they love. I see what losing my son has done to my other two children, my husband, and my family, and would not want them to go through a great loss again, my children and husband especially.

I cannot bring Jason back. I have to live for everyone I have here who I love so much. I do believe I will see Jason again when it is my time, and that brings me peace.

Carfentanyl, a synthetic opioid, has clinical potency
up to 10 times that of morphine
and 100 times that of fentanyl.

~NATIONAL INSTITUTES OF HEALTH

CHAPTER SEVENTEEN

How do we stop the epidemic?

It's an epidemic. And I don't pretend to
have the answers for it. ~JAMIE LEE CURTIS

In 2017, more than 70,200 Americans died from an overdose, and the statistics continue to climb. The numbers are staggering yet we're still struggling to find answers. Since losing your loved one, what do you think should be done about it?

*

KIMBERLY CALAIS
Kim's 23-year-old daughter Emily died from a multiple drug
overdose including heroin and methamphetamine in 2016

Although numbers differ, they say that over a hundred Americans are lost every day to overdose. When you add the number of people touched by their battles and their ultimate losses, the number grows exponentially. Yet, what's being done?

Not nearly enough.

I often listen and discuss the news about this crisis, and usually state, "I don't have a horse in this race anymore, but..." and then give my two cents as to what I believe needs to change.

To me, it feels like society and those in control are decades late and billions of dollars short. It's like closing the barn door after the horses have escaped. We're trying to control the bleeding but not how to cure the cause or prevent the injury. While the headlines scream about the epidemic of fentanyl and other fatal opiates in defining today's crisis, I feel we should take a step back and look at overdose of any kind. The crisis, in my opinion, is less about the substance and more about what led our loved ones to use in the first place.

I've learned that the majority of lost loved ones began using some form of a substance around thirteen or fourteen years of age. While this age is usually considered the casual adolescent experimentation phase, there is nothing usual about casual use anymore. Kids today are certainly not the kids of generations gone by.

Access to so many substances are limitless. A person need not travel to the proverbial street corner to get whatever drug they want. They can now just log on and have it delivered to their—or your—doorstep. Add peer group pressure and the mindset of invincibility that most kids have, and the combination is quite daunting.

If I had the ability, I would start the reform of awareness with middle school children and their parents. Ideally, every school would be staffed with at least one mental health professional who would meet and establish relationships with the kids. This same professional should also meet with the parents, as a direct line of communication should exist between those who are essentially raising our children.

School-sponsored and organized events could be held where former addicts and families who lost a loved one come speak, with the recovering addicts sharing their own journeys, identifying their own feelings of invincibility, simply relating to them in their own words. The families can speak openly to the parents and provide valuable insight as to what to look for, and provide resources I wish I had. An alliance between school and home, without judgment, is critical, particularly as those kids move to high school, and the peer group and social media pressures become even more overwhelming.

The expression, "It takes a village to raise a child," certainly applies and, in my view, it takes that same village—and more—to save a child from the disease of addiction.

I do not want to sound jaded, but I believe that under the current structure of rehabilitation and treatment, it is very difficult to make any appreciable difference in the lives of those suffering from the monster of addiction. We haven't begun to scratch the surface to change this tide that is exterminating our young people in record numbers. I believe the greatest impact occurs in the beginning.

If I could go back in time, my wish list would have included the presence of mental health professionals in the school who could tap into what's happening in the school and, together, form an action plan that would help Emily succeed on all levels. A lot of attention has been given to bullying, which has been linked to teen suicide and school shootings. That same environment of exclusion or pressure often results with kids turning to substance to fit in or tune out.

Would an honest talk with a recovered addict have scared Emily straight? I'll never know. But if it could impact even one person, it's more than worth the effort. I believe I would also have benefited from hearing from parents and families of those suffering from mental health and addiction issues. I wouldn't have been so quick to write off Emily's experimentation with marijuana and alcohol to be just that—experimentation—and conclude that she'll grow out of it like I did.

She didn't. And now she's gone.

If I could talk to families who are in danger of running this race, I'd tell them to look behind the veil and listen for what is not being said. Are your kids changing friends? Are you meeting their friends? Are they changing the way they dress and wear makeup? Are they dropping out of activities and hobbies they enjoyed? Are they defensive when you ask them about time spent with friends? Are they becoming more secretive? Are they moodier? Spending more time alone? Has their schoolwork suffered? Are they spending too much time on social media? Are you fighting with each other? Have you caught them in lies? Have they stolen anything from you? Do they look or smell off when coming home from time out with friends?

I would strongly caution any parent who can answer yes to any of these questions to not write it off as traditional adolescence.

I did. And now she's gone.

*

SUSAN CARLYON
Susan's 22-year-old son Adam died from
an overdose of carfentanyl in 2016

Suboxone should be readily available and given to addicts. The wait time to get into a rehab facility must be considerably shortened. Rehabs need to be available to everyone, not just those people who are wealthy or have good insurance. The stigma of addiction must be eliminated. People need to understand that addiction is a brain disease.

*

MARYBETH CICHOCKI
MaryBeth's 37-year-old son Matthew died
from a Percocet overdose in 2015

Long-term treatment must be affordable and covered by the insurance industry. We must recognize substance use disorder as a chronic brain disease, and treat it as we treat any other disease.

I wish I had the contacts with my state legislatures that I have now through my advocacy work. I would have had the opportunity to get Matt into longer treatment and would have had better knowledge of the disease. I would know that it would always be in our lives.

I tell people to always tell their children they love them. Even through the craziest ugliness, let them know you are there for them. Tough love is not the answer. You should always be understanding and continue to open the door for conversations that could lead to treatment. Never give up. If they don't make it, at least you will not have regrets 😢

*

KIM DELONG
Kim's 29-year-old son Tyler died
from a fentanyl overdose in 2017

I think on a national level we need to stop drugs from entering the country. Locally there needs to be more police presence in neighborhoods where drugs have been known to be available. They need to be on foot and possibly on horseback on a daily basis. The HIPAA laws need to allow parents of overdose victims to be contacted. Free or low-cost treatment must be available. I didn't know that I could ask my son to give me legal permission to view his medical records and talk to his doctor. The HIPAA laws prevented me from knowing how serious my son's addiction really was. I was clueless. If I could do it over, I would have taken time off through the Family Medical Leave Act to get my son to an inpatient program far away from his friends.

*

ELAINE FAULKNER
Elaine's 25-year-old son Jacob died from
an overdose of opiates and Xanax in 2017

That's a very good question. I don't believe there is an easy answer. Drug use in our culture is deeply ingrained. When I say drug use, I mean all of it; over the counter medications, prescriptions, and illegal drugs. Compulsive behaviors are encouraged and exploited for profit. Parts of our culture glorify drug and alcohol use, and substance abuse is blatantly or passively promoted in music, movies, and other media.

Supply of illegal drugs has shown no signs of slowing, despite one trillion dollars having been spent in the past forty years fighting the war on drugs. As a society, we were not prepared for the fallout of unintentional addiction following the pharmaceutical companies' promotion of the medications they assured us were safe.

Doctors and dentists are starting to reduce narcotic prescriptions, although Vicodin remains one of the top prescribed drugs in the U.S. I believe Jake was at the forefront of a dangerous new trend of deaths involving benzodiazepine combined with other substances.

It breaks my heart that Jake is another overdose statistic. My heart goes out to all the parents raising children and doing the best they can. You love your child, that is a given. Some factors are not controllable when your child becomes an adult. They may, or may not, follow your suggestions.

Refer your loved one for treatment and counseling. Get help for yourself through counseling and support groups. Educate yourself on all your options. Know where the treatment centers are located and your insurance coverage options. Be prepared, as best you can, to act when needed. If, like myself, you can't have the outcome you desire, be at peace with yourself and your efforts.

*

SHANNIE JENKINS
Shannie's 31-year-old son Kyle died
from a heroin overdose in 2017

I felt like I knew a lot about addiction because of Kyle being so

SURVIVING LOSS BY OVERDOSE

upfront and honest. But there was so much I didn't know, and it is such a confusing disease. People will always have their opinion of it being a choice vs a disease, but it is just that...an opinion.

I don't wish this nightmare on anyone. My goal since even before Kyle passed was to take the shame out of addiction. No one WANTS to be an addict. They carry so much shame with them when they fall back into the darkness of addiction. But no one hates it more than themselves. And us parents carry so much guilt and shame. Trust me, I did it myself and still struggle with that. What-if . . .

As parents, we love our children and want them to always be safe. To know we can't save them is the worst feeling ever. I see so many posts in Facebook groups about cutting all ties from their kids and not enabling them. It is such a fine line between love and enabling, what is right and wrong? All I know is that I always wanted my son to know how much I love him. Even in his darkest days, he knew how much I loved him, and I know how much he loved me.

I wish I had an answer to a cure. I just know that there is a cure out there, but are any doctors or scientists working on one? Addiction needs a cure! It is so connected to the brain. How can a brain be reset to pre-addiction? Is that possible?

The one drug that gave my son a life for a short time after prison was Vivitrol. At the time Kyle had the implant, little was known. Now it comes in a shot form and I believe in a pill form. It only helps for opiates and not for meth and other drugs though. Kyle was thirty-one and made the decision to go off the implant after a year of being on it.

We respected his decision and kept in close contact to make sure he was doing well. He didn't want to be on it forever. Now I wish so much that we would have talked to him more and asked him to stay on it.

Other diseases need medications for the rest of a person's life, and I believe this is one also at this point. To see our son be so healthy and happy and starting a new life with a fiancée and going to be a daddy, and his brain getting hijacked was so heartbreaking. I know Kyle didn't want to die. But the draw to the drug is so powerful.

*

LORI LATIMER
Lori's 29-year-old son Greg died from
alcohol and fentanyl-laced cocaine in 2019

Since Greg's death, I realize how little people know about the severity of the drug/opioid/fentanyl epidemic. I was naïve. I thought that since I never did drugs, my sons' father never did drugs, and we talked to them about drugs, that my children wouldn't do them.

I didn't know the warning signs. I didn't know the danger of the poison that is fentanyl. I didn't know that synthetic fentanyl mainly comes from China and into Mexico, and then into the United States (some does come through Canada as well, but it mainly comes through Mexico). Some of it is produced in Mexico.

It's much cheaper than other drugs (cocaine, heroin, etc.). It's cheap to produce so it makes other drugs go further and gives a stronger effect than pure heroin, cocaine, marijuana, black market pills, or whatever else it's laced into.

The stigma of drugs and addiction needs to end. I saw a Facebook post by someone I went to high school with about addicts deserving whatever happens to them. That's heartless and cruel, yet far too common. It's a big part of why people are afraid to talk about what's happened to them or someone close to them. People of all ages need to be made aware of the truth of drugs and addiction, and of the very real threat of fentanyl. Only by shining a light on the true scope of this issue will people understand and stop being naïve like I was.

I also believe that people who have been affected by this epidemic such as addicts, family members, and friends, need to speak out. If Greg had been an addict, I would have no problem saying so because let's face it, what do I have to lose at this point? But I know many people are ashamed to talk about this because of the judgment and criticism they endure. Only by telling real stories of real people and the impact this has had on real lives will we begin to shift the stigma that still surrounds drugs and addiction.

I went to Washington, D.C. in September 2019, and spoke to several senator offices as well as the House of Representatives, and people in charge of agencies like Customs and Border Patrol. This issue transcends politics, political parties, age, gender, socioeconomic status, or anything else. I wanted to hear from them about what they're doing about these issues.

There are people from both political parties who are working on a bipartisan basis to create legislation on these issues. Unfortunately, we don't hear about that in the news because it isn't polarizing or sensational enough. People don't tend to listen to politicians unless they're screaming about the outrage of the moment. There's relatively little attention given to the drug/opioid/fentanyl issue in the media, and if any is given, it's usually only a twenty- or thirty-second story in the middle of a newscast.

People are a little more aware of fentanyl now due to the deaths of the Los Angeles Angels baseball player Tyler Skaggs, as well as the rapper Mac Miller, who both died from fentanyl that was laced in other drugs, as did the pop singer Prince. But even when they've heard of these people, most people still don't understand the horror of fentanyl.

I believe the only way to bring awareness to all this is through sharing our personal stories, like the brave women in this book. People are always captivated by stories. When we can weave facts and statistics into our stories, people listen. I saw it on Capitol Hill. I've seen it in the faces of people I've spoken with locally.

We need to address the root cause of all of it. I don't pretend to have any answers. I do know that ignoring it isn't working. Just Say No hasn't worked because it doesn't address the root cause. We need better mental health options and treatment options. And our legal system needs to enforce the laws related to illegal drugs. We need to stem the flow of illegal drugs coming into our country.

Finally, pharmaceutical companies and many doctors need to be fined and/or legally punished for their role in this epidemic. Someone else very close to me almost died from prescription opioid addiction just a few years ago. He was taking eight 80 mg oxycodone pills a day for several years. The pain management doctor he was seeing was prescribing them without hesitation. The pharmacy was filling them without hesitation. He was clearly addicted and not fully functioning, yet they continued to hand him the pills like they were candy.

The numbers vary, but between one hundred to two hundred people die every day from drugs in the United States. That is not acceptable. Teachers in middle schools need to talk about opioids and fentanyl and the dangers and warning signs. Too many children begin experimenting with drugs when they are thirteen or fourteen, and sometimes even younger. Unfortunately, many middle school teachers don't even know what fentanyl is. They have the opportunity to make a huge difference in the lives of their students, and should be required to do so through education on these topics.

*

AMANDA MARIE
Amanda's 30-year-old brother Cory
died from a heroin overdose in 2015

I don't know how to stop the drug-overdose epidemic, but it is more than obvious that what we are doing now isn't working. Things need to change. Things have to change.

Addiction doesn't play favorites and its effects are far-reaching. While studies show that some are more at risk than others due to specific environmental and genetic factors, all you have to do is use. Even if you are lucky enough to have every resource at your disposal, once you start, you can't just stop. If it were that simple, we wouldn't have over one hundred families per day repeating the same narrative. We wouldn't have this book.

*

DIANA MITCHELL
Diana's 18-year-old daughter Brooke died from
a mix of fentanyl, ecstasy, and cocaine in 2017

We need more placements in the schools. Better connection from rehab to home. We find that a lot of people are lost when they come home after rehab. There are no reinforcements until a couple weeks after they've been home. By that time, we lose them.

*

WHITNEY O'BRIEN
Whitney's 23-year-old brother Michael died from
a heroin/cocaine/benzodiazepine overdose in 2016

There needs to be change in this country. Addiction is a chronic, relapsing brain disease and it should be regarded as such. The stories shared in this book can and will serve a purpose. Our loved ones have suffered and died for a cause; their deaths will not be in vain. By sharing their stories, it puts a face to this epidemic and will help to destigmatize substance use.

Since my brother's death, I have felt obligated to stand up for this disease and defend its victims. Perhaps I'm motivated by the guilt I carry, or maybe it's the sympathy I feel for others who are in the trenches fighting this disease. I'm not sure where this altruistic urge manifests from, but whatever the reason, I will not rest and will not stay silent until there is change.

One of the simplest and easiest things that can be done to help curb society's view of addiction is to start altering the language we use to describe this disease. The people in the grips of this epidemic are often suffering from unresolved trauma and/or untreated mental illness, making them vulnerable to addiction. They are not junkies. So, please stop using this term. It's derogatory, archaic, and carries a heavy negative connotation. It only feeds the stigma. The stigma that keeps people from seeking help.

This disease is not a result of character flaws or moral failings. When sober, they are not clean, nor are they dirty while using. They are not criminals. They are our brothers and sisters. Our mothers and fathers. Our children. Our spouses. Our friends.

Society's majority use words and phrases that perpetuate biased and punitive attitudes that imply willful misconduct. The correct term is "substance use disorder" or "opioid use disorder." I implore you let go of the verbiage that bolsters harmful judgments.

Since Michael's passing, I've spent a lot of time researching areas such as harm reduction and medicated assisted treatment (MAT). These are things I knew virtually nothing about when my brother was alive. This knowledge has yielded a newfound understanding of treatment and recovery. In his final weeks, Michael tried relentlessly to get on Suboxone. By and large, I was agreeable to whatever he thought would help him get sober. However, my impression was that he was trading one addiction for another. This is a common American prejudice. Treatment for addiction is just as stigmatized, if not more, as the addiction itself.

Methadone and Suboxone are medications that consist of naloxone and buprenorphine, and are used to prevent withdrawal and stave off cravings. When given the appropriate doses, people are not high, as I once ignorantly assumed. They are functioning citizens who are less likely to relapse and more likely to achieve long-term recovery. They are not substituting one drug for another. These are lifesaving medications; not replacements.

Taking a medication to manage illness is the standard treatment for any chronic disease. We have to stop forcing people to jump through unnecessary and unreachable hoops in order to obtain evidence-based care. It took four days for my brother to get on Suboxone. He was given a prescription which he promptly took to our local pharmacy where they had to wait for approval from insurance. Once it was granted, it then had to be ordered because Suboxone is not a routinely stocked medication (go figure!). It was finally ready for pickup on day four. He died the next day.

Availability of methadone and Suboxone is met with excessive barriers and dangerous hindrance. If this remains, people will die while waiting for treatment, just like my brother.

For many, ongoing medication therapy is what enables them to achieve and sustain sobriety. These medications are scientifically proven to be the most successful pathway to long-term recovery. Not detoxification. This is a huge pill for some to swallow (no pun intended). I'd like to reiterate that I support whatever recovery route is effective and I believe treatment is an individual choice. But I trust what science tells me. Opioid tolerance decreases rapidly during cessation. Those who have recently detoxed can die from the usual dose of heroin they used prior to detox. Individuals who are utilizing medication treatment are just as sober as those who choose an abstinence-based approach to recovery.

The abstinence versus harm reduction debate is ongoing and controversial. Harm reduction strategies can reduce overdoses and prevent the spread of disease. These methods are often met with resistance and criticism. If we can clear some of the misconceptions surrounding harm reduction, we can start saving lives.

In essence, harm reduction encourages recovery in a step-by-step approach starting with ways to make drug use safe. Needle exchange programs provide users with clean, hypodermic syringes and other intravenous paraphernalia to reduce infection and abscesses, as well as the transmission of diseases such as HIV/AIDS and hepatitis. So why wouldn't we provide new, sterile supplies to those in need? Because needle exchange is viewed as condoning drug use and making it easy for users to shoot up.

In actuality, studies have not shown an increased likelihood that individuals will start using drugs intravenously. It's also financially feasible. If you consider the fact that preventing HIV/AIDS and hepatitis with needle exchange will save our country countless dollars in medical costs, it just makes sense. So, if we can all agree to start distributing safe, sterile supplies, where are these individuals going to go to use their substances? Since many of our loved ones are dying in public restrooms, parks, or in locked bedrooms, let's provide them with a safe place to use. Safe injection facilities (SIF) prevent overdose deaths by taking drug use out of the public. In doing so, the discard of used syringes in the community will decline and the opportunity to seek treatment and other medical care will be readily available. In these sites, addicts inject themselves under the supervision of trained medical professionals, who can intervene and administer naloxone (Narcan—an opioid reversal agent). Safe injections sites are a radical approach to opioid addiction but there has never been an overdose death in a SIF, ever. I repeat: ever.

SIFs save lives, period. Keeping people alive is the humane and ethical thing to do and it gives them the opportunity to seek treatment and achieve recovery.

In an effort to curtail heroin use, we must crack down on the overprescribing of painkillers in this country. After all, more than half of heroin users claim to have abused prescription opioids first. As a nurse, I see this firsthand. Every time I hand a narcotic to a patient, it takes everything in me to not spout off on a substance use rant. But these medications have become mainstreamed and expected.

Nowadays, hospitals are reimbursed based on patient satisfaction scores. So, if a patient comes in for pain medicine and we don't give it to them, we won't get paid. It's no wonder they're overprescribed. We hand them out like candy. A Percocet for you. A shot of morphine for you. A Vicodin for you. It's disturbing and I shoulder some of the blame as a healthcare worker. But eliminating access is not the answer either. Nurses and doctors have an obligation to be explicit when educating patients on the potential dangers of prescription painkillers. When applicable, non-opioid alternatives should be considered, and patients should be routinely monitored for signs of misuse.

These stories of real experiences and relationships can influence serious policy changes. After all, political leaders often site personal relationships as grounds for lobbying drug reform. Currently, there are stringent limitations placed on physicians prescribing privileges. Doctors must first obtain certification to prescribe Suboxone. Once permitted, they may only care for a maximum of thirty patients within their first year of accreditation. After the first year, their capacity expands to one hundred patients. These restrictions prevent access and delay treatment. We would never limit a doctor's ability to prescribe antihypertensive medication to a patient with uncontrolled blood pressure. It's also time to stop considering jail time as treatment.

I want to be clear—in no way do I condone drug use. But when a person's only offense is possession or ingestion of substances, I hardly consider them criminals. Addiction is a brain disease characterized by compulsive use despite negative consequences. When you jail an addict and force them into abstinence, you are doing them an injustice.

Drug-related felonies often result in court-supervised treatment. Many states ban medication-assisted treatment in drug court. If we are going to offer those convicted of drug-related crimes only abstinence-based approaches, then we're putting them in a position to fail. Only when our country begins to understand that the majority of damage comes not from the disease but the laws that criminalize it, can we begin to generate change, distinguish the stigma, and reel in this epidemic for good.

To those of you who have not yet lost your loved one to this disease, my advice is to hang in there. Easier said than done, I know, but hear me out. You probably feel as though you have already lost your loved one. They're lying to you, stealing from you, manipulating you—they aren't the person you know and love. So, you've chosen to write them off and consider them dead to you. Let me just say that being cheated and deceived is painful, trust me I know. But it hurts way less than the pain of guilt and regret.

One day, you'll wish you had tried harder. One day, you'll wonder what could have been if you would have reached out more. If I could do things over again, I would have stayed more open and available to him. But as a way of protecting myself, I withdrew and became distant. Rather than checking in with my brother, I would call my parents for updates on him. I was so worried about enabling him that I wasn't there to support him.

So, answer that call and respond to that text, because what if it's your last? The knowledge I've gained has given me understanding and hope—two things I desperately wish I had while he was alive. There was so much I could have offered him, my family and myself, had I put in the manhours before he died. Drown your pain and feelings of helplessness in knowledge, my friends. Because knowledge is power.

*

ALICE RICH
Alice's 42-year-old brother Gary
died from a fentanyl overdose in 2015

I just feel like more could be done to find out where the drugs are coming from. We can take down drug dealer Johnny all day, but there are just more dealers to pop up and take his or her place. Drug dealers are a dime a dozen. Go big or go home. I just cannot believe that it's impossible to take down the heads of drug operations. Having said that, the police know who the dealers are and what houses the drugs come from. Longer sentences and stricter consequences for dealers.

I know—funding, overcrowded jails, blah blah blah. Check the costs of treating thousands of people per day who are overdosing across the country. How much does it cost for funerals, burials, cremations? Rehab centers are full. How about rehab in prison? Inmates have to do something while they're in there; rehab classes sound good. Education, counseling, twelve-step meetings. I don't know the answer, but nothing else seems to be working.

I also think we need more support and education for those dealing with addicted loved ones. I hear a common theme of, "He was such a funny person, hard worker, liked by all, etc." While they are special people, the addict can be cunning, manipulative and unintentionally play on the false hope of their loved ones. How do we cope with that?

CHAPTER EIGHTEEN

Finding hope in the aftermath

Be like the birds, sing after every storm.
-BETH MENDE CONNY

Hope is fuel that propels us forward. It's the promise that tomorrow will be better than today. Each breath we take and each footprint we leave is a measure of hope. But traumatic loss has a way of redefining hope. What does hope mean to you today?

*

KIMBERLY CALAIS
Kim's 23-year-old daughter Emily died from a multiple drug
overdose including heroin and methamphetamine in 2016

Hope. Such a simple yet powerful word. The prospect of hope was the message of Barack Obama's presidential bid of 2008, which caused millions to vote for him. Without even the smallest presence of hope, most people are not likely to get out of bed each day or leave their homes. Living becomes existing.

During one of my GRASP meetings, we discussed how harm reduction, although not a solution, allows the existence of hope for those battling addition. Conversely, those lost to overdose no longer have hope. My hope died on January 2, 2016, with Emily.

At that time, my vision of hope had been that Emily's life would turn a corner and her demons would finally be cast behind her for the rest of her life. I hoped she would embrace all the beauty and magic that made her so wonderfully unique, and that she would reach each and every dream she had for herself, and touch the lives of others she met along the way whenever she shared her journey.

She used to call herself a warrior, and she was. I told her she was like the phoenix rising out of the ashes, destined for the amazing life that awaited her. In fact, I gave her a pendant with the phoenix rising for Christmas 2015. It was red—her favorite color—and she wore it immediately. Two weeks later it was in the bag of her possessions returned to me by the coroner.

My hope for all that was Emily's life has now, as you would expect, changed. For the longest time, hope was gone. It was all I could do to get out of bed. Conversely, I could not sit still. I did not want to provide myself any opportunity to think—or feel. I still don't, but I've become more welcoming to my thoughts and emotions. I have loved Emily since the day I found out I was pregnant with her. I have loved her for over twenty-seven years now. That love will never go away. Just like my grief. My grief is commensurate with my love. I love her deeply. I grieve for her deeply.

There are so many metaphors to the grief journey. The unpredictable tides of the ocean is a good one. You never know when the winds will shift and whether you'll be relatively safe during the calm, or catapult toward demolition due to the sudden change of an unpredicted storm. There is no predictability in life for me anymore. I take absolutely nothing for granted. Not even tomorrow. Not even in five minutes. And I'm okay with that. This mindset allows me to be truly present in each moment of my life, no matter how painful those moments are. It is in this same way that I embrace the concept of hope.

I've learned so much since Emily left my world. As mentioned earlier, I'm amazed at how glib we are as a society. We take for granted that we'll live to x age, we'll marry, have x number of kids, retire, and travel. We will bury our parents just like our children will bury us. I used to think this way. I don't anymore.

I wake each day with hope that I will be able to savor the beauty and handle the pain of whatever moments await me, as I include Emily in all my experiences. I talk to her all day long. And I look for signs of her wherever I go. I try not to hold any grudges or hold on to any anger. I communicate all my feelings—good, bad or indifferent—as needed in real time. I live with compassion toward others, knowing that everyone is someone's child and should be treated with dignity. I have ended relationships that serve no purpose or hurt me.

While I do not see a life of advocacy before me, I did find a way to embrace a new type of hope for the others who are still battling. Not long after joining the GRASP Facebook group, I read a post about a project from lighthouseofhopefulhearts.org, Lighthouse of Hopeful Hearts, a project created to honor those lost to a substance passing. Families and friends can submit the name of their loved one, which is then embroidered on a patch and sewn on to a backpack filled with basic necessities. These packs are then distributed to those who are surviving in the margins of society including those fighting addiction and mental issues, those without homes, those leaving treatment facilities, and those with nothing.

This nonprofit organization was started by a California mom who lost her son to an overdose death. Throughout the year, she and volunteers prepare and fill some five hundred packs for distribution on Christmas Day. It is a herculean task borne on the shoulders of a true angel, bringing a form of comfort of those who grieve, and a sense of hope to those who still battle.

Participants of this project are asked to write a letter about their person, connecting the story of those who have lost hope with those who are so desperately trying to find it. I financially contribute to this necessary and worthwhile project on Emily's birthday and Christmas, as well as monthly throughout the year. I believe in the help and hope it offers. I was able to assist in a small distribution in San Francisco in 2018, handing over a few of the Emily packs and connect my little girl with someone else's little girl or boy. The gratitude these people exhibited was truly humbling.

I am cautiously optimistic and hold a small amount of hope that this epidemic of substance use will soon wither and ultimately die;

however, I don't foresee it in my lifetime. That being said, I am hopeful that moments of pain or despair can be eased by sharing Emily's story. Submitting our story for this book has been a very emotional experience and, while not apparent, much of what I've shared comes with an abundance of tears. I've revisited memories I had pushed to the side. Strangely enough, the words flowed despite the tears or, perhaps, because of them.

Writing is cathartic in and of itself. Giving life to such debilitating pain allows me to have hope that a difference can be felt. Emily was one of two treasured lights of my life. I don't want her flame to be extinguished. I want her beautiful and brilliant light to guide others through their journey through the desolate and anguish-filled rubble which they are forced to walk when losing their loved one to overdose.

*

SUSAN CARLYON
Susan's 22-year-old son Adam died from
an overdose of carfentanyl in 2016

I don't have a definition of hope. However,

I HOPE that my son is happy and at peace.

I HOPE that my son's name and face are never forgotten.

I HOPE that some really positive things happen in my life.

I HOPE that all drug dealers are put in jail for a long time.

*

MARYBETH CICHOCKI
MaryBeth's 37-year-old son Matthew died
from a Percocet overdose in 2015

Hope is carrying on my son's legacy by helping other grieving parents. Hope is starting "A Hug From Matt," and giving out bags of food and hygiene items plus Narcan to the homeless.

*

KIM DELONG
Kim's 29-year-old son Tyler died
from a fentanyl overdose in 2017

Hope is believing in someone and having faith that they will overcome addiction to live a happy and productive life.

*

ELAINE FAULKNER
Elaine's 25-year-old son Jacob died from
an overdose of opiates and Xanax in 2017

My hope is based on finding out that Jake is not so very far away! His spirit is near and communicates with us. We just don't have his physical presence here in our reality. I believe our separation is just a temporary situation, and we will be reunited someday. That gives me hope! It may be many years before we see each other again, but it will eventually happen! I hope that my pain can be put to good use by sharing my journey with others. I hope to offer support to those who are walking, or will walk, the same path. I intend to honor Jake by living my life in a kinder and more compassionate way. Jake encouraged and helped others. That's my inspiration. I hope I can leave a lasting impact. Jake made the world a better place. He showed kindness and love, and his legacy will live on through the lives he touched and the lessons he taught us.

*

SHANNIE JENKINS
Shannie's 31-year-old son Kyle died
from a heroin overdose in 2017

The evening I sat outside Kyle's apartment waiting for the coroner, I posted on Facebook that Kyle just overdosed and died. I always told Kyle if the disease ever took him, I would not be silent.

Three days later at his candlelight vigil, we announced it openly and honestly on the local news channel. Almost two years later, and I still am surprised when people are not honest how their loved one died when it is an overdose. There is nothing to be ashamed about. The addict fighting the disease is probably the strongest person you will ever meet.

My hope is that we continue to talk out loud, that we continue to take the shame out of the disease, that there is a cure to help this generation. So many young people are dying. How far will this go?

I know a lot of work has been done even in the last couple years, but there is so much more to do. It breaks my heart to welcome newcomers to a Facebook group for parents who lost their child to an overdose. How do you welcome them into this group? I don't want to welcome more parents, knowing that their journey has just begun.

I don't want to see the next generation having to deal with this epidemic. I will never give up hope, and I hope the world doesn't either.

*

LORI LATIMER
Lori's 29-year-old son Greg died from
alcohol and fentanyl-laced cocaine in 2019

Hope changed for me on January 6, 2019. Prior to that day, my hope was that I would leave a legacy my sons and grandsons would be proud of. My hope was that I would leave this life with my sons and grandsons at my side, like my mom had done.

Now I find hope in knowing that Greg is okay, that he's still with me, and that I will see him again one day when my life is complete. He continues to give me hope through the many signs I receive from him.

I waited several months after Greg died before posting publicly on Facebook about his cause of death. It wasn't that I was ashamed of it—my reasons were personal and confidential due to the nature of his death. I knew that making my post public would potentially open me up to some negativity.

Instead, I received nothing but love and support from people I know, as well as many I don't know. I find hope in my belief that by me speaking out, I can affect just one person so that one family does not have to live with the hell that my family and I will live with the rest of our lives.

And I find hope in my family. Steve and his family are my constant reminder that there are blessings in life. Greg's friends still tell me stories of the wonderful, loving things he did for others in his short life. That gives me hope that he did make a difference, and that he will not be forgotten because he left a legacy that many only wish they could leave. And I have hope and a knowing that Greg knew how very much I loved him, and how proud and honored I am that he chose me to be his mom in this life.

*

AMANDA MARIE
Amanda's 30-year-old brother Cory
died from a heroin overdose in 2015

I feel hope every time I am presented with the opportunity to connect with others who have suffered such an unbearable loss. I find hope nestled inside each space I hold for their grief. There is hope in every chance I have to share his story. There is hope in each possibility that sharing my sorrow might keep someone else from having to experience it themselves.

*

DIANA MITCHELL
Diana's 18-year-old daughter Brooke died from
a mix of fentanyl, ecstasy, and cocaine in 2017

Hope is seeing the number of overdoses coming down. I fight every day trying to get the correct things put into place and hope our government will actually spend the money on recovery.

*

WHITNEY O'BRIEN
Whitney's 23-year-old brother Michael died from
a heroin/cocaine/benzodiazepine overdose in 2016

Three years ago, I was completely stripped of all hope. What was supposed to be the happiest time of my life was suddenly the worst. I remember feeling very alone. I still have moments of isolation when the world is blissfully unaware of my pain. At first, it was dark—very dark. I am starting to see a light of hope flickering in the distance. Hope is something I experience every day through the eyes of my children. My son exudes liveliness. He wakes every morning with a hunger to play and learn. Energy oozes from his every pore; he is bursting with joy and verve. This child does not realize the purpose he is serving in our lives during this anguishing time. He inspires me, and fills me with hope and faith.

I truly believe my daughter was sent to mend my broken heart. My hope for her is that she will fulfill many destinies in her lifetime. But she had a mission before she was even born. She is my angel on earth who was sent to restore my happiness and nourish my soul.

*

ALICE RICH
Alice's 42-year-old brother Gary
died from a fentanyl overdose in 2015

Gary's friend who overdosed in the Taco Bell parking lot has been clean almost two years. That is my definition of hope. Sobriety can be obtained and maintained. Success stories give me hope.

CHAPTER NINETEEN

Surviving the Journey

I don't want my pain and struggle to make
me a victim. I want my battle to make me
someone else's hero. -ANONYMOUS

Though every journey is unique like a fingerprint, we are never truly alone for more people walk behind, beside, and in front of us. In this chapter are answers to the final question: What would you like the world to know about your journey?

*

KIMBERLY CALAIS
Kim's 23-year-old daughter Emily died from a multiple drug overdose including heroin and methamphetamine in 2016

Tragically, there are thousands of stories like ours. While each has a common theme due to its outcome, the particulars are as unique and individual as a fingerprint or snowflake. No two are alike. How could they be? Each and every person lost to overdose was a human being with irreplaceable value. They loved and they were (and are) loved. They had dreams and talents. I hear repeatedly how creative these lost lives were. So very tenderhearted with gentle souls. They felt pain as much, if not more, than the rest of us. I know Emily was very much like this. Even as a toddler, she had such an explosive curiosity about life and loved to create. She would sing for hours, make up plays (assigning out parts, of course), dressing up her dolls to outfits she designed and made. She always had a smile on her face and a twinkle in her eye. She said she wanted to make it on Broadway, and I believed she could do it. She was that special.

But her tender heart and little girl dreams were bruised by the cold reality which is life. She tried her entire life to fit in with others, to elevate herself to social groups she thought were more important, all the while turning away from her true self, something that must have caused her soul such pain, a pain so deep that she sought solace in drugs. I remember her telling me that using drugs helped her to be more comfortable in her own skin, distancing herself from the social anxiety that she suffered from.

It broke my heart then and it breaks my heart now.

In the beginning I wondered whether Emily intended to end her life, or if it ended accidentally. After a few months, the answer didn't matter as much, as I believe that she rolled the dice each time she filled that syringe. She knew the risks on every level. The pain she endured was worth that risk to her. An escape of whatever length to escape a life that overwhelmed her and slip into what she described as the all-encompassing love and warmth of her high from heroin. For me, there is no difference if her death was intentional or not. She is gone because she suffered and ached for relief.

I'm reminded of the song "Vincent," by Don McLean. While the song is about Vincent Van Gogh and his death by suicide, it is my belief that drug use and addiction can in some ways be viewed as a very slow form of suicide. These verses resonated with me and touch my broken heart deeply:

> And now I understand what you tried to say to me.
>
> How you suffered for your sanity. How you tried to set them free. Perhaps they'll listen now.
>
> For they could not love you. But still your love was true. And when no hope was left in sight, on that starry, starry night,
>
> You took your life as lovers often do; But I could have told you Vincent
>
> This world was never meant for one as beautiful as you.

Emily was and is beautiful. So is your loved one. I wish the world knew the strength it takes to have one heart that beats for two. I wish they could see the additional and unnecessary despair the specter of stigma causes. We should not have to walk these horrific and dark roads alone. We should not have to hang our heads in some form of shame due to the manner our loved ones left this earth. While my head may have hung in those first weeks, it was not to protect me. I didn't want her memory to be diminished by judgment of the masses. But that was then.

Now I share Emily's story. She was right. When you have a child, you're a mother for the rest of your life. What she didn't know was

SURVIVING LOSS BY OVERDOSE

that continues even when the child is gone. I refuse to let her be forgotten. The light from her life will continue to shine for as long as I live. She did not die in vain. Love is immortal. Love never dies.

I want to end by sharing something I wrote a few months ago. I shared it on the GRASP site, and believe it touched the hearts of many who read and shared it. It came to me while I was trying to describe what this grief feels like.

> SKIN
>
> I think . . . a lot. Especially when I drive. And I drive . . . a lot. Today I was thinking about the constant presence of my grief, consciously or subconsciously. I then thought about how all-encompassing it is. And then a new analogy popped into my head. All the manifestations of my grief are like a new layer of skin that surrounds every part of me. Every cell. Every bone. Sleeping. Waking. Inhaling. Exhaling. It is the largest organ of my human body. It bleeds. It burns. It is scarred. It has disfigured all that was once me. It is completely unique with the unmistakable and irreplaceable imprint of my daughter's life. And her death.
>
> No one can see the difference this additional layer of skin makes in my existence and it takes incredible strength to navigate life inside of it. I didn't ask for this new skin. I ache and feel so alone inside my skin. Most no longer recognize me inside this skin. I am seemingly unknowable and untouchable in this skin. It is a permanent barrier which separates me from all who knew me before, yet sadly unites me with others who wear their own new skin.
>
> Others like you.
>
> I will continue to live in this skin until my last breath. Then, and only then, will this grieving end.

You are not alone.

*

SUSAN CARLYON
Susan's 22-year-old son Adam died from
an overdose of carfentanyl in 2016

It has been an extremely difficult journey losing my son to an overdose. No parent should ever have to bury their child. We have lived longer than our children. That doesn't seem fair.

Substance abuse is a whole different ballgame than losing someone to a disease that society accepts. Addiction is a brain disease, but few take that into account.

We had no idea Adam was using drugs. I knew something was wrong with him but was completely blindsided when he told us about his drug use. We didn't see that coming.

The stigma for us as parents, as well as the way people looked at and acted toward Adam, was extremely hurtful and changed the way people interacted with us.

In addition, I endlessly blamed myself. Was I a bad mom? Is that why Adam turned to drugs? How could I have prevented this? What more could I have done?

To this day, I desperately want to talk to Adam in person and tell him how very sorry I am that I didn't understand his struggle to its full extent, that I feel so badly for him and everything he had to go through each and every day. I would have taken on all his pain for him in a heartbeat. I love and miss my son tremendously, and I so badly want to hug him one more time.

*

MARYBETH CICHOCKI
MaryBeth's 37-year-old son Matthew died
from a Percocet overdose in 2015

Losing my child has been the most painful experience of my life. I've found time does nothing for the grief. I've learned that by losing Matt, I've lost a future of having a daughter-in-law and future grand-babies. I've lost watching my two sons grow old together. The losses are so profound and so numerous. I still find myself breathless when reality hits. Holidays are painful. Mother's Day is unbearable. I now understand what it's like to live without a piece of your heart. I know I will grieve Matt forever.

*

KIM DELONG
Kim's 29-year-old son Tyler died
from a fentanyl overdose in 2017

My son was raised in a very loving family. He was educated and highly intelligent. We discussed drug use many times while he was young. He took good care of himself and wanted nothing to do with drugs. By all accounts he was happy but let his guard down when he met a pretty girl who was an addict, and that was his downfall.

He thought he was invincible. I never imagined or suspected that my son would use fentanyl. It happened so quickly that it was over before we knew what was happening. I thought I could fix my son by nursing him back to health and loving him. I was wrong. Don't attempt it on your own. If you find yourself in this situation, get your loved one into treatment immediately or it will be too late.

*

ELAINE FAULKNER
Elaine's 25-year-old son Jacob died from
an overdose of opiates and Xanax in 2017

Through the difficult and strong emotions, the triggers and the pain, I have survived. I would never have wanted to bear this, but it was put on my shoulders. I pray not for an easy load, but rather a strong back.

I am grateful I followed suggestions to attend support groups and seek professional help. I have leaned on others and have tried not to do this alone, although sometimes it's a struggle to be around people. I share my feelings with those close to me. Some days the pain seems manageable, other days the pain is unbearable and I don't think I can get through it, but I do.

I go to counseling weekly. My counselor helps me to recognize and work through the complex emotions of grief. Counseling helps me not get stuck in resentment, anger, regret, fear, shame, and other emotions that lead to depression or bitterness. I still feel those emotions, but now I recognize them and let them pass.

I work to accept what happened. I will always hate it, I will always feel pain around it, but I accept that I can't change it. When I stay in acceptance, I find the peace I crave. Being in a peaceful state allows me to consider Jake's entire life span and enjoy the memories without overly focusing on the end.

I have an increased appreciation for life, and loved ones, and take them less for granted. I'm grateful that my family is stronger and closer through our loss, rather than torn apart by it. I was given back my childhood's magical view of nature that I lost on the way to adulthood; a rare gift. I'm truly charmed by clouds, trees, flowers, and scenery. From the sharing of our story, I hope to help others receive the message that they are not to blame for the loss of their loved one.

Forgiveness is something that I work hard to practice. I forgive myself for my imperfect parenting and my mistakes. Practice giving yourself the love and care you deserve. I set boundaries with people who drag my spirit down. One of the most loving things you can do for yourself, and others, is to reach out and seek the company of those who understand. We are brothers and sisters in grief. May we find peace.

*

SHANNIE JENKINS
Shannie's 31-year-old son Kyle died
from a heroin overdose in 2017

I feel very blessed that God has used me as a vessel to speak out against addiction. The opportunities to share the story of Kyle's life and his struggles. To share his beautiful picture and his soul with so many. I know the purpose in Kyle's death is not for me to know, but my heart is totally open to what God wants us to do from here.

Yes, Kyle's life was cut way too short, and he doesn't get to be a daddy to his son Knox, but I feel so lucky that God chose me to be Kyle's mom. I got thirty-one years with this beautiful son and we built such a wonderful mom-son friending. The relationship we had was a gift that not all parents get to have with their child.

I remember after I spoke with our county commissioner declaring this an epidemic for our county, I was driving home and was crying. I shouted out to God, "Okay, God. I have done everything you have wanted me to do, but I want my son back!"

I had such an overwhelming feeling that said, "He wasn't yours to keep. I know your pain because I had to give my son to save others also." It was like a slap in the face to wake up. How true is that?

We dedicated Kyle to the Lord when he was four weeks old in 1986. We promised to raise him in a Godly home, and raise him the best we could. Was life perfect? Absolutely not. But we always kept God close in our lives. Kyle was lent to us to be his parents. How do I question God's timing when it was time to take Kyle home? And why wouldn't God want Kyle as an angel? Kyle had something special about him. He loved people and his heart was huge. He felt like an angel here on earth, but God had a plan for Kyle. I trust in that.

I honestly do not know how I would ever get through losing my son without my faith. It is what I hang on to each day. I know I am still in shock and still in a fog, yet feel that I am where I need to be in my grief. I lost a child. But I do believe that God is not done with me yet. If and when He calls for me to share or help others, I will be there.

When an opportunity comes up, I take an internal look and see if it is calming or stressful. When it is calming, I feel that it is what I am supposed to do. I look forward to the day when I can hug Kyle again but until then, I know he is with me and his family. And I thank God for Kyle every day.

*

LORI LATIMER
Lori's 29-year-old son Greg died from
alcohol and fentanyl-laced cocaine in 2019

When you lose a child unexpectedly, it changes you. There is so much collateral damage that no one anticipates. It's unimaginable and surreal, even when you're living it. There are days I want to crawl out of my skin, days I feel like I'm living in a dream, in someone else's life, and I just want mine back. Most days, it doesn't seem real.

There are so many layers to losing a child that makes this grief different than other types of grief. I've been divorced (more than once). I've lost both my parents. Absolutely nothing prepared me for this. There are physical layers to this level of grief that I never knew existed.

Adding in the horror of drugs takes it all to whole new level. First there was the shock that Greg had died. Then came the shock that he was doing drugs. Then came the shock of his death being caused by a combination of cocaine and fentanyl. And then came all the research and education. It's like going down a deep, dark hole with no end in sight.

Greg had an insatiable appetite for life from the minute he was born. He had a thirst for knowledge and experiences that transcended most people I've met in my life. He touched more people than I had any idea he had touched. His life was filled with love, curiosity and adventure. He was smart and kind. He loved deeply and could always be counted on. My mom fell and broke her hip six days before her ninetieth birthday and was in the hospital on her birthday. We had a party in her hospital room, and although she was basically in a coma, we all bought her birthday cards and had a cake. Greg wrote her the most beautiful letter in her card. It was so profound that we had him read it at her memorial service. Part of it read, "As long as I'm alive, your daughter will be taken care of."

That was my son. I know he wrote those words from his heart and meant them with every fiber of his being, deep down in his soul. And now, he's gone.

If you or anyone you know is using drugs, let them know they are literally playing Russian Roulette with their lives—and they most likely don't even know it. Talk to those you love about the hidden dangers of fentanyl. It only takes a couple grains of fentanyl to kill someone. The result can be fatal and will shatter the lives of those you love. I know my son never intended to die that night—he just thought he'd have fun. That fun turned into a nightmare that my family and I will live with the rest of my life.

What I have left of my beautiful, loving son are memories… and ashes. I wear some in a spiral formation in a pendant around my neck every single day. Some are in a tattoo I had done on his birthday this year. The tattoo is identical to the rose he had over his heart with my name. Over the rose over my heart is his name, and under the rose is my son, Steve's, name. Greg's ashes are in the ink. Greg's best friend, Jay, went to Maui to visit one of their mutual friends, Travis, in March, just two months after Greg's death. Greg had visited Travis in

Maui several times and loved it there. I asked Jay if he would take some of Greg's ashes and spread them in the place Greg had loved so much. After they scattered Greg's ashes, they sent me a photo of where they scattered them. An hour later I looked outside my patio door, and there was a beautiful double rainbow. I know that was Greg's sign saying he approved. In August, a group of Greg's friends, Steve, his wife, my oldest two grandsons and I floated down the river Greg loved so much near where he lived. Greg and his friends have been doing this since high school. We stopped along the way and scattered some of his ashes there. The rest of his ashes are in beautiful wooden boxes in Steve's home and in Jay's home, and in beautiful urns in his father's home and my home. That's what's left of my son. The pain that we all feel is one I wouldn't wish on anyone.

At the end of it all is choice.

Every day I have a choice. Will I choose to live or simply exist? How do I choose to live and honor Greg's life?

Choosing hope isn't always the easy path, and there are some days when it seems completely out of reach. On those days I hear Greg's voice. I know without a doubt that if I choose to simply exist, he would be mad at me, and if I make that choice, I'm not being the mom that he knows and loves. So even on the hardest of days, I choose to honor Greg's life.

I choose to live.

I choose to love.

*

AMANDA MARIE
Amanda's 30-year-old brother Cory
died from a heroin overdose in 2015

People will give their unsolicited advice about what you should do when a loved one is an addict. They will tell you to practice tough love, give ultimatums, and force interventions. I am going to do the same and tell you what to do: **love them anyway.**

The reality is that some of those who struggle with addiction will not make it. No matter how hard they try, no matter what we do to help them, some of them will not recover. Some of them will die.

There is only one thing I wish I would have done differently: I wish I would have told Cory more often that I love him. I couldn't save my brother, but I could have done that. My greatest fear is that he died with the same feeling that made him use: the loneliness of pain and the pain of disconnection.

Johann Hari, author of "Chasing the Scream: The First and Last Days of the War on Drugs" said, "The opposite of addiction is not sobriety. The opposite of addiction is connection."

So, connect. Don't hide your eyes from the ugly parts of humanity because it reflects something in yourself that hurts too much to deal with. Instead, look closer. The energy between your differences is available for your growth. It is available for healing. If you keep looking away, it will manifest itself over and over until the lesson is learned. I think I learned mine. I hope Cory did too.

*

DIANA MITCHELL
Diana's 18-year-old daughter Brooke died from
a mix of fentanyl, ecstasy, and cocaine in 2017

Losing someone to overdose . . . there are really no words. You're in an exclusive group. You're judged on what a bad parent you are, like we did something wrong. I just take it one day at a time and push myself to actually get out of bed.

*

WHITNEY O'BRIEN
Whitney's 23-year-old brother Michael died from
a heroin/cocaine/benzodiazepine overdose in 2016

The only physical piece of my brother left on this planet is a lock of hair gently snipped by the funeral director from the nape of Michael's neck. There were three taken—one for myself, one for my parents, and one for Erika. Each is about eight inches long and delicately coiled, held together by a clear, elastic band. I keep mine a velvet drawstring bag, tucked away among other mementos. I save it for moments when I'm drowning in sorrow and can no longer ignore the colossal ache gnawing at my heart. I sit and gently comb through it with my fingers. I am always amazed by the endless shades of red; no two strands are the same hue.

I remember when the funeral director—Chrystle was her name, and I will never, ever forget her—asked if we would like a lock of his hair. A resounding and harmonious, "Yes!" escaped both mine and my mother's mouth. It's one of the most precious things I have. If my

344

house were burning down and I only had time to grab a few things, this would be one of them. I will cherish and safeguard it always.

Michael's death is palpable. But to a stranger walking into my parents' home, not so much. Ignore the shrine on the coffee table and one would assume there are three people living in that house, not two. Well, and the long dead peace lily sent to the funeral home by a family friend which sits pathetically in the corner of the living room, whose only purpose is to serve as a constant reminder that nothing lives forever.

Aside from the shrine and the dying plants, it's hard to tell Michael's truly gone. Sometimes I swear I can hear him clearing his throat. His shoes are resting at the foot of his bed. His clothes are hanging in the closet. His toothbrush is still perched in its charger on the bathroom sink. I've even noticed a few those remarkable red hairs on the wall of the shower.

His room remains intact barring some rummaging my parents and I have done. I make a point to put everything I touch back exactly as I found it. I find a great deal of comfort in his room. It's the place I feel closest to him. It still smells like him: a combination of strawberry-flavored vape, Polo Black cologne, and just the musk of Michael.

His childhood treasures have been claimed by my son, his safe has been cracked by my dad, and my mom washed his sheets and made his bed. It all really feels like an enormous invasion of privacy. And yet I constantly find myself meandering into his room searching for signs. I beg him to send me something.

I found a poem scribbled in a spiral notebook that is very telling of his emotional outlook:

I've fallen in a well

This life is worse than hell

You can see it in my eyes

if you look deep down inside that

this life has destroyed me and everything I know

But I still continue with no pain even though

Now I'm in ruins, I hope to god you'll see

That tonight is the night,

there's no turning back for me.

Losing my brother has irrevocably changed my life. I will never be the person I once was; a reality I am slowly learning to absorb. Michael's death has carved me into a different, softer, kinder creature. I feel a calling to help educate others and spread awareness. His death has triggered a benevolent itch. I want to act. To help. To give.

I will never get over losing my brother. It will never be okay that he died. My grief will last as long as my love for him lasts: forever. It's taken some time, but I am learning to surrender to my grief rather than fight it, and just let this pain run its course.

Grief is like an earthquake—it shakes you at your core until you crumble and fall, leaving you in utter ruin. The aftershocks continue to rattle your life on a daily basis. The fault line indicates your life before and after.

We should count ourselves lucky in life if we have someone who would do anything for us, no questions asked. Someone who relishes in your accomplishments and feels the defeat of your failures. Who brags about you. Who can fight tooth and nail with you, but would defend you until the end. Someone to harbor all your secrets and skeletons. Someone who feeds off your happiness and holds you up during times of sorrow. Who is tethered to your soul and woven to your heart. Who bleeds the same blood and knows the ins and outs of your family's roots. Someone who, no matter how long it's been since you last talked, can pick up right where you left off. Who accepts you for all your faults and loves you more because of them. Not because they have to, but because you are worth loving.

This is the unspeakable bond of a brother and sister. The only person in the world who shares the love that binds you together.

My brother, my angel, let this be a testament of my love for you. I will never stop telling your story. In doing so, you will help so many others who are tortured by this disease. You will accomplish in your death what you didn't have time to do in life. You will spread goodness and arouse change. Your death will not be in vain, I promise you.

*

ALICE RICH
Alice's 42-year-old brother Gary
died from a fentanyl overdose in 2015

It sucks. Heroin sucks. Senseless death sucks. There is a better life. Drugs are never the right answer. I don't know a drug user that is happy and carefree. An addict's life is full of secrecy, urgency, loneliness, isolation, and grief.

Where others see just a junkie, we see sons and daughters, wives and husbands, brothers and sisters, moms and dads, and friends whom we love. We see a part of our life that we do not want to live without. We feel powerless and frustrated over the situation, over heroin. There are no words to explain the pain and loss felt. The pain is way worse than I expected and is lasting way longer than I expected. I have lost grandparents and aunts and uncles whom I loved dearly. Why is this different? Perhaps because his death was tragic and senseless.

Gary was an amazing guy. So handsome, so funny; he just had a way about him, and I love him so much. With pain in my heart and tears running down my cheeks, I say to you now, talk openly with your loved one. Hug them harder, kiss them more often, and talk to them as long as you can. Hate the drug, not the addict. There is nothing you can do but make sure they know that they are loved and be supportive to their efforts to come clean; no matter how many times that is.

CHAPTER TWENTY

Meet the writers

We need to teach each other that they're human beings, and they deserve exactly what you do: a warm bed, a warm meal, a warm blanket, a pillow to lay their head on.

~MARYBETH CICHOCKI

*

KIMBERLY CALAIS

Kim's 23-year-old daughter Emily died from a multiple drug overdose including heroin and methamphetamine in 2016

Kimberly Calais was born in San Francisco, and raised in Pacifica, California. She worked in the superior courts in the courtroom and administration for twenty years prior to retiring in 2001. She went on to earn a paralegal certification in 2006.

She is the proud mother of two beautiful daughters. Kim enjoys a close relationship with her surviving daughter, Kelly, and she currently lives in Toronto, following her marriage in 2012.

In an effort to keep Emily's memory alive and hopefully make a difference in the lives of those who still battle,

she is a fervent supporter of Lighthouse of Hopeful Hearts (www.lighthouseofhopefulhearts.org), an organization working toward bringing awareness, removing prejudice, and eliminating the stigma associated with addiction, overdose and mental health issues.

*

SUSAN CARLYON
Susan's 22-year-old son Adam died from
an overdose of carfentanyl in 2016

Susan Carlyon is a mom, wife, and teacher. She was born and raised in Kent, Ohio, and lives in Stow, Ohio. She earned her Bachelor of Arts Degree in Teaching from Hiram College. She has taught two and three-year-olds for twenty years. She is married and has two children, a daughter Amanda and a son Adam, who is forever twenty-two. Susan and her family were completely devastated when her son died in 2016, from an accidental overdose.

Susan is a founding member of the Akron, Ohio, NOPE Task Force (Narcotics Overdose and Prevention Education). She and her daughter go out into the schools in Northeast Ohio and speak to seventh through twelfth graders, telling them Adam's story. In the first year after Adam's death, they spoke to ten thousand students. Susan is determined to keep Adam's name and face at the forefront of her life both through NOPE and all the things she does in honor of her son, such as many random acts of kindness in Adam's name.

*

MARYBETH CICHOCKI
MaryBeth's 37-year-old son Matthew
died from a Percocet overdose in 2015
mothersheartbreak.com

MaryBeth Cichocki, R.N. is a wife, mother, grandmother and dog rescuer in Delaware. She lost her son, Matt, to an overdose of prescription drugs on January 3, 2015. After his death she was unable to return to caring for ill babies in the neonatal ICU and now spends her time advocating and writing about the disease of addiction. She started a blog which tells the story of Matt's addiction and her journey through complicated grief. MaryBeth also facilitates a support group for those who have lost a loved one to addiction.

Passionate about sparing others from her grief, MaryBeth testified about her difficulty finding comprehensive treatment for her son at the state capitol during the Joint Finance Committee hearings. She works with legislators to implement changes in how to treat the disease of substance use disorder and played a pivotal role in the passing of six bills in Delaware, related to treatment for those suffering from substance abuse disease.

*

KIM DELONG
Kim's 29-year-old son Tyler died
from a fentanyl overdose in 2017

Kim DeLong grew up in Beverly, Massachusetts, where she lived a happy life with her parents and two sisters. She married at age twenty-two and had two sons. She worked in the finance industry for almost twenty years before changing careers to work in the construction industry.

She loved being a mother and raising her boys, of whom she is very proud. The death of her oldest son has turned her life upside down. She is thankful for her loving family and friends for holding her up. She hopes that telling her story will help others.

*

ELAINE FAULKNER
Elaine's 25-year-old son Jacob died from
an overdose of opiates and Xanax in 2017

Elaine Faulkner has been married to her husband Jack for thirty-six years. Together they raised three children in the Pacific Northwest.

After completing the chemical dependency program at Northwest Indian College, Elaine became certified as a Drug and Alcohol Counselor and Case Manager. She has worked in outpatient treatment center, a community detox center, juvenile detention, and a needle exchange program.

All her life and work experience did not prepare her for the sudden loss of her middle child, Jacob, when he died of an accidental overdose in the summer of 2017. Elaine is rebuilding her life with her husband, daughters, and son-in-law. She continues to work in the chemical dependency field as a case manager for Whatcom Therapeutic Court (Drug Court). Elaine has a passion for using her knowledge and experience and hopes to help others. She can be reached at emf820@gmail.com.

*
SHANNIE JENKINS
Shannie's 31-year-old son Kyle died
from a heroin overdose in 2017

Shannie Jenkins was born and raised in the Grays Harbor area of Washington State. She moved to Olympia, Washington, in 1975 where she graduated in 1978. She had two sons, Ryan in 1984 and Kyle Brinton in 1986. Shannie worked at the elementary school that her boys attended. She and the boys' dad divorced in 1992, but remained friends and raised their boys together. She worked at the school district for seventeen years and has worked for the transit system for the past eleven years. She remarried in 2010. She enjoys spending time with family and her grandkids.

*
LORI LATIMER
Lori's 29-year-old son Greg died from
alcohol and fentanyl-laced cocaine in 2019

Lori Latimer was born and raised in southern California. She moved to Atlanta when her oldest son, Steve, was four. In 1989, she was blessed with another son, Greg.

Lori has a Bachelor's in Psychology from Georgia State University. While working as a freelance family law paralegal, Lori started her own business which has evolved into her current work as a spiritual mentor and soul navigator, helping people clear blocks and restrictions and release karmic patterns that have been holding them back.

After the unexpected death of her son, Greg, she started Grief with Grace to help other mothers who have lost children. Her work can be found at www.lorilatimer.com. She's also involved in bringing awareness to this crisis through speaking and working with legislators at the state and federal levels. She is passionate about preventing any other mothers from the heartache and grief she lives with. Lori's son, Steve, has blessed her life with her beautiful grandchildren.

*

AMANDA MARIE
Amanda's 30-year-old brother Cory
died from a heroin overdose in 2015

Amanda Marie studied integrated, interdisciplinary arts and psychology and received her bachelor's in 2016 from Eastern Illinois University. She earned a Master's of Science from the University of Illinois, with a focus on the role and impact of leisure on the overall quality of life, and fostering, improving and sustaining socio-economic order through recreation in a culturally diverse society.

She works for a nonprofit legal aid foundation assisting victims of domestic violence. She is committed to helping others recover their health, hope, and faith in themselves and people around them.

She currently resides in Illinois with her two sons, one of whom is a metal-head computer whiz and the other a hip-hop loving basketball player. In her free time, she loves to write. Her work can be found at www.givingupmyghosts.com.

*

DIANA MITCHELL

Diana's 18-year-old daughter Brooke died from
a mix of fentanyl, ecstasy, and cocaine in 2017

Diana Mitchell was raised by
military family. She and her
husband are both blue-collar
workers who worked very hard
and long hours to make sure their
children had everything they
needed to succeed in life.

*
WHITNEY O'BRIEN
Whitney's 23-year-old brother Michael died from
a heroin/cocaine/benzodiazepine overdose in 2016

Whitney O'Brien resides in Peoria, Arizona with her husband and their three young children. She graduated from Grand Canyon University with a bachelor's in nursing and has spent the majority of her career working as a labor and delivery nurse. She is also a mental health clinical adjunct for a local community college. In her spare time, she volunteers with a local harm reduction group that distributes Narcan to drug users in the community. She is an advocate for drug policy reform and the legalization of syringe exchange in the state of Arizona. You can find more of her writing on Medium.

*
ALICE RICH
Alice's 42-year-old brother Gary
died from a fentanyl overdose in 2015

Alice Rich was born and raised in Akron, Ohio. She earned her B.A. in nursing from Ohio University and has worked more than twenty years in the field of obstetrics. She lives in a small town with her husband and six children, not far from where she grew up. She enjoys spending time with her family, kayaking, and spending time outdoors.

*

CAROL WALL
Carol's 29-year-old son Jason died
from a heroin overdose in 2016.

Born in Glasgow, Scotland, Carol is a mother of three and grandmother of five. She has been married to Tom, her high school sweetheart, for thirty-seven years. Carol and Tom reside in St. Catharines, Ontario, where she works as a business manager for a large car dealership. Her husband Tom is a real estate broker. Since the passing of her son, Jason, Carol is advocating to stop the stigma and trying to spread the word on this opioid epidemic. Her mantra is to educate with compassion.

362

Thank you

Words cannot express the gratitude I have for the writers and coauthors Whitney O'Brien and Shannie Jenkins, who courageously share their stories in this book. It required tremendous courage to pen such painful memories for the purpose of helping others, and they have my utmost respect and gratitude.

Addiction runs deep in my family, and I promised my only brother I would do everything in my power to advocate for a cure so future generations don't have to suffer the way he has. It is my sincere hope that these stories, as raw as they are, help open the dialogue, raise awareness, and remove the stigma associated with substance use disorder until a cure is found.

Drugs and addiction are rampant in today's world, yet nobody has answers. But they will. If we can find treatment for AIDS, we can find a cure for addiction. Until then, we will continue to share our stories to educate and advocate for past, present, and future loved ones.

Warm blessings to you all.

Lynda Cheldelin Fell

SURVIVING LOSS BY OVERDOSE

Shared joy is doubled joy;
shared sorrow is half a sorrow.
SWEDISH PROVERB

*

LYNDA CHELDELIN FELL

Lynda Cheldelin Fell is an international bestselling author of over 30 books including the award-winning Grief Diaries series. After losing her daughter in a car accident in 2009, Lynda discovered that helping others was a powerful balm for her wounds—a catalyst that changed her world. She became an international bestselling author in 2013 and founded AlyBlue Media soon after.

Today Lynda is founding partner of the International Grief Institute, an educational consulting firm that provides professional certifications and training to the funeral and bereavement industry. She has earned five national literary awards and five national advocacy award nominations for her work. Learn more at www.LyndaFell.com.

lynda@lyndafell.com | www.lyndafell.com

Humanity's legacy of stories and storytelling
is the most precious we have.

DORIS LESSING

*

Grief Diaries: Surviving Sudden Loss
Grief Diaries: Surviving Loss by Cancer
Grief Diaries: Surviving Loss of a Spouse
Grief Diaries: Surviving Loss of a Child
Grief Diaries: Surviving Loss of a Sibling
Grief Diaries: Surviving Loss of a Parent
Grief Diaries: Surviving Loss of an Infant
Grief Diaries: Surviving Loss of a Loved One
Grief Diaries: Surviving Loss by Suicide
Grief Diaries: Surviving Loss of Health
Grief Diaries: How to Help the Newly Bereaved
Grief Diaries: Loss by Impaired Driving
Grief Diaries: Loss by Homicide
Grief Diaries: Loss of a Pregnancy
Grief Diaries: Hello from Heaven
Grief Diaries: Shattered
Grief Diaries: Project Cold Case
Grief Diaries: Poetry & Prose and More
Grief Diaries: Through the Eyes of Men
Grief Diaries: Will We Survive?
Grief Diaries: Victim Impact Statement
Grief Diaries: Hit by Impaired Driver
Grief Diaries: Surviving Loss of a Pet
Real Life Diaries: Living with a Brain Injury
Real Life Diaries: Through the Eyes of DID
Real Life Diaries: Through the Eyes of an Eating Disorder
Real Life Diaries: Living with Endometriosis
Real Life Diaries: Living with Mental Illness
Real Life Diaries: Living with Rheumatic Disease
Real Life Diaries: Through the Eyes of a Funeral Director
Real Life Diaries: Living with Gastroparesis
Color My Soul Whole
My Grief Diary
Grammy Visits From Heaven
Grandpa Visits From Heaven
Faith, Grief & Pass the Chocolate Pudding
Heaven Talks to Children
A Child is Missing: A True Story
A Child is Missing: Searching for Justice
Grief Reiki

To share your story, visit
www.griefdiaries.com

PUBLISHED BY ALYBLUE MEDIA
Real stories. Real people. Real insight.
www.AlyBlueMedia.com

Made in the USA
Monee, IL
02 June 2024

59271482R00225